THE ANCIENT FUTURE OF THE ITZA

... ual uyotemai y ... vaan tical ...
poken. bulue otabsan v mehen ah ...
leinen pe Kinil val, v chera ne ... ka ...
anuche zhac memal ... huan uchi ...
yab xooc, tu kin amol baxax, ti vla haa
y la yoch, oe lu hi ox ox Kinin vale, ...
hilp ya hauhil ah hun nau kahen

Oxil cauac val ukin v pe hi chenil ...
yu tumil binel u cah utzacle hauil binelut
opim balte akab. okoly ka tix ual lukic ...
tuchi val ouiie ya lavah, ti cha bi upuc ...
tumen ah ouc te cui. ah ouc chapat ti ta
tuhenil tihatunil vale, vuiil che, vuiil ...
nich, yokol cu lan hechenil ti yac hunil, niete
bal cu nuchub, nic te ual u nah ti Jahau hil da ...
vuah loe, tu kin uchā cuch, hey a pis ...
le, ti touil ah ox hun ahau vale, bulucc ...
bulue ahau, bolon ahau, ai ula ... ...
cuch, taix tie uso col ca bal kol honte ol ...
tateuki tiJahauJhil lai uki nil oxil cauac

Canil kan val ukini tukelep kahan ti hu
ahau, kekin tuhatunil - Oxkol be ...
bat nom yax cach, tu ho cam be, tu ho can ...
tetsan tate tihil, auat nom Cui auat ...
Kim, auat nom ah ya, ulom u kat chac ...
vayab yoo c, hom che, hom tunich, ...
yan ah vucchu uah, ulom vuich te ...
chenil, auat nom chum kin v go ...
ti Canil Kan, ucha bal hal utzar, u ...
vyanaktsan, yokol sac boc, yokol che ...
yokol may cuc, ti val tiho pis tun ...
ahau, v pe ah bulue otabpan, ta lute ...
utzan kin, utzan vooh y tich p ...

The Ancient Future of the Itza

The Book of Chilam Balam of Tizimin

Translated and annotated by Munro S. Edmonson

 UNIVERSITY OF TEXAS PRESS, AUSTIN

The Texas Pan American Series

The Texas Pan American Series is published with the assistance of a revolving publication fund established by the Pan American Sulphur Company.

International Standard Book Number
0-292-70353-8
Library of Congress Catalog Card
Number 81-1208
Copyright © 1982 by the University
of Texas Press
All rights reserved
Printed in the United States
of America

First Edition, 1982

Requests for permission to reproduce material from this work should be sent to Permissions, University of Texas Press, Box 7819, Austin, Texas 78712.

The publication of this volume was assisted in part by a grant from the National Endowment for the Humanities, an independent federal agency whose mission is to award grants to support education, scholarship, media programming, libraries, and museums in order to bring the results of cultural activities to the general public. Preparation was made possible in part by a grant from the Translations Program of the endowment.

T u men ah miatzob Ba Cabob:
Sir J. Eric S. Thompson,
Don Alfredo Barrera Vásquez,
Yum Ralph L. Roys,
Y etel Robert Wauchope,
U y Ahau Tulan,
May Cu.

Pathih hun ten e;　　　　It could happen once;
Bey he u patal u lac e.　　The like could happen again.

　　　　　　　　　　　　　　　　　—Mayan proverb

Contents

Acknowledgments

I have many debts. The first is to the U.S. Postal Service for having lost my Roys *Chumayel* in the mail. Without that, my collaboration with Victoria R. Bricker might have been less close and less productive. She can now have her Roys back together with my gratitude for her tact and energy as critic, adviser, and colleague. I am also returning Harvey M. Bricker's pocket calculator with equal gratitude for his getting hooked, however briefly, on the Mayan correlation problem.

For help with the Mayan language I am indebted to Eleuterio Poot Yah of Hocaba and Merida, Moisés Romero Castillo, Marshall Durbin, Francesca Merlan, and the late Robert Wauchope, who, as director of the Middle American Research Institute of Tulane, provided funds from a Ford Foundation grant to help with the formation of a working dictionary. Thanks go also to the students who worked on that project—Thomas Langdon, Robert Moore, Maurice Onwood, and James H. Rauh—and to a number of other stimulating students, particularly Marla Hires, whose interest got me started on the Tizimin, as well as Malcolm Shuman, Philip Thompson, and Marcia Jordan Thompson, whose research in Yucatan has provided me with a form of vicarious fieldwork.

I am grateful to Tulane University and the National Endowment for the Humanities for a summer grant that enabled me to complete the translation and to Arthur Welden for including me in the Tulane Yucatan Colloquium that got me to parts of the peninsula I had never visited. The generosity, hospitality, and assistance of Alfredo Barrera Vásquez and Joann M. Andrews during my visits to Yucatan are profoundly appreciated. The helpful and creative labor of the late Marjorie LeDoux, director of the Latin American Library at Tulane, has been invaluable to me over many years, specifically so on this project.

Finally, I should like to thank my wife, Barbara Edmonson, for letting me make free of her time and intelligence over many years, with the promise that I'll get back to cutting the hedge (and she can get back to her own research) before another *uinal* goes by.

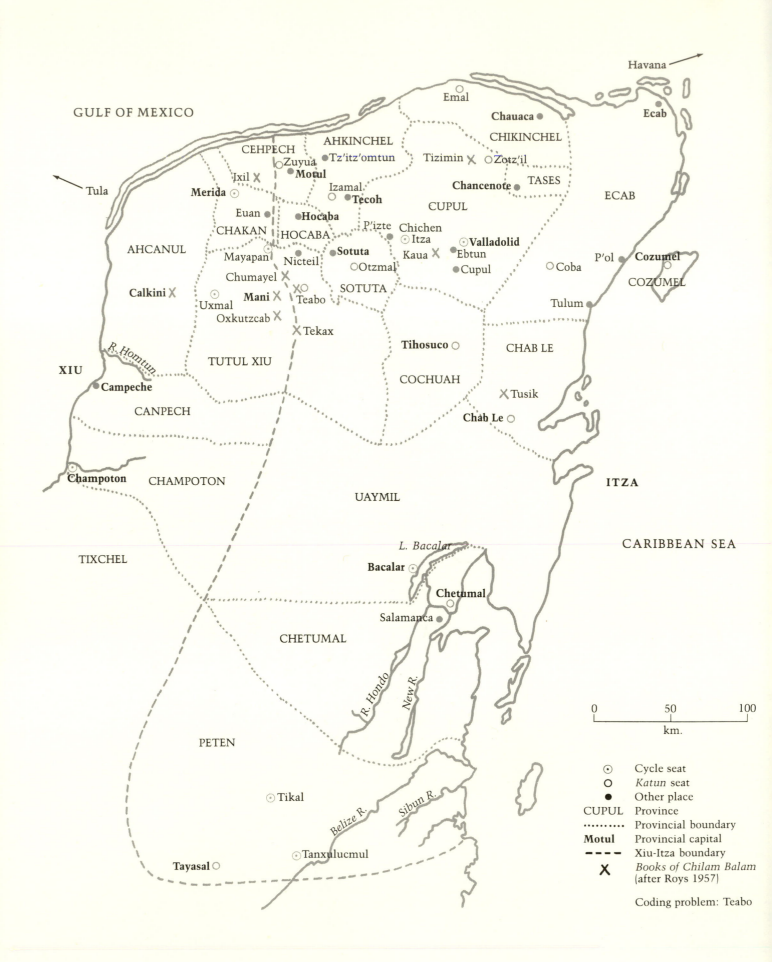

GULF OF MEXICO

Havana

Tula

Emal

CEHPECH

AHKINCHEL

Chauaca

Ecab

CHIKINCHEL

Zuyua

Tz'itz'omtun

Tizimin

Zotz'il

TASES

ECAB

Ixil

Motul

Merida

Izamal

Tecoh

Chancenote

Euan

Hocaba

CUPUL

CHAKAN

HOCABA

P'izte

Chichen
Itza

Valladolid

Mayapan

Sotuta

Kaua

Ebtun

Nicteil

Otzmal

Cupul

Coba

P'ol

Cozumel

Chumayel

COZUMEL

Calkini

Mani

Teabo

SOTUTA

Tulum

Uxmal

Oxkutzcab

Tekax

Tihosuco

CHAB LE

XIU

R. Homtun

TUTUL XIU

COCHUAH

Campeche

CANPECH

Tusik

Chab Le

CHAMPOTON

Champoton

CHAMPOTON

UAYMIL

ITZA

CARIBBEAN SEA

TIXCHEL

L. Bacalar

Bacalar

Chetumal

Salamanca

CHETUMAL

R. Hondo

New R.

0   50   100

km.

PETEN

Belize R.

Sibun R.

Tikal

⊙ Cycle seat

○ *Katun* seat

● Other place

CUPUL Province

.... Provincial boundary

Motul Provincial capital

– – – Xiu-Itza boundary

✗ *Books of Chilam Balam*
(after Roys 1957)

Coding problem: Teabo

Tayasal

Tanxulucmul

Introduction

The *Book*

The *Books of Chilam Balam* (Spokesmen of the Jaguar) of the Yucatecan Maya constitute a treasure-house of historic and ethnographic information collected by the Maya themselves over a period of many centuries. They are exasperatingly difficult to translate and interpret for a number of reasons. They are largely composed in archaic and elliptical language. Their chronology is obscured by esoteric numerological, astrological, and religious assumptions. The orthography of the surviving texts leaves a great deal to be desired. But most of all the *Books* reflect a world view and a sense of history that are distinctively Mayan.

An additional complication to the comprehension of these *Books* is the fact that they are by no means purely Mayan. They have been shaped by almost a thousand years of cultural confrontation—five centuries and more of ideological friction between the Yucatecan heirs to the Classic Mayan civilization and the invading groups of Nahuatl speakers from Central Mexico, followed by an almost equal period of conflict and accommodation between the Mexica-Mayan cultures and the European civilizations of Spain and Republican Mexico. The resulting history is dramatic and dynamic and reflects the influence of at least three thoroughly different cultures.

Among the twelve surviving *Books*, the *Book of Chilam Balam of Tizimin* is the most historical. Others come from Mani, Calkini, Ixil, Chumayel, Kaua, Teabo (three of them), Tekax, Oxkutzcab, and Tusik. The Tizimin was collected by the parish priest of Tizimin, Manuel Luciano Pérez, who sent it to his bishop in Merida in 1870 with the remark that it had been in his possession for a number of years (*muy buenos años*) (Barrera 1948:291). The original is now in the Museo Nacional de Antropología in Mexico City. I have worked from a photostatic copy in the Latin American Library at Tulane University. All of the forty-two texts of the Tizimin except chapters 9 and 22 to 25 are parallel to passages in one or more of the other *Books*—those of Mani, Chumayel, or Kaua, all of which include additional materials of a less historical order: medical, exegetical, astronomical, liturgical, or literary. Taken by itself, however, the *Book of Tizimin* constitutes an outline history of Yucatan from the seventh century to the nineteenth, with explicit coverage of each *katun* (approximately twenty years) from 1441 to 1848.

This is history in the Mayan manner. It is dominated by a sense of cyclical repetition and by a profound faith that correct calendrical calculation will enable the priests to predict the fate of the next cycle. In most instances the cycle in question is that of the *katun*, a period of 7,200 days

opposite: Tizimin geography

(or twenty *tuns* of 360 days each). It was to be expected that each *katun* would repeat the fate of the preceding such period with the same numeral coefficient, there being thirteen sacred numerals to the count (see the appendix). The Tizimin itself makes it clear that the priests were expected both to predict and to record the events of each *katun*. The predictions (chapters 6, 9, 14, and 15) were taken seriously as guides to policy, and the recordings of recent events were taken seriously as guides to further predictions. The predictions, customarily drawn up five years before the beginning of the *katun*, were announced at his inauguration by the Jaguar (*Balam*)—its ruling lord. But it was also his duty (or that of his Spokesman—*Chilam*) to write the history of the *katun* five years after leaving office, as a basis for future prophecy. The burden of the *Book of Tizimin* may thus be accurately described as prophetic history—as the ancient past and the ineluctable future of the Mayan people.

Given these highly Mayan assumptions, the history of any one *katun* may be taken as equivalent to that of any other with the same number. There is no linear order to prophetic history. Nonetheless, I have found it possible to identify the primary reference of each passage of the Tizimin in European linear time, at least to the nearest twenty years, and I have therefore rearranged the passages in at least approximate historical order. A reader who wishes to follow the order of the original manuscript may do so by reading my chapters in the sequence listed in the table. Folio numbers are indicated together with corresponding passages in Barrera 1948 and Roys 1967, and folios are also indicated in the Mayan text of the present edition. There is usually, however, no way of judging the priority of several texts relating to the same *katun*. The plausibility of this reordering is indicated in the figure, which demonstrates that the incidence of Nahuatlisms (see "Nahuatl" in the index) appears to be roughly constant through (linear) time, while the incidence of Hispanicisms (see "Spanish" in the index) increases exponentially throughout the reordered text. Those texts I have placed as preconquest may have been preserved in oral or hieroglyphic form, and it is my belief that none of them was written in Latin letters before *katun* 9 Ahau (1559–1579).

Immediately after the Spanish conquest (that is, around 1548), the Franciscan missionaries to Yucatan, like those in the Valley of Mexico somewhat earlier, began instructing the children of the nobility in Spanish, Latin, and Mayan, and the Mayas promptly became literate in European alphabetic writing. The earliest surviving text known to me is a passage of the Chumayel written in 1556 (Edmonson 1976), but sections of the Tizimin were not written much later. The extant manuscripts of the *Books* are, however, later copies, and internal evidence (see note 5155) places the final composition of the Mani, Tizimin, and Chumayel manuscripts around 1824 to 1837. Various parts of the manuscripts are included in these extant versions in different orders, and some may have circulated independently for a time in oral, glyphic, or alphabetic form. There are consequently lexical, orthographic, semantic, and syntactic discrepancies among the texts that are suggestive of their varying histories. Thus, where the Tizimin has *ahau* (line 5368), the Chumayel has *rey*, a lexical substitution. Where the Tizimin has *Hauana* (line 5366), the Chumayel has *Havana*, an orthographic one. Where the Tizimin has *hum pis katun* (line 5202), the Chumayel has *lahun piz katun*, a semantic change (from

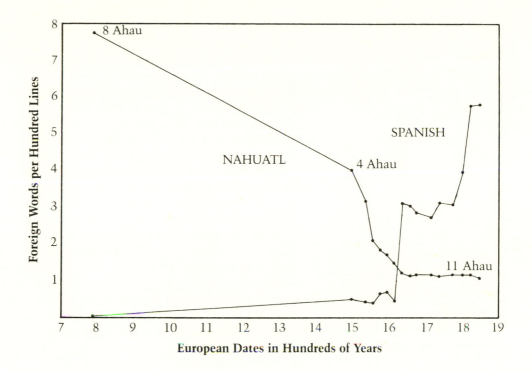

'one *katun*' to 'ten *katuns*'). And, where the Tizimin has *conolbil* (line 5304), the Chumayel has *conbil*, a syntactic variation (implying something like 'marketing places' rather than 'marketplaces'). Obviously a close comparative study of these texts would be most rewarding, but such a study has not been undertaken here.

The Translation

With minor exceptions, the orthography of the Mayan text is that of the original manuscript. To facilitate typesetting I have changed *c̄h* to *ch'*, *ɔ* to *tz'*, and *ɣ* to *y etel*. With the exception of some marginal notes (see chapter 24) apparently added in the mid nineteenth century, the Tizimin appears to have been recopied in a single hand, probably between 1824 and 1837 and probably in or near Tizimin itself. Word divisions are not standardized in the manuscript and I have made my own, but in no case have I altered the original order of the letters.

Some of the late texts (chapters 24, 25, 39, 40, and 41) are written in a relatively straightforward style. But all of them are in the poetic form of couplet parallelism that is customary in formal Mayan discourse (Edmonson 1971). They have been so transcribed and translated. Except in the chapters just cited, there is an additional poetic element: the extensive use of kennings or *difracismos* (Garibay 1953). Each particular couplet has both an obvious and a synthetic or esoteric meaning, which sometimes applies to many couplets at a time. Examples are listed in the index under "kennings." Hence I have found it necessary to prepare an interpretative prose translation, which is presented first and which is keyed to the corresponding numbered lines of the literal translation and the Mayan text and to the notes that follow. My surmises as to the meanings of the

Concordance

Chapter	Folio	Barrera	Roys
22	1r–7r	167	
42	7r–8v	158, 220	120
	9r–9v missing (see note 5514)		
15	10r		166
6	10r	196	166
14	10r	196	167
29	10r–10v	197	167
9	10v–11r		
10	11v	144	
12	11v–12v	147	
2	12v–13r	223	
11	13r	95	133
16	13v	98	
18	13v–14r	99	
21	14r	104	
26	14r	106	
27	14r–14v	110	
30	14v	112	
33	14v–15r	113	
34	15r	115	
35	15v	117	
37	15v–16r	118	133
13	16r	124	147
17	16r	126	149
19	16r–16v	128	151
20	16v	129	152
23	16v	131	153
28	16v–17r	133	155
31	17r–17v	137	158
32	17v	139	159
3	17v	140	160
4	17v	140	161
5	17v–18r	140	161
7	18r	141	162
8	18r	121	
38	18r–18v		
1	18v–19r	57	135
36	19r		
39	19r–19v	119	134
41	19v–20r	121	134
40	20v–21r		
25	21r–22r		
24	22r–27v		

complex puns, metaphors, and traditional religious symbolisms that are involved are mostly based on the repetitive contexts in which they appear within the Tizimin itself (see the index under "metaphor" and "pun"). I do not pretend to understand them all, but perhaps this mode of presentation will enable others to understand the basis of my judgments and to push on to further clarifications.

The scansion of Mayan poetry is complex because the principle is semantic. When it waxes lyrical, as in prayers and dramas, the couplet structure may be tightly signaled by a strict parallelism of syntactic form, with analogous or identical noun and verb inflections in the paired phrases. In other cases the structure may become quite loose. For example, a locative adverb like *te* 'there' may be paired with a locative noun phrase like *ti ho* 'at Merida'. Since one cannot scan it until the meaning is clear, scansion and translation form a kind of dialectic. If one of them becomes derailed, the other is bound to. I am aware that I have achieved neither perfect scansion nor perfect translation, and there are cases in which I have been poetically inconsistent. I remain uncertain, for instance, whether direct discourse falls inside or outside of the couplet structure, and I have sometimes made two lines in one context of an expression which appears as one line elsewhere. I remain persuaded that Mayan formal discourse tends strongly to couplets, whether or not they are syntactically marked. There are good and bad couplets, but I believe searching for them is in either case a significant aid to translation and an important aspect of the translator's task.

The *Book of Tizimin* has not been adequately translated before. The only other complete translation (Makemson 1951) is so seriously flawed that I have not tried to use it (see note 1570 and the review in Thompson 1951). Barrera Vásquez has a draft translation which I have not seen. I have consulted a transcription and a partial translation and notes by Roys (n.d.). The most relevant published works are Barrera's 1948 translation of the reconstructed text, based on the Tizimin, Chumayel, Mani, and Kaua versions, and Roys' 1967 translation of the Chumayel. In addition, the First Chronicle (chapter 1) has been translated and published by Brinton (1882) and Martínez Hernández (1940). I have commented on these translations where relevant in the notes.

Students of the *Books of Chilam Balam* will have noted the really extraordinary discrepancies between one translator and the next (see notes 579, 1239, and 1570). I cannot but agree with Barrera that these are texts of quite unusual difficulty. The *Popol Vuh* is a model of explicitness and clarity by comparison. All scholars who wrestle with colonial texts in the Indian languages of Middle America must cope with archaism and homonymy—multiplied by textual, orthographic, and lexicographic inadequacies. But these texts are purposely obscure. They are not intended to make sense to outsiders—and they don't.

I have the highest regard for the previous scholarship in this field, particularly for the contributions of Barrera and Roys. It is with diffidence that I dare to disagree with them. But it may be that many of the discrepancies are a consequence of method. I have chosen to translate the Tizimin blind, without prior consultation of the previous attempts or prior knowledge of the detailed parallel Spanish history of Yucatan. My endeavor was to gain an unbiased and presumably Mayan—or at least endogenous—view of the work. I believe I have done that. While my confidence has been shaken or my interpretation changed by some items of subsequent reading, others have encouraged me to stick to my guns.

In learning Yucatecan Maya, I depended first on the production of a general dictionary incorporating all entries in Brasseur 1872, Pío Pérez 1866–67, Swadesh, Alvarez, and Bastarrachea 1970, Blair and Vermont-Salas 1965, and Solís Alcalá 1949, plus additional vocabulary from Roys 1931 and 1967, Redfield 1941, Tozzer 1941, and a substantial part of the Motul dictionary. I then prepared a root dictionary of my own (Edmonson n.d.b). I have also consulted Martínez Hernández 1929, Pacheco Cruz 1969, and Pío Pérez 1898. I lay no claim to speaking the language, but the language of the Tizimin is no longer spoken in any case.

Besides the problems presented by the copyist's errors, the manuscript gives no reliable indication of vowel length and no real phrase or sentence punctuation or word division. Furthermore, the language is archaic. Even the latest passages are about 150 years old, and the earliest ones may go back 500 years or even more. In the First Chronicle, for example, we read: *uac Ahau chuc cu lumil Chakan Putun* (lines 49–52). If my translation is correct, this would be expressed in modern Maya something like: *tz'oc u cubsic u lumil Chakan Putun e le uac Ahau i* 'six Ahau finished the seating of the lands of Champoton'. The form *le* 'the', which is ubiquitous in modern Maya, does not occur at all in the Tizimin. The rare verb *chuc* strikes me as archaic in comparison with *tz'oc* 'finish'. Modern Maya would almost certainly use some form of *cub, cul,* or *cut* for 'sit, seat' rather than *cu,* which is also an archaism, and it would make freer use of pronouns (*u*) and demonstratives (*e, i*). While the verb-object-subject ordering of noun phrases is not compulsory in modern Maya, it is much the commonest.

Verbs with aspect markers (*c, h, t*), which I believe to be the only true verbs in Maya, together with fully expressed pronominal subjects and objects, are the exception rather than the rule in the Tizimin. There is instead a marked addiction to participial and substantival constructions depending for their verbal force upon the Mayan lack of the verb 'to be'. Thus (lines 170–175): *ox lahun tun man i tz'ulob u yax ilc ob u lumil Yucatan* 'thirteen (Ahau) then (was) the passing (of) the foreigners; (it was) their first sighting of the lands of Yucatan'.

The style of the older texts particularly is terse but elegant. They are meant to be read and pondered rather than skimmed over or recited. I have tried to translate as literally as possible, representing every linguistic element of the Mayan text in English to the degree I could. Although indications of subject and object are often delayed for several phrases or clauses, leaving a literal translation quite stilted in English, I have nonetheless followed the Mayan order of things in order to preserve the couplet structure of the original. Every couplet in turn is represented in my interpretative translation, also in order, although I have felt free to alter the syntax to render more clearly what I think the text means. I have not changed the order of the ideas, but I have changed passive and participial to active constructions, broken the sentences at different points, and introduced my own paragraphing. Not all details are preserved in the interpretation, but they will be found in the literal translation, the Mayan text, and the index.

The Itza

What follows is a summary of the substantive content of the *Book of Tizimin*. It is not footnoted because the *Book* itself is the documentation for the assertions made. Specific points may be tracked down in the index, and additional references are provided in the notes to particular passages. If aspects of this treatment sound unfamiliar to Mayanists, that is because I find reason to disagree with a number of traditionally accepted viewpoints. Specifically, these include the interpretation of the colonial calendars, the nature of the post-Classic and colonial political and religious systems, and the relationship between the Xiu and the Itza. The *Books* differentiate clearly between the Chichen Itzas and the Peten Itzas, but they call them both Itzas.

The story of the Tizimin is the story of the Itza or Water Witches, a group of elite lineages who dominated the eastern half of the Yucatan Peninsula in the post-Classic and colonial periods. It is also the story of the *katun*, since the Itza claim to have established Chichen Itza as the seat of the thirteen-*katun* cycle (*may*) in *katun* 8 Ahau (672–692). According to the Tizimin, the Itza were joined a century later by the Toltec Xiu, a grouping of similarly elite lineages who dominated western Yucatan and Campeche until the seventeenth century and who claimed an ancestral seat at Tula itself. I believe these traditions to be essentially mythological as they relate to the Classic period but find no reason to mistrust the account from the tenth century on.

The Itza and the Xiu agreed that the right to seat the cycle conferred upon the city that did it dynastic and religious primacy over the whole country for 260 *tuns* (approximately 256 years). At the end of that time the primate city and its road and idols were ritually destroyed, and a new cycle seat was established. The Itza and Xiu disagreed, however, on the correct timing of the cycle, the Itza maintaining that it ran from 11 Ahau to 13 Ahau and the Xiu insisting that it went from 6 Ahau to 8 Ahau (see the appendix and the index under "calendar" and "cycle").

In 6 Ahau (948–968), the Itza seated the cycle in Champoton, where they ruled until the following 8 Ahau (1185–1204). Presumably under Xiu pressure, they destroyed Champoton and spent forty years wandering in the wilderness, finally settling at Chichen Itza. In 2 Ahau (1244–1263), the Xiu of Uxmal and the Itza of Chichen Itza compromised and agreed to seat the cycle at Mayapan, which was centrally located and was to be ruled jointly. This alliance, known as the League of Mayapan, lasted until 1451.

When the fateful *katun* 8 Ahau came around again (1441–1461), the Xiu governor of Mayapan, Hunac Ceel, entered into a conspiracy with the illegitimate Itza lord of Izamal, Can Ul, overthrowing and sacrificing the Itza rain priest of Chichen Itza, Xib Chac, and capturing and destroying Mayapan in 1451. The Tizimin gives a *katun* by *katun* account of Mayan history from this time down to the *katun* before the Caste War of the middle nineteenth century.

In addition to the mystique of the *katun* cycle, the *katuns* themselves were religiously and politically important. The seat of the cycle enjoyed an overall preeminence, but the actual rule of the country was vested in the lord of the *katun*, the Jaguar (*Balam*) and his Spokesman (*Chilam*), and was supposed to rotate among the subsidiary cities. Commonly more than one city claimed the honor, which conferred tribute rights, control of land titles, and appointments to public office. Even the ruined cities lent their prestigious names to the seating of the *katun*, and at various dates between 1461 and 1539 the privilege was claimed by Chichen Itza, Izamal, Uxmal, Tihosuco, Coba, and Emal.

Early in the sixteenth century, the war of the *katuns*—or *katun* of the wars (*u katun katunob*)—between the Xiu and the Itza was exacerbated by the arrival of the Spanish. The result was a formal bifurcation of the politico-religious system and, coincidentally, a major calendrical reform, which was promulgated at the beginning of 11 Ahau: 11.16.0.0.0 (1539). The Itza continued to consider Mayapan to be the seat of the cycle, and they seated the *katun* at Emal. The Xiu established Merida as the seat of both the cycle and the *katun*. In effect, the peninsula was divided into eastern and western jurisdictions along a north–south line running right through Mayapan. A new calendar was announced at Mayapan, with new yearbearers, a new count of the twenty-day *uinals* (from 1–20 instead of 0–19), and a count of the *katuns* by initial date rather than by terminal date (see the appendix). This calendar, universally used by the colonial Yucatecans from 1539 to 1752, is in agreement with Landa's statement that the Mayan new year fell on Sunday, July 16, 1553 (see Edmonson 1976).

The Flower *katun* 11 Ahau thus initiated a new Itza cycle, which was also the cycle of the Spanish Empire and ended very nearly with the empire in 1824, at the end of 13 Ahau. The Itza of the sixteenth century found themselves embattled on several fronts, being opposed by the Spanish secular and religious authorities, the Xiu nobility, who found it convenient to become Christians, and the merchants and peasants of both the east and the west (often also Christianized), who objected to paying tribute to the Itza as well as taxes to the Spanish. Lowborn claimants to the lordship of the *katun* sprang up everywhere, supported by rebellious guerrilla companies in the woods who made it dangerous and eventually impossible for the legitimate lords to complete their ceremonial visits to collect tribute and confirm titles. Few lords of the *katun* completed their terms of office. The military companies were not brought under control until the middle of the seventeenth century, and peasant rebellions continued long after that.

The Xiu had a long-standing tradition of accommodating foreign culture. They were considerably more Mexicanized than the Itza even in the post-Classic period. After the conquest they accommodated similarly to Christianity and attempted to justify their stance in terms of Mayan prophecy. By the early seventeenth century, they apparently had lost interest in the Mayan political game and did not claim to seat the *katun* after 1 Ahau (1638–1658). Merida had become the Spaniards' city.

The Itza were more resistant. From the outset of the Spanish conquest they were troubled by the possible implications of the European calendar, particularly by the seven-day week, which (leap years being ignored) appeared to represent a new class of yearbearer that the Maya hadn't thought of. While the Xiu tried to accommodate the Mexican fifty-two year divinatory cycle and the Christian year by inventing a twenty-year (rather than twenty-*tun*) "*katun*" (see chapter 22), the Itza clung to the

Pencil drawing of restored structures at Mayapan, Yucatan, by Tatiana Proskouriakoff. Courtesy of the Peabody Museum, Harvard University. Photograph by Hillel Burger.

traditional *katun* and sacrificed the false lords whenever they could lay hands on them. Even the Itza had to give way, however, and in 1611 the Itza lord of the *katun*, Ol Zip of Emal, converted to Christianity. This was in the fourth *katun* after the corresponding conversion of the Tutul Xiu of Mani, but the Xiu and the Itza had always been four *katuns* apart.

By 3 Ahau (1618–1638), the Itza had managed to incorporate the Christian week into their cosmology, and the Tizimin gives the auguries of the days and the detailed divinatory significance of each day as a yearbearer (see chapter 25). While the Xiu were being assimilated as a peasant proletariat in and around Merida, the Itza lords were becoming independent peasant farmers in the eastern areas, increasingly preoccupied with weather, harvests, and the agricultural calendar. Nonetheless, they retained a lively interest in theology and in the traditional *katun* calendar, and they continued to read and ponder their prophetic histories.

The Itza took their prophecies very seriously indeed. One group which had fled south after the fall of Mayapan and resettled at Tayasal on Lake Peten rejected as calendrically premature the efforts of Cortés in 13 Ahau (1539) and of Fuensálida and Orbita in 3 Ahau (1618) to Christianize them. But when the appropriate *katun* 8 Ahau approached (1697–1717) they knew the time was right, and in 1695 they sent an embassy to Merida to ask the governor to convert them. Obliging with their usual obtuse alacrity, the Spaniards arrived before 8 Ahau began and forced the Indians into armed opposition. But true to the prophecy it was in 8 Ahau that Tayasal was conquered. (For a detailed documentation of this event, see Bricker 1981.)

In 1752, five years before the end of *katun* 4 Ahau, the Itza resolved upon another calendrical revision. It happened that in that year the name day of the *katun* fell on the second day of the Mayan year. Furthermore, the Itza cycle was due to end two *katuns* later, in 13 Ahau, with apocalyptic implications. The priests calculated that, if they redefined the *katun* as a period of twenty-four years instead of twenty *tuns*, they could always celebrate the seating of the *katun* on its eve, on the Mayan new year. If they further redefined the cycle (*may*) as twenty-four such *katuns* beginning from the 11 Ahau of the conquest, it would not end until 2088, a distinct advantage over surrendering legitimacy in 1776. *Katun* 4 Ahau was therefore reseated in 1752, hence lasting for thirty-nine years, and Valladolid (Zaciapan) was made the seat of the new cycle and also the seat of *katun* 2 Ahau (1776–1800). Just as the Mayapan calendar of 1539 adjusted Mayan terminal dating to Mexican initial dating, the Valladolid calendar of 1752 adjusted the Mayan calendar to the Julian one. The cost was the final abandonment of the true *katun* and hence of the Classic Mayan Long Count dating (see the appendix).

Despite the brilliance of the Valladolid calendar, there may well have been Mayas, including Itzas, who remained uneasy about 13 Ahau, the traditional end of the Itza cycle. One such may be responsible for the aberrant fifty-two-year calendar of chapter 41, which appears to have been designed in 1758 and may be identified with Coba. It retains the yearbearers of the Mayapan calendar but alters their numeral coefficients by twenty-one years (presumably the twenty-one years between the beginning of 4 Ahau in 1737 and the writing of chapter 41 in 1758). There is no evidence that this calendar was adopted by anyone but its author. Other similar experiments occurred sporadically in Mayan history: see the twenty-eight-year cycle of the early seventeenth century (lines 3531 ff.). A further experiment of this type may be implied by the marginal notes to chapter 24, probably added in 9 Ahau (1848–1872), which give Type I yearbearers and an ecclesiastical calendar attuned to the Gregorian one (see the appendix and Satterthwaite 1965).

The final chapter of the Tizimin continues to identify itself as Itza in the very last line. But this is a new Itza cycle that is initiated in 1824—or so its author appears to believe. It claims the mantle of all the gods, the privilege of prophetic vision, the tradition of the Spokesmen of the Jaguar Priest of the *katun*, and the aegis of the 4 Gods, yearbearers and rain giants of the four directions. It honors Mayapan and Christianity. And it predicts and records the ending of tribute to the Spaniards as well as the Caste War.

Perhaps the most startling aspect of the *Book of Tizimin* when it is viewed historically is the autistic disjunction between Mayan and Spanish views of the same broad epoch. There are consistent correspondences on numerous points, but the focus of attention is totally different. The Spaniards chronicled their *entradas*, the sequences of their officials, their laws, discoveries, and conquests. They themselves appear in Itza history, however, as an annoying but shadowy and largely irrelevant presence, alluded to by nicknames. Their tribute was regarded as a temporary burden, destined to be returned at the appropriate time. The thrust of Mayan history is a concern with Indian lords and priests, with the cosmology that justified their rule, and with the Indian civil war that was perceived as the real dimension of colonial history.

In effect, this is a secret history. Certainly the Spaniards remained largely oblivious to the continued existence of a traditional Mayan government in Yucatan and ignorant of the ideology that supported it. It is astonishing to learn from the Tizimin that the ancient Mayan cities— Mayapan, Uxmal, Chichen Itza, Coba, even Merida itself—continued to serve as symbolic reference points for a lively and indigenous religious and political life centuries after their pyramids had fallen into ruins. It is startling to find Chichen Itza still collecting tribute in the middle eighteenth century!

Even though these pages depict its decline, Mayan civilization here presents us with a strong sense of continuity, sophistication, and vitality. While we cannot read Itza history as a direct guide to events of the Classic period, the ideology of cyclic history doubtless both preceded and followed the period that is here described. And the end of the cycle is not yet.

THE SEVENTH CENTURY

8 Ahau

---

1. The First Chronicle

From the end of the Xiu cycle in 692 to 751, and then came the end of the Itza cycle in 771. (10)

(18v) Uaxac Ahau* 8 Ahau (692),
  Uac Ahau   6 Ahau (711),
Can Ahau 4 Ahau (731),
  Cabil Ahau   Second Ahau (751)
Ca kal hab* 5 Forty years,
  Ca tac   And then followed
Hum ppel hab One year,
  T u hum pis tun   Which was the first *tun*

Ah ox lahun Ahau Of 13 Ahau (771).
  Ox lahun Ahau.* 10   It was 13 Ahau.

---

1. This text, together with the two other early chronicles in the Mani and the Chumayel (Barrera 1948: 68 ff.; Roys 1967: 139 ff.), is unquestionably the oldest sketch of Mayan history we have. While the Chumayel contains one text that can be dated to 1556 (Edmonson 1976), it is likely that nothing in the Tizimin was transcribed from glyphs before 9 Ahau (1559). A glyphic version of this chronicle could have been composed in 13 Ahau (1539) but could also have drawn on glyphic predecessors. I consider the claim of the Itza to have ruled Chichen Itza (and that of the Xiu to have come from Tula) in 8 Ahau (692) to be legend or myth, but the tale seems to be substantially historical from the following 8 Ahau (948) on. See the appendix on chronology.

All the earliest chronicles are preoccupied with the sequence and dates at which various cities became the seats of the cycle. Taken together, the sources provide us with the following outline.

Date	Xiu	Itza	Other
8 Ahau (692)	Tula	Chichen Itza	Bacalar
8 Ahau (948)		Champoton	
2 Ahau (1263)	Uxmal	Mayapan	
8 Ahau (1461)			Tayasal
11 Ahau (1539)	Merida		
4 Ahau (1752)		Valladolid	

5. Barrera 1948: 59 has eighty.

10. The significance of this date is that it ends the Itza *may*, or cycle of thirteen *katuns*. The Itza counted from 11 Ahau to 13 Ahau; the Xiu count ran from 6 Ahau to 8 Ahau, as does the Chumayel text. The Tizimin and Mani chronicles

(note continued on following page)

From 692 to 751, then the
East priest Bi Ton arrived, the

····   ·· ·   ⟨⟨⟨   ⟨⟨⟨   ⟨⟨⟨

Uaxac Ahau*   8 Ahau (692),
 Uac Ahau   6 Ahau (711),
(Can Ahau)*   (4 Ahau) (731),
 Caa Ahau   2 Ahau (751).
Kuchc i   15 Then arrived
 Chac Na Bi Ton*   The East priest Bi Ton,

(note continued from preceding page)

begin with 8 Ahau rather than 6 Ahau but otherwise agree with the Xiu. The beginning date is thus the end of *katun* 8 Ahau on 9.13.0.0.0 8 Ahau 8 Uo, March 18, 692.

11. The count now repeats.

13. 4 Ahau has been omitted.

16. Chac Na Bi Ton: the East priest (Chac) and chief of the Toltec Xiu. The prefix Na 'mother' commonly introduces the matronymic, in this case Bi 'roll', and the patronymic comes last: Ton 'lame'. Barrera 1948: 59 and Brinton 1882: 144 consider this a place-name.

The place-names of Yucatan are difficult to identify and often difficult to locate (see Roys 1935). Frequently they are introduced by the locative *ti* 'at', and the names of many of the smaller towns follow this with Ix 'little'. A few towns have monosyllabic names; more commonly the name is inflected or compounded, and names of four or more elements are not unknown (ti Ix Peton Cah, ti Ix Kil Itzam Pech). Numeral prefixes of unknown significance occur occasionally: Hun Uc Ma, Cabil Neb A, Ox Cum, Can Uat Hom, Ho Tzuc Chakan, Uuc y Ab Nal, Uaxac Tun, Bolon Ch'och', Lahun Chab Le, and Ox Lahun Zuyua. Numbers above 13 do not seem to occur. Otherwise, since there appear to have been eighteen provinces (see note 777), I would be tempted to guess that they were numbered in relation to the *uinals*. The numeral prefix is invariant over time for any one town.

Classificatory elements are common in place-names: A or Ha 'water', Cab or Luum 'lands', Hol Tun 'water hole', Tun 'rock', Cah 'town', Ch'een 'well', Puc 'hill', and Tz'onot 'cenote'. Animal and plant names are frequent descriptive elements: snail, deer, turkey, iguana, alligator, puma, squirrel, bat, rabbit, dove, and skunk in the first category, gourdroot, balche, guano palm, caoba, custard apple, banana, chile, nance, corn, and ceiba in the second. Construction features occur occasionally: mounds, walls, ovens, and plazas. Color names with directional associations are frequent. There is a surprising dearth of Nahuatl place-names. I have found only five: Tizimin (*Tzimentlan*), *Mayapan*, Yucatan (*Yucatlan*), Valladolid (*Zaciapan*), and *Zuyua*.

The interpretation of personal names presents several difficulties (Roys 1940). While it seems likely that calendrical names were used even after the conquest, they are extremely rare. Examples are 7 Eb and 5 Xochitl. Numeral elements are sometimes prefixed to surnames without any accompanying day name, as in 8 Ol Kauil, 11 Ch'ab Tan, or 7 Sat Ay. I believe these to be priestly titles. Occasionally a numeral appears to be used as a surname, as in Lahun Chan, Cab Bech', or Hun Pic. The typical naming system is binomial, and most commonly both names are monosyllabic, the first being a matronym and the second a patronym, as in Yax Cutz, Can Ul, Kak Mo, or Can Ek. Often the matronym is preceded by Na—Na Pot Xiu, Na Ahau Pech, or Na Puc Tun—but this appears to be optional. Sometimes the name is preceded by Ah, as in Ah Muzen Cab or Ah Kin Chil, implying priesthood or a collective: the man and his family. Women's names may *very* occasionally be identified by the prefix Ix, as in Ix Tab or Ix Kalem, but I believe that this element is far more commonly the simple conjunction 'and'. Both Roys and Barrera have in my opinion provided us with an entirely excessive list of goddesses.

Very commonly either surname may take the suffix -*il* or -Vl, an abstractive, again with collective meaning, but this is also optional: Chac Hub, Chac Hubil or Ul Ahau, Ulil Ahau. Additional elements may precede or follow the name, apparently for differentiating people of similar names. These may be prefix titles, such

(note continued on following page)

chief of the Toltec Xiu. It was
710. (20)
   From 692 when Chichen Itza

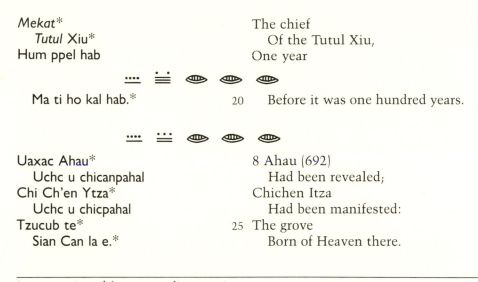

Mekat*	The chief
Tutul Xiu*	Of the Tutul Xiu,
Hum ppel hab	One year

Ma ti ho kal hab.*   20   Before it was one hundred years.

Uaxac Ahau*	8 Ahau (692)
Uchc u chicanpahal	Had been revealed;
Chi Ch'en Ytza*	Chichen Itza
Uchc u chicpahal	Had been manifested:
Tzucub te*	25 The grove
Sian Can la e.*	Born of Heaven there.

(note continued from preceding page)

as Ahau 'lord', Ah Kin 'sun priest', Chilam 'spokesman', Ah Bobat 'prophet', Ah Miatz 'sage', or Nacom 'captain'. Color words and numerals may also serve as titles, referring to the directional priesthoods or those of the numeral gods: (1) Chac 'red, east', (2) Zac 'white, north', (3) Ek 'black, west', (4) Kan 'yellow, south', (5) Yax 'green blue, center', (6) Uac Chu Uah, (7) Uuc Sat Ay, (8) Uaxac y Ol Kauil, (9) Bolon y Oc Te, (10) ?Lahun Chan (Lah Hun Chan), and (11) Buluc Ch'ab Tan. Again, higher numerals do not appear.

Following the patronym, additional elements of a similar kind may be appended, as in Na Tzin Yabun Chan: Tzin Yabun the Younger, or Hun Pic ti Ax: Hun Pic from Ax. A considerable ambiguity is created by the overlapping of categories of personal names, titles, place-names, day names, and colors. Thus Chac is a lineage name, a title (rain priest), a color (red), a place, a god, and an epithet (strong). Many of the traditional surnames have been continued into modern times, which is sometimes helpful in identifying them: Xiu, Ay, Pot, Bak, Pat, Puc, etc. The commonest lineage names in the Tizimin are Can, Ku, Ay, Ahau, Hun, Tun, and Chan in that order. The runners-up are Chac, Hub, Ol, Nab, Pat, Puc, Ul, Tz'itz', and Yan.

17. *Mekat* 'chief' from Nahuatl *mecatl* 'tumpline', implying a cargo bearer or bearer of the burden of the *katun*. The title appears to be restricted to the Xiu, but the concept is Mayan as well: public office is a 'burden' (*cuch*).

18. Tutul Xiu 'Toltecs', traditionally the rulers of Uxmal 'windfall'. The name is significantly bilingual: Nahuatl *totollin* 'many reeds', with the Mayanized Nahuatl explanation *xiu* 'grasses'. It identifies an elite ethnic group rather than a lineage or a person. The Xiu were the nobility of the western half of the Yucatan Peninsula and were more influenced by Nahua and Spanish ideology than were the eastern Itza. They claimed identification with Nonohualco, Zuyua, Chiconauhtla, and "the great city of Tula" (Barrera 1948: 57–58).

20. That is, Bi Ton arrived in Yucatan one year before the end of 13 Ahau (771). Barrera 1948: 59 adds these ninety-nine years to 2 Ahau to arrive at 5 Ahau (1106).

21. We return to the starting date for the second time: 692.

23. Chi Ch'en Itza 'mouth of the well of the witches of water', the best known of the Mayan cities and the traditional seat of the Itza. Like the Xiu, the Itza were an elite ethnic group. Together they dominate the history of Yucatan in an east–west, quasi-moiety political system.

25. Tzucub Te 'grove of trees', a sacred grove, the most famous of which was always at the cycle seat, in this case Chichen Itza.

26. Siyan Can 'born of heaven' was the traditional sobriquet of the primate city of the cycle, here Chichen Itza. Barrera 1948: 59 cites the Motul translation of the phrase as 'accounts and words from the histories of serious sages' and identifies it with Bacalar. It is elsewhere applied to Mayapan, Merida, Valladolid, etc.

was the seat of the cycle to 731 to 771, the end of the Itza cycle, to 810 to 849 to 889, Chichen Itza ruled two hundred years. Then it was destroyed and they went to Champoton, the home of the imperial Itza. By 968 they finished subjugating the

(Uac Ahau)*	(6 Ahau) (711),
Can Ahau	4 Ahau (731),
Cabil Ahau	2 Ahau (751),

···· ≡ ⬬ ⬬ ⬬

Ox lahun Ahau	30	13 Ahau (771).
Lai tzolc i*		That was the counting
Pop		Of the mats.
Buluc Ahau		11 Ahau (790),
Bolon Ahau		9 Ahau (810),
Uuc Ahau	35	7 Ahau (830),
Ho Ahau		5 Ahau (849),
Ox Ahau		3 Ahau (869),
Hun Ahau*		1 Ahau (889).

···· ≡ ⬬ ⬬ ⬬

Lahun kal hab		Two hundred years
C u tepal Chi Ch'en Ytza*	40	Chichen Itza ruled.
Ca pax i		Then it was destroyed.
Ca bin ob		Then they went
T cahtal*		To the settlement
Chakan Putun*		Of Champoton,
Ti y anh i	45	Where there were then
Y otochob*		The homes
Ah Ytzaob		Of the Itza,
Ku y an uinicob i*		The gods who own men.
Uac Ahau		6 Ahau (968)
Chuc cu*	50	Completed the seating

27. Uac Ahau has been omitted.

31. The mats were counted at the end of the (Itza) *katun* cycle. Since mats were symbols of authority, frequently paired with thrones, counting them was a ritual confirmation of inherited ranks. Succession was not automatic; it involved an examination in ritual knowledge.

38. Barrera 1948: 60 continues this count down to 8 Ahau, which he interprets as 692.

40. That is, 692 to 889.

43. I read *ti cahtal*.

44. Chichen Itza was the primate city for 200 years. Then it was destroyed and the primacy was moved to Champoton. This occurred at the end of 8 Ahau or the beginning of 6 Ahau (ca. 948). A period of 40 years in the wilderness may have intervened. Being the seat of the cycle (*may cu*), as opposed to the seat (*hetz'*) of the *katun*, theoretically established dynastic preeminence for a period of 260 *tuns* (ca. 256 years). The Chumayel gives Chichen Itza the full 260 *tuns*; the Tizimin awards it 200; the Mani strips it to 120. Doubtless, political differences are involved, but the terminal date is not affected. Chakan Putun 'meadow swamp' is the modern Champoton. Barrera 1948: 140 translates the name as 'plain of *putun* chiles'. *Putun* also means 'Chontal' (Roys 1935: 4).

46. *Otoch* 'home' contrasts with *na* 'house' as a dwelling place as opposed to a residence. One implication may be that the Itza formerly lived in Champoton.

48. Barrera 1948: 60 has 'religious men'; Brinton 1882: 145 says 'holy men'. *Kuyan* 'bent' could also mean 'sacrificed people'.

50. The Chumayel places this in 4 Ahau. It must have been around the end of 6 Ahau and the beginning of 4 Ahau (968).

territory of Champoton. From 968 to 1047 to 1086 to 1125 to 1165 to 1204, then Champoton was destroyed, having been ruled for a cycle by the Itza, who then destroyed their home again and its road. For two katuns the Itza wandered in the wilderness, suffering: from 1204 to 1244, forty years. Then they resettled in Mayapan and destroyed the road of Champoton.

Lumil	Of the lands
Chakan Putun	Of Champoton.
Can Ahau	4 Ahau (987),
Cabil Ahau	Second Ahau (1007),

= = ◁ ◁ ◁

Ox lahun Ahau	55	13 Ahau (1027),
Buluc Ahau		11 Ahau (1047),
Bolon Ahau		9 Ahau (1066),
Uuc Ahau		7 Ahau (1086),
Ho Ahau		5 Ahau (1106),
Ox Ahau	60	3 Ahau (1125),
Hun Ahau		1 Ahau (1145),
Lah ca Ahau		12 Ahau (1165),
Lahun Ahau		10 Ahau (1185),

= ≡ ◁ ◁ ◁

Uaxac Ahau		8 Ahau (1204).
Paxc i	65	Destroyed
Chakan Putun*		Was Champoton.
Ox lahun kal hab		Two hundred sixty years
C u tepal Chakan Putun		Champoton was ruled
T u men Ytza uincob		By the Itza people.
Ca tal ob	70	Then they came on
U tzacl ob y otochob		And returned to their homes
T u ca ten		For the second time.
Ca u satah ob be*		They destroyed the road
Chakan Putun		Of Champoton.
Ca tz'it u katunil	75	For two parts of the *katun* cycle
Bi(n)ci ob Ah Ytzaob		The Itza went on
Y alan che		Beneath the trees,
Y alan haban		Beneath the bushes,
Y alan ak		Beneath the vines,
Ti num yaob	80	Where they suffered.
Uac Ahau		6 Ahau (1224),
Can Ahau		4 Ahau (1244):
Ca kal hab		Forty years,
Ca tal ob		Then they came
U hetz'	85	And established
Y otochob t u ca ten		Their homes again.
Ca u satah ob be		Then they destroyed the road
Chakan Putun		Of Champoton.

---

66. Coming to the end of its (Xiu) cycle, Champoton was destroyed in 1204. Another chronicle (Barrera 1948: 72) attributes the destruction to Kak u Pacat 'fire glance' and Tecuilli 'brazier', presumably Xiu. The Xiu did not believe that the Itza were programmed to rule Champoton any longer, so they drove them out to wander and suffer for forty years before establishing a new seat at Mayapan in 1263. This was the occasion for the founding of the League of Mayapan, allying that city with Uxmal (Xiu) and Chichen Itza (Itza). The rule of Mayapan itself was supposed to be shared.

73. Barrera 1948: 61 and Brinton 1882: 145 have 'lost the road'.

From 1204 to 1323 to 1362 to 1401 to 1441 they lived on the lands of Zuy Tok, a Toltec Xiu of Uxmal, which had been established for two hundred years. (104)

From 1283 to 1362 to 1401 to 1441, and in the final katun of the Xiu cycle, they destroyed the governors of Chichen Itza by the conspiracy of Hunac

Cabil Ahau		Second Ahau (1263),
Ox lahun Ahau	90	13 Ahau (1283),
Buluc Ahau		11 Ahau (1303),
Bolon Ahau		9 Ahau (1323),
Uuc Ahau		7 Ahau (1342),
Ho Ahau		5 Ahau (1362),
Ox Ahau	95	3 Ahau (1382),
Hun Ahau		1 Ahau (1401),
Lah ca Ahau		12 Ahau (1421),
Lahun Ahau		10 Ahau (1441).
U hetz'c i		They established
Cab Ah Sui Tok*	100	The land of Zuy Tok,
Tutul Xiu		A Tutul Xiu
Uxmal		Of Uxmal.
Lahun kal hab c uch i		Two hundred years had passed
Ca hetz'h ob lum Uxmal*		Since they established the land of Uxmal.
Buluc Ahau	105	11 Ahau (1303),
Bolon Ahau		9 Ahau (1323),
Uuc Ahau		7 Ahau (1342),
Ho Ahau		5 Ahau (1362),
Ox Ahau		3 Ahau (1382),
Hun Ahau	110	1 Ahau (1401),
Lah caa Ahau		12 Ahau (1421),
Lahun Ahau		10 Ahau (1441).
Uaxac Ahau		8 Ahau (1461)
Paxc i		They destroyed
U hal ach uinicil*	115	The governors
Chi Ch'en Ytza*		Of Chichen Itza
T u keban than*		By the sinful words
Hunac Ceel*		Of Hunac Ceel.

100. Zuy Tok 'flint knife', the Xiu lord of Uxmal in 1263 and the founder of a two hundred–year dynasty there. Barrera 1948: 61 reads this as meaning that Zuy Tok established himself in Uxmal in 2 Ahau (1007).

104. The text does not say so, but the preceding count of two hundred *tuns* leads up to 8 Ahau again. This is the critical 8 Ahau (1461) of the fall of Mayapan. The following lines return to Itza chronology and count down to the same date.

115. *Hal ach uinic* 'true virile man', the governor of a province or city, in this case the rain priest Xib Chac of Chichen Itza.

116. Brinton 1882: 146 has 'the ruler deserted (depopulated) Chichen Itza'.

117. The "sin" of Hunac Ceel was Xiu calendrical arrogance.

118. The fall of Mayapan was the epochal event of the preconquest period. See the discussion in Tozzer 1941: 32–34. Two different versions put the blame on

(note continued on following page)

Ceel, Cinteotl the Younger, Tzontecome, Tlaxcallan, Pantemitl, Xochihuehuetl, Itzcoatl, and Cacalacatl, the eight of them conspiring with Ul Ahau of Izamal. One full cycle—and they were destroyed by Hunac Ceel because of betrayal of information. From 1461 to 1500, in forty years, they finished off the part of Mayapan inside the

Ah *Sinteyut* Chan*
  Tzum Tecum
Taxcal
  Pantemit
Xuch Ueuet
  Ytzcoat
Kakalcat
  Lai u kaba
U uinicilob la e
  Uuc tul ob
T u men u uahal
  Uahob*
Y etel Ytzmal
  Ulil Ahau*
Ox lahun uutz'
  U katunilob*
Ca pax ob
  T u men Hunac Ceel
T u men u tz'abal
  U nat ob*
Uac Ahau
  Can Ahau
Ca kal hab
  Ca chuc i
U lumil ych paa
  *Mayapan**

Cinteotl Chan,
120   Tzontecome,
Tlaxcallan,
  Pantemitl,
Xochihuehuetl,
  Itzcoatl,
125 Cacalacatl:
  These are the names
Of the people there,
  The seven of them,
Because they were patting
130   Tortillas
With Izamal
  And Ul Ahau.
Thirteen folds
  Of the *katun* cycle,
135 Then they were destroyed
  By Hunac Ceel
Because of the giving away
  Of their knowledge.
6 Ahau (1480),
140   4 Ahau (1500):
Forty years.
  Then it was completed,
The land within the walls
  Of Mayapan,

(note continued from preceding page)

Hunac Ceel and on Can Ul, the usurping Itza governor of Izamal. The primacy of the *katun* cycle was at stake. The sequence of events is far from clear, but it involved the elimination of Xib Chac (who was succeeded by Kukul Can as governor of Chichen Itza) and a related dynastic dispute in Izamal. It culminated in an internal rebellion within the walls of Mayapan by seven Xiu lords, and Mayapan was destroyed in accordance with the Xiu time schedule. The Mani gives the most precise date for the destruction of Mayapan: 1451 (Barrera 1948: 71). All sources agree that it occurred in *katun* 8 Ahau (1461), though Barrera 1948: 62 puts Hunac Ceel in 1204. Tozzer 1941: 32–34 identifies Hunac Ceel with Kukul Can.

119. The Mani makes it clear that the seven "Hummingbird" or "Highland" (Uitzil) lords, Xius resident in Mayapan, were responsible for the destruction of the city in 1451 (Barrera 1948: 64). They are not named in the Chumayel, but they all bear binomial ones in the post-Classic Mayan fashion: Cinteotl 'corn god' Chan 'the younger', Tzontecome 'skull grandfathers', Tlaxcallan 'tortilla house', Pantemitl 'flag bearer', Xochihuehuetl 'flower elder', Itzcoatl 'flint snake', and Cacalacatl 'crow cane'. Barrera 1948: 62 gives Cacaltecatl 'crow people'.

130. "Patting tortillas with" implies "playing footsie with": conspiring. Barrera 1948: 63 and Brinton 1882: 147 convert this into banquets.

132. Ulil Ahau 'snail lord', governor of Itzmal 'lizards' in the 1450s. Both the Ul and the Ahau lineages remained prominent at Izamal into the seventeenth century. Barrera 1948: 63 has Ulmil, implying 'turkey people'.

134. Brinton 1882: 147 translates this as 'thirteen divisions of warriors'.

138. Barrera 1948: 63 has 'to teach the Itzas a lesson'.

144. *Mayapan*: Mayan *may* 'cycle' plus Nahuatl *-apan* 'water place', the holy and primate city of the Itza from the end of the Classic period (ca. 987–1007),

(note continued on following page)

walls, Ul Ahau and the Itza, because of the deceit of Hunac Ceel. (148)

From 1244 to 1323 to 1362 to 1401 to 1441, then in the katun ending in 1461, Mayapan was dismantled by the mob that had seized the walls of the city. (166)

From 1461 to 1533: then the

T u men Ytza uincob
  Y etel Ulmil Ahau
T u men u keban than
  Hunac Ceel

Cabil Ahau

  Ox lahun Ahau
Buluc Ahau
  Bolon Ahau
Uuc Ahau
  (19r) Ho Ahau
Ox Ahau
  Hun Ahau
Lah ca Ahau
  Lahun Ahau

Uaxac Ahau
  Uchc i*
Puch' tun ich paa
  Mayapan
T u men u pach tulum*
  T u men mul tepal
Ich cah
  Mayapan

Uac Ahau
  (Can Ahau)
Cabil Ahau
  Ox lahun tun

145 By the Itza people
  And Ul Ahau
  Because of the sinful words
    Of Hunac Ceel.

Second Ahau (1263),

150   13 Ahau (1283),
  11 Ahau (1303),
    9 Ahau (1323),
  7 Ahau (1342),
    5 Ahau (1362),
155 3 Ahau (1382),
  1 Ahau (1401),
  12 Ahau (1421),
  10 Ahau (1441).

8 Ahau (1461)
160   There was
  Crushed stone inside the walls
    Of Mayapan
  Because of the seizure of the walls
    By crowd rule
165 In the city
  Of Mayapan.

6 Ahau (1480),
  (4 Ahau) (1500),
Second Ahau (1520),
170   The thirteenth *tun*,

(note continued from preceding page)

when it was first called Born of Heaven, to 1752, and perhaps to 1824 for at least some Itzas. Barrera 1948: 99 translates the name as 'deer standard'. It was the largest walled city of the post-Classic period; hence it is often referred to as Pa Cabal 'fort of the lands' or just as Pa 'fort'. After its destruction in 1451, it continued to be a ceremonial center, but the ceremonies were often held "outside the walls," and it acquired a new nickname: Tzucub Te, or Sacred Grove. Centrally located, it was the storm center of Mayan politics during the post-Classic and colonial periods. The modern name of the Maya may be derived from Mayapan but does not appear in the Tizimin until 4 Ahau (1737), despite the fact that it was known to Columbus and used constantly in the Chumayel. See Tozzer 1941: 7 on the origin of the name.

160. Barrera 1948: 63 has 'the land of Ichpa-Mayapan was seized by those from outside the walls—because of the multiple government inside Mayapan'. Brinton 1882: 147 says 'fighting took place in the fortress of Mayapan, on account of the seizure of the castle, and on account of the joint government in the city of Mayapan'.

163. Tulum 'walls' is a dramatic Mayan site on the Caribbean coast; here, however, the reference is to the walls of Mayapan. The walled city of Tulum is not mentioned in the Tizimin.

Spanish first saw Yucatan, eighty years after the fall of Mayapan, in the final katun *of the cycle. From 1539 to 1618 to 1658 to 1737 to 1800 to 1848! (192)*

Man i	There came
Tz'ulob	The foreigners,
U yax ilc ob	And first saw
U lumil	The lands
Yucatan*	175 Of Yucatan
Tzucub te	And the grove,
Can kal hab	Eighty years (after the fall of Mayapan),

Ca tac ox lahun pis i	And then was the thirteenth measure.
Buluc Ahau	11 Ahau (1539),
Bolon Ahau	180 9 Ahau (1559),
Uuc Ahau	7 Ahau (1579),
Ho Ahau	5 Ahau (1598),
Ox Ahau	3 Ahau (1618),
Hun Ahau	1 Ahau (1638),
Lah ca Ahau	185 12 Ahau (1658),
Lahun Ahau	10 Ahau (1677),
Uaxac Ahau	8 Ahau (1697),
Uac Ahau	6 Ahau (1717),
Can Ahau	4 Ahau (1737),
Cabil Ahau	190 Second Ahau (1776),
Ox lahun Ahau	13 Ahau (1800),
Buluc Ahau.*	11 Ahau (1824).

175. *Yucatlan*: Nahuatl 'plantation place', first seen by the Spaniards perhaps in 1507 (Aguilar) and 1511 (Valdivia), more definitely by Ponce de León in 1513. There were additional *entradas* by Córdoba (1517), Grijalva (1518), Cortés (1519), and Montejo (1526). In the 1530s it was approached from the west via Campeche. See Closs 1976 for a partial summary and discussion. The *katun* of the fall of Mayapan ended in the Mayan year 1461. The text is dating the distance from that to the end of 13 Ahau, which is eighty *tuns*.

192. This last count takes us from 1539 to 1816 in the preconquest chronology (1824 in the calendar of Valladolid) and ends on the first *katun* of a new Itza cycle. The whole chronicle shows a mixture of Xiu and Itza influences, but the Itza view predominates.

THE FIFTEENTH CENTURY

8 Ahau

---

2. The Fall of Mayapan

By 1461 it was the Xiu time to decorate the city for the 13 Gods.

(12v) Uaxac Ahau*
　U kin
U mis kiuic
　Ix chan cab*
Ca em i
　U than ox lahun ku

8 Ahau
　Was the time
195 To sweep the marketplace
　And the little plazas,
　When there descended
　The word of the 13 Gods.

---

193. Although this text was written after the conquest in 9 Ahau (1559), it refers mainly to events of the period of the fall of Mayapan in 8 Ahau (1461) from the Itza point of view. From this 8 Ahau to 13 Ahau (1800), the Tizimin dutifully records the seats of the *katun*. Other early chronicles (Barrera 1948: 72) start even earlier, in 12 Ahau (1421). The primary seats of the *katun* (in a period of almost continuous revolts) were as follows.

Date	Xiu	Itza	Other
12 Ahau (1421)			Otzmal
10 Ahau (1441)			Sisal
8 Ahau (1461)	Champoton	Chichen Itza	Kan Caba, Izamal
6 Ahau (1480)	Uxmal	Chichen Itza?	Hunac Thi
4 Ahau (1500)		Chichen Itza	A ti Kuh
2 Ahau (1520)		Tihosuco	Chacal Na
13 Ahau (1539)	Merida?	Coba	Euan
11 Ahau (1539)	Merida	Emal	Kin Colox
9 Ahau (1559)	Merida	Teabo	
7 Ahau (1579)	Merida	Mayapan	
5 Ahau (1598)	Merida	Zotz'il	
3 Ahau (1618)	Merida	Zuyua	
1 Ahau (1638)	Merida	Emal	
12 Ahau (1658)		Valladolid	
10 Ahau (1677)		Valladolid	
		Chab Le	
8 Ahau (1697)		Chab Le	
6 Ahau (1717)		Teabo	
4 Ahau (1737)		Teabo	
2 Ahau (1776)		Valladolid	
13 Ahau (1800)		Coba	

196. They swept the main plaza and the smaller plazas for the *katun* ceremonies and announced the prophecy of the *katun*. Barrera 1948: 223 reads Ix Chancab as the name of a female personage.

*In 1461 it was at Chichen Itza,
and the 13 Gods provided poor
fare. That was the fate of the
time according to their own
word in 1461. (210)*

*And Chichen Itza summoned
the lord of Uxmal to celebrate
the date under the East priest
Xib Chac and the priest of
Quetzalcoatl, Kukul Can. Then
the Itza were betrayed, which
led to fighting and slaughter
and shooting and sin. (230)*

And, because it was time for

Uaxac Ahau
  T u Ch'i Chen
Ox lahun ku*
  U ich
Ox te
  Sa cum
Lai
  Hi u tepal
Ti tal i
  T u than
Ox lahun ti ku
  Uaxac Ahau uchc i
T u Ch'i Chen
  Ca tz'ibtab i*
U y ahau
  Ah Uxmal
Ca tal i
  U chek eb*
T u pach Chac
  Xib Chac
T u menel Ah *Nacxit*
  Kukul Can*
Ca em i*
  U katlam Ah Itza e*
Ca tal i
  Hoc*
Mucuc tza
  Homol tza
Tz'on
  Bacal tza
Ti ca oc i
  Keban ul i
T u men Ah Uaxac Ahau xan e
  Ca uchic

8 Ahau
200   Was at Chichen Itza.
    The 13 Gods'
      Aspect
    Was breadnut tree
      And atole gourd.
205 That was
      Exactly its rule,
    Which was spoken
      In the words
    Of the 13 Gods.
210   8 Ahau occurred
    At Chichen Itza.
      Then it was written
    To the lord
      Of the people of Uxmal.
215 Then came
      The pacing of the pyramid
    Behind the East priest
      Xib Chac
    For the priest of Quetzalcoatl,
220   Kukul Can.
    Then befell
      The betrayal of the Itza.
    Then came
      Uprooting
225 And removal by burial,
      Removal by dart shooting,
    And blowgun,
      And removal by shot.
    When that started,
230   Sin arrived.
    Also because of 8 Ahau
      There was then

---

201. Barrera 1948: 223 has 'where he was the most elaborately worshipped face'. I can't follow his reasons.

212. Barrera 1948: 223 has 'then it happened that a painting was sent to the Lord of Uxmal and he came to leave the imprint of his feet on the back of the Red Fearsome Chac'.

216. The ritual began with the "pacing of the pyramid" of the seat of the *katun*, in this case Chichen Itza. The Xiu were invited to participate.

220. The lord of the *katun* was the East priest Xib Chac. He was to be assisted by the priest of Quetzalcoatl, Kukul Can. Nacxitl (Nahuatl *nahui icxitl* 'four leg') is one of the names of Quetzalcoatl. Kukul Can 'quetzal snake' is the Mayan equivalent but is also in this instance a personal name. The Can lineage was prominent in Chichen Itza and Izamal.

221. The Itza were double-crossed and war broke out over the lordship of the *katun*.

222. Barrera 1948: 223 says 'the exodus of the Water Witch'.

224. Barrera 1948: 223 says 'there came fighting in hiding, fighting with fury, fighting with violence, fighting without mercy'. At lines 321 ff. he translates the same words as 'there will come snatching of bags and rapid and violent war'.

the ceiba sacrifices to end the cycle, all at once Chichen Itza's term ended and Izamal's began. It was ended by Ul Ahau three years early, the priestly office. Itzam Can and Ahau Can appeared, and Hapay Can was named priest designate. Ul Ahau was lord of Izamal, whose gods collected the tribute. Then the katun *ended, and the rule of Izamal with it, and Hapay Can was sacrificed. The Izamal Rabbits and the Center priest Bol Ay arrived among the*

Hul yax che*
  Bai ca uch t u ca ten
Hi uilbal u cuch*

  T u kinil ual e
Hun uatz'
  Hun tz'on ual e
Uaxac Ahau ca uch i
  Ulel Ytzmal
Tabtab i
  T u men sipc i
Ah Ulil Ahau
  Lai*
U hetz' katun uch i
  Ichil uuc lahum pis katun

U than
  U tepal kul
Ytzam Caan hok i
  Ahau Caanil
Y etel Hapai Caan
  Ti tabtab i*
Ah Ytzmal
  Ul Ahau
Ti uch i
  Patan u mehen kul Itzmal

(13r) Ca hok i
  U tah katun
Ti uch i
  Tepal Itzmal ca tz'oc i
Hapai Can e*
  T an u num ya
Ah Ytzmal Thul ca ul i*
  Yax Bol Ai ca ul i*

Kuch
  Tan y ol caan

The appearance of the ceiba,
  And thus it occurred again.
235 It may have been the moon phase of
the burden
  At the time of the return,
One turn,
  One shot returning.
8 Ahau was over.
240 Coming up was Izamal,
To be all tied up
  By the fault
Of Ul Ahau,
  Who
245 Was the seating of the *katun*
  In the seventeenth measure of the
  katun:
The word,
  The rule of the gods.
Itzam Can appeared,
250 Ahau Can,
And Hapay Can,
  Who was all tied up.
The lord of Izamal
  Was Ul Ahau.
255 Then occurred
  The tribute of the sons of the gods
  to Izamal.
Then came
  The division of the *katun*.
That happened:
260 The rule of Izamal then ended.
Hapay Can then
  Had his suffering.
Itzmal Thul then appeared;
  The Center priest Bol Ay then
  appeared,
265 Arriving
  In the middle of the Cans

---

233. Barrera 1948: 223 reads 'weakening of the ceiba'. He loses me, but I think the scansion precludes his interpretation.

235. Barrera 1948: 223 has 'but who will know the burden he will bring when he has completely turned around?'

244. From some other text, Barrera 1948: 224 adds 'for the sin he had committed with the espoused wife of another lord his friend, which brought on war'.

252. Barrera 1948: 224 has Ul Ahau tied up. I think the terminative *i* precludes this.

261. Hapay Can 'swallowing snake' was arrow sacrificed at Uxmal, according to Tozzer 1941: 35.

263. Barrera 1948: 224 reads this as a place-name.

264. Barrera 1948: 224 translates *yax bolay* as 'great butcher beasts' and *kuch t an y ol caan* as 'celestial buzzards in the center of the Heart of Heaven'.

Cans with the East priest Bol
Ay and the East priest Xib
Chac, the three victims who
were sacrificed at Izamal. (274)
It ended with the crime of

Y etel Chac Bol Ai
  Y etel Chac Xib Chac
Ox num
  Ti ya*
U pixan
  T an u mansic u num yail
Uai
  Itzmal
Tabtab i
  T u men u keban
Y ahau
  Can Ul e*

With the East priest Bol Ay
  And the East priest Xib Chac:
The three victims
270 In pain
Whose souls
  Underwent suffering
Here
  At Izamal,
275 All tied up then
  Because of the sin
Of the lord
  Who was Can Ul.

---

270. Barrera 1948: 224 has 'great was the suffering'.

278. Can Ul 'snake snail', a lord of Izamal and a member of the Can lineage on his mother's side and the Ul lineage on his father's, hence a relative of the Cans of Izamal and Chichen Itza, including Kukul Can. The squabble here was significantly dynastic. With patrilineal succession and lineage exogamy, the successor to Ul Ahau should have been an Ahau, but none appears in this account. Can Ul's claim to patrilineal legitimacy rests on what may have been an incestuous union. The closest kinship relations between him and Ul Ahau would reconstruct as:

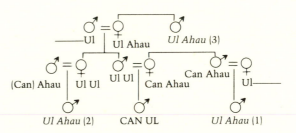

A legitimate series of marriages could have made Can Ul the father's sister's son of the retiring lord, Ul Ahau (1). If preferential cross-cousin marriage obtained (Eggan 1934), Can Ul's mother's brother might have married his father's sister, producing a relationship through his father, as the text claims, to Ul Ahau (2). Such a relationship would be either too close (incestuous) or too distant to warrant succession: Can Ul's father and his father's sister would have to be Ul Uls. As the retiring lord was presumably older, it is also possible that Ul Ahau (3) was the brother of Can Ul's paternal grandmother who married incestuously.

All the Cans could be as close as half brothers, sons, or grandsons to one another and, given polygyny, some of them very likely were. Any one of them could have been Can Ul's father's sister's son, but not if Can Ul had any close relationship to Ul Ahau. Finally, one of them, Ahau Can, could have been Ul Ahau's mother's brother's son or sister's son's son without incest. The genealogy of this would have been:

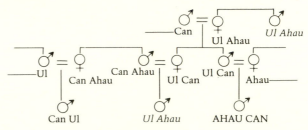

(note continued on following page)

Can Ul, dividing the heirs of
Hapay Can. And Kukul Can
found out and killed and tortured the nobles and did in the
Hapay Cans for the sin of their
lord. Itzam Can was named
designate; then came the usurpation of Can Ul. Ahau Can
was the candidate with the
Chichens. Who was Can Ul? He
was announced as lord in his
final office by inheritance from
his father. It was another triumph for the orders of Ants,

Lei tah mehen*
   Hapai Can la e
Ca natab i
   T u men Kukul Can e
Ca xot i
   U cal
U y i ob
   U y ub ob
T u lacal y al
   U mehen
C u pactic
   U luk Hapai Caan
Lei ah cuch teob
   U cuchah u keban y ahau ob*
Ca tun hopp i
   U tumtic Itzam Caan*
Ca tal y ocol
   U keban y ahau Can Ul
Ca hok i
   Ahau Caan
T u Chi Ch'enob
   Uai
Max
   Can Ul?*
T u chican e*
   Ti hok i
Ahau i
   Ox lahun te u cuch
Ca sihsab i
   T u men u yum
Lai hun ppel cu*
   Yubil
Sinic
   Balamil

This was the division of the sons
280   Of Hapay Can.
   Then it was understood
      By Kukul Can.
   Then were cut
      The throats,
285 The eyes,
      The ears
   Of all the born
      And engendered children.
   Then he folded
290   The removal of the Hapay Cans,
   Who were made to be the bearers,
      And bore the sin of their lord.
   And then began
      The renewal of Itzam Can.
295 Then came stealing,
      The sin of the lord Can Ul.
   Then appeared
      Ahau Can
   With the Chichens
300   Here.
   Who
      Was Can Ul?
   He was manifested then
      And appeared
305 As lord,
      His thirteenth burden,
   To which he was engendered
      Through his father.
   This was one more seat
310   And mantle
   Of the Ants
      And Jaguars,

(note continued from preceding page)
Both Can Ul and Ahau Can could have had a claim to patrilineal succession
through their fathers' mothers, who could well have been sisters of Ul Ahau, but
Ahau Can's grandmother neglected to marry incestuously. Presumably Can Ul
went to better schools.

279. Barrera 1948: 224 reads *tah* as 'tribute'.

292. The text makes no distinction between the plural -*ob* and the third person
plural pronoun *ob* or between the possessive use of the pronoun and its use as
subject or object of a verb. I have made the first distinction where possible by
treating the plural as an attached suffix and the pronoun as a separate word. It
makes a difference, as in this case: *u keban y ahauob* 'the sin of the lords' or *u
keban y ahau ob* 'the sin of their lord'. See also line 5160.

294. Barrera 1948: 224 has 'test'.

302. Barrera 1948: 224 sees this as a place-name: Maxcanú 'guardian monkey'.

303. Barrera 1948: 224 says 'at the beginning of the mountains'.

309. Barrera 1948: 225 has it as 'but he was valiant in war and had the Wooden
Mask of the Breath Squeezer and was Flint Powerful'.

Jaguars, Coral Snakes, Wooden Masks, Stabbers, and Little Flints who assembled for the calendar round sacrifices. There was to be slaughter, shooting, and usurpation of the lordship into the Christian period, at the 1539 sacrifices for the final end of the Itza cycle, but the real end was 1461, which over-whelmed the Itza governors. (338)

Defeating the Spanish will be another matter: in 1559 there will be a war in the correspond-ing katun. (346)

Calam
  Koh Che
Y etel Ah Cacap
  Chan Tokil*
Oc na
  Kuchil
Ma ya cimlal
  Kin tun y abil
Hoc*
  Muc tza
Tz'on
  Bacal tza
Ah cootz*
  Ah sitz'
U cuch katun
  T u kinil *xp̄tianoil**
T u kinil nicte unicil
  T u kin u chac tun num ya

Uchom u uutz'
  Katun
T u y ox lahun te
  Ah uaxac Ahau ual e*
U lubul
  U than
Y okol u hal ach uinicil
  Y ahau Ah Ytza
Ma cetel
  Bin tz'ocbal nicte uinicil

Lai bolon Ahau*
  Ti pak i
Chimal kal
  Y etel halal kal
Lai bin uchuc t u nup katun
  Hun tz'am ual e.*

Coral Snakes,
  Wooden Masks,
315 Stabbers,
  And Little Flints,
Coming to the house
  And appearing
With the painless death
320   Of the calendar round:
Uprooting
  And removal by burial,
The blowgun
  And removal by shot,
325 Pluckers
  And lusters
After the burden of the *katun*
  In the time of Christianity,
In the time of the Flower people,
330   In the time of the red stone
    suffering
Occurring on the fold
  Of the *katun*,
On the thirteenth:
  The return of 8 Ahau,
335 The posting
  Of his word
Over the governors,
  Lords of the Itza.
Otherwise
340   Will be the ending of the Flower
    people.
That is 9 Ahau,
  Who plants
His shield bundle
  And arrow bundle.
345 That will occur on the opposite *katun*:
  They are a pair returning.

316. That is, the explanation of Can Ul's de facto success was a deal with the military orders.
321. See note 224.
325. Line repeated in the text by error.
328. *Xp̄tianoil* is an anachronism of the time of transcription. It is virtually the only Spanish word in any of the texts I have placed as preconquest. See also line 480.
334. That is, 8 Ahau (1461) was the thirteenth (Xiu) *katun*.
341. The ending of the Flower *katun* was the beginning of 9 Ahau (1559).
346. "Pairs" of *katuns* are not elsewhere attested, and the concept of pairing within a cycle of thirteen is difficult. 8 Ahau and 9 Ahau are six *katuns* apart, and the Maya sometimes divided their cycles of thirteen into six plus seven. Barrera 1948: 225 reads this as 'when the *katun* may close completely'.
From 8 Ahau (1461) on, the Tizimin makes a conscientious effort to keep track of the lords of the *katun*. Some pretenders are hard to identify, but the principal

(note continued on following page)

(note continued from preceding page)
claimants were as follows. Items in parentheses are not mentioned in the Tizimin.

Date	*Katun* Lords	Other Events
8 Ahau (1461)	Can Ul of Izamal, Xib Chac and Kukul Can of Chichen Itza, Hunac Ceel of Mayapan	Fall of Mayapan
6 Ahau (1480)	Kak Mo of Uxmal and Champoton	
4 Ahau (1500)	Kukul Can of Chichen Itza	Ahau Pech Spokesman (Aguilar, Valdivia, De León, Córdoba, Grijalva, Cortés *entradas*)
2 Ahau (1520)	(?) of Tihosuco	(Montejo *entrada*)
13 Ahau (1539)	Kin Chil (?) of Coba (Bach Can), Pot Xiu of (Merida?), (Can Ek of Tayasal)	Xopan Nahuatl Spokesman
11 Ahau (1539)	Zulim Chan of Emal, Yax Chac of Merida	Tzin Yabun Spokesman, Ho Za Bac and Muzen Cab revolt
9 Ahau (1559)	Uac Nal of Teabo, (?) of Merida	Kauil Ch'el Spokesman (Landa)
7 Ahau (1579)	Chu Uah of Mayapan, Yax Chac and Amayte Kauil of Merida	Bech' Kab revolt
5 Ahau (1598)	Puz Hom and Kaua Hom of Zotz'il, Zuhuy Zip and Ol Zip of Emal, Hun Uitzil of Uxmal, Ahau Can of Merida, (Can Ek of Tayasal)	Kauil Ch'el and Puc Tun Spokesmen, Ma Zuy and Ben Pal revolt
3 Ahau (1618)	Yax Coc Ay Mut of Zuyua, Ek Coc Ay Mut of Merida	Bol Ay revolt
1 Ahau (1638)	Ol Zip and Ol Ha of Emal, Amayte Kauil of Merida	Ual Icim, Za Bac Na, Muzen Cab, Can Ul, and Hun Pic revolt, Chan war
12 Ahau (1658)	Yax Chuen and Pat Ay of Valladolid, Hun Pic of Ax	
10 Ahau (1677)	Pat Ay of Valladolid, Hun Chan of Chab Le	
8 Ahau (1697)	Amayte Kauil of Chab Le, (Can Ek of Tayasal)	Kak Mo revolt
6 Ahau (1717)	Kak Mo of Teabo	Chic Kalac revolt
4 Ahau (1737)	Mac Chahom of Teabo	(Canek 1761 revolt at Cisteil)
2 Ahau (1776)	Yopoc Ik of Valladolid	
13 Ahau (1800)	Kin Chil of Coba	Miz Cit revolt (Independence)

3. The Conspiracy Collapses

Katun 8 Ahau was the ninth in the Itza cycle of katuns. Izamal was its seat. And again they made war on Champoton and left carvings on its walls to end the attempt of the great Kak Mo to seat the katun. (366)

⸪ ⸪ ⬯ ⬯ ⬯

(17v) Uaxac Ahau*
  Katun
U bolon tz'it katun
  C u xocol
Itzmal
  U hetz' katun*
Y ulel ob
  T u ca uatz'
Emom *chimal* e
  Emom halal
Y okol Chakan Putun*
  Ti
U pakal
  U polob ich pak i*
U tz'oc
  U sitz'il
Kin Ich*
  Kak Mo*
U hetz'
  T u katunil ual e.

8 Ahau
  Katun
Was the ninth part of the *katun*
350   To be counted.
Izamal
  Was the seat of the *katun*.
They were to arrive
  For the second occasion.
355 Descended are the shields;
  Descended are the arrows
Over Champoton,
  Where
They are planting
360   Their carvings in the walls
To end
  The desire
Of Sun Eye
  Kak Mo
365 To be the seat
  Where the *katun* cycle returns.

347. The calendrical battle between the Itza and the Xiu is reflected in two cycles of *katun* prophecies (Barrera's first and second wheels) running from 11 to 13 Ahau. The "first wheel" is Itza and goes from 1539 to 1824. The "second wheel" is Xiu. It goes from 1539 to 1677 and then adds the prophecies for the preceding cycle, 1441 to 1539. The Itza cycle corresponds to my chapters 3, 4, 5, 7, 8, 10, 16, 18, 21, 26, 27, 28, 30, 31, 32, 33, 34, 35, 37, 39, and 41; the Xiu cycle comprises chapters 11, 13, 17, 19, 20, and 23. The first eight *katuns* in both cycles correspond chronologically and depict the Xiu devotion to Merida and the Itza devotion to Mayapan as seats of the cycle. In the first seven of these *katuns*, Merida claimed to seat the *katun* as well and was opposed by one or another Itza center. When 8 Ahau was reached, the Xiu priests returned to the preceding *katun* of that name and gave us the text before us. There is no reason to suppose that it is not a transcription of a preconquest glyphic prophecy, probably made in 9 Ahau (1559).

352. Can Ul of Izamal succeeded Kukul Can as lord of the *katun* and Ul Ahau as governor of Izamal late in 8 Ahau (1461). His lordship did not last long, and the following *katun* was seated at Uxmal. An extensive note on the history of Izamal is given in Tozzer 1941: 172–173.

357. Champoton apparently asserted a claim to seat the *katun* but was unsuccessful. It contended with Uxmal in the next *katun*.

360. Barrera 1948: 140 reads *polob* as 'heads'.

363. Kin Ich 'sun eye' is a metaphor for divine or glorious. It was later applied to Christ (line 1590). Landa 1929: 2: 26 considers it the name of a god.

364. Kak Mo 'fire parrot' of Uxmal overthrew Amayte Kauil of Chab Le ca. 1710, retaining the lordship into the following *katun*. He was probably imitating the events of the preceding cycle, even to changing his name. Kak Mo was a god name, particularly at Izamal, where it was equated with Itzam Na. See Tozzer 1941: 144, 146, 173.

6 Ahau

---

4. Uxmal and Chichen Itza

Katun 6 Ahau was the tenth in the Itza katun cycle. Uxmal was its seat. They held the procession separately and announced their prophecy to their lords, but they lied and fornicated and raised taxes and cut throats. Thus was 6 Ahau. (386)

(17v) Uac Ahau*
    Katun
U lahun tz'it katun
    C u xocol
Uxmal
    U hetz' katun
Oclis
    T u ba ob*
Chic ix u u ich ob
    Chic ix u than ob
T u y ahaulilob
    (. . . . .)*
Bin u tus ob
    Coil than
Tzuc
    Achil
Ca emec u koch ob
    Xotic u cal ob*
Lai u cuch uac Ahau
    C u cutal t u katunil ual e.

6 Ahau
    Katun
Was the tenth part of the *katun*
370   To be counted.
Uxmal
    Was the seat of the *katun*.
They were made to steal
    From themselves
375 And shameful were their faces
    And shameful were their words
In their lordships
    (. . . . .)
There will be lies
380 And madness,
And also lust
    And fornication.
Then their taxes will come down
    To cut their throats.
385 That is the burden of 6 Ahau,
    Who is seated in this *katun* period
    again.

---

367. This text is probably from 9 Ahau (1559) from a glyphic original of 4 Ahau (1500) or, perhaps, a little earlier. I believe Kak Mo (formerly of Champoton) to have been the Xiu lord of the *katun*, opposed by Kukul Can of Chichen Itza.

374. Barrera 1948: 140 has 'in which it was placed by itself'.

378. Line missing. The preceding lines may imply a sort of truce: the Xiu and Itza lords of the *katun* were to proceed independently in their ceremonial circuits and see how it went.

384. It didn't work, and taxes had to be raised considerably, presumably to support soldiers.

4 Ahau

---

5. Trials of the Itza

---

4 Ahau was the eleventh in the Itza katun series. Chichen Itza was its seat. For both the Xiu and the Itza attended, and there was a plague. And Kukul Can came for the fourth Itza term. For the fourth time he ruled the katun. (400)

(17v) Can Ahau*
  U buluc tz'it
Katun
  C u xocol
T u Chi Ch'en Ytza
  U hetz' katun
Ulom kuk
  Ulom yaxum*
(18r) Ulom Ah Kan Tenal
  Ulom xe kik*
T u can uatz'
  Ulom Kukul Can t u pach Ah
Ytzaob
T u can ten
  U than katun ual e.*

4 Ahau
  Was the eleventh part
Of the *katun*
390 To be counted.
At Chichen Itza
  Was the seat of the *katun*.
Come is the quetzal;
  Come is the blue bird;
395 Come are the yellow deaths;
  Come is blood vomit.
For the fourth time
  Come is Kukul Can after the Itzas.
For the fourth time
400 Is the word of the *katun*'s return.

---

387. This is probably a glyphic text of late 4 Ahau (1500) or a little after, transcribed in 9 Ahau (1559). Kukul Can continued as lord of the Itza *katun*, apparently without Xiu competition, an astonishing longevity in that office (ca. 1461–1500): even the author is amazed at what he describes as a fourth term.

394. *Kuk* 'quetzal' (*Pharomachrus*) was the emblem of the Itza as *uitzil* 'hummingbird' (*Archilochus*, Nahuatl *huitzitzillin*) was for the Xiu. I believe *yax um* 'blue bird' is a euphemism for the hummingbird, which had astonishingly ferocious theological implications for the Nahuas—Huitzilopochtli, for example. The couplet is frequent in the Tizimin.

396. *Kan tenal* 'yellow deaths': jaundice? hepatitis? yellow fever? Barrera 1948: 140 has 'he of the yellow tree'. There is still considerable controversy about preconquest diseases. *Xe kik* 'blood vomit': tuberculosis? smallpox? The latter, generally considered a European introduction, would hardly be expected before 1500.

400. Barrera 1948: 141 says 'the fourth time the *katun* speaks'.

6. Hopes of the Xiu

The prophecy of Ahau Pech from start to finish: on the day of the ancestors, the end of the term after four katuns, *the divination of the holy day is announced. Let me take office whom you know, O Itza Fathers of the Land, and acknowledge and reverence the sun priest Ahau Pech from beginning to*

(10r) U *profesia**
   Na (A)hau Pech
T u kin i
   Uil
U natabal kin e
   Yum e
Ti y oksah ich
   Ah tepal ual e*
Can tz'it u katunil uchom i
   Ual e*
Hahal pul
   T u kin ku e*
Y oktah
   Ua u ba*
In kuben e
   Yum e
Ti au ich ex
   T u bel
Au ulah ex Ah Ytza e
   U yum cab*
Ca ulom
   Lai ca a tz'a t au ol

Tal i
   T u chi
Na (A)hau Pech
   Ah kin*

The prophecy
   Of Ahau Pech
On the sun
   And moon,
405 Of the day of remembrance
   Of the fathers
Which removes the face
   Of the returned ruler.
Four parts of the *katun* cycle are done
410   And returned.
The true cast
   On the day of the god
Is removed
   And stands up.
415 Let me be seated then,
   Fathers,
Whom you saw
   On the road.
Welcome Him, O Itzas,
420   Fathers of the Land.
When He is come
   That will be when you give up your hearts
And come
   Before
425 Ahau Pech
   The sun priest

---

401. An interesting prophecy which seemingly tries to mediate between the Xiu and Itza cycles by setting up one that is halfway between them. It was probably written in glyphic form early in 4 Ahau (1500) and perhaps transcribed in 9 Ahau (1559). Na (A)hau Pech 'lord tick' was an Itza prophet, a sun priest, and, according to the Mani, *gran sacerdote* of the late fifteenth century at Chichen Itza. See also Tozzer 1941: 42. The Ahau lineage was prominent there and at Izamal, and the Pech lineage is notable slightly later at Merida.

408. The time of remembrance of ancestors is the end of one *katun* and the beginning of the next. *Katun*-ending monuments were regarded as ancestral commemorations (*natabal*).

410. The fourth *katun* in a cycle ending on 1 Ahau. I find no other evidence for such a cycle.

412. The omission of true (*hahal*) suggests that it is the Mayan God who is implied. Lines 419–422 appear to confirm this.

414. Literally, 'erects itself so that I may sit there'.

420. Ba Cabs were obsolescent by *katun* 4 Ahau (1737). Hence I believe this prophecy to be preconquest (1480).

426. The concept of priesthood among the post-Classic and colonial Maya centers on the office of sun priest (*ah kin*), a prerequisite to all political or religious authority. The office required both birth and training, being inherited

(note continued on following page)

end, and 4 Ahau will finish a
cycle which is neither Xiu nor
Itza. (432)

T u kin i   In the sun
 Uil   And moon

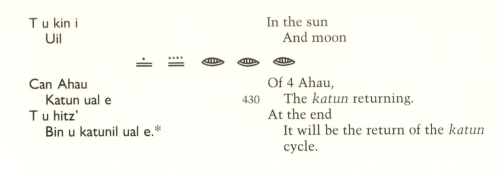

Can Ahau   Of 4 Ahau,
  Katun ual e   430   The *katun* returning.
T u hitz'   At the end
  Bin u katunil ual e.*   It will be the return of the *katun*
                                                   cycle.

(note continued from preceding page)

patrilineally but requiring appropriately high-ranking credentials in the maternal
line as well. Sun priests were nobles in both lines: *al mehenob,* women's children
and men's children of known lineage. They also underwent extensive training and
were ranked by achievement as well as birth. The less distinguished were rele-
gated to the practice of medicine, sorcery, and consultative divination. Those of
higher rank became lords (*ahauob*) and took on the burden of public office.

The highest-ranking priesthood was that of the Jaguar (*Balam*), who governed
the entire country for one *katun* as the representative of the Sole God (*Hunab
Ku*). Landa 1929: 1: 72 calls him the sun priest of the cycle (*ah kin may*). He was
seconded by his Spokesman (*Chilam*), and together they manifested the comple-
mentarity (and friction) of variously named dualistic gods. On a different time
scale were the rain priests of the four (or sometimes five) directions, who represented the yearbearers or Fathers of the Land (*Ba Cabob*), also identified with the
rain gods (*Chacob*). Each city had its own directional priesthoods. More obscure
are the priesthoods associated with the 9 Gods of the underworld and the 13 Gods
of heaven, but these too were local, as were the priesthoods of the high gods who
were patrons of the twenty sacred days.

Few of these gods or priesthoods are clearly specified in the Tizimin, nor is
their rank explicated, though they were almost certainly ranked. They included
the priests of Itzam Na, Quetzalcoatl, Ah Puch', Ix Tab, Uayab Zotz', Itzam Cab
Ain, Ix Ch'el, and Muzen Cab, all of whom are mentioned, and there may be a
number of others whom I have failed to recognize. These various priesthoods
were no doubt subject to considerable local variation in iconography, rank, and
calendrical association. Some of the gods, for example, were also considered tute-
lary, as Itzam Na was for Izamal, Quetzalcoatl for Chichen Itza, and Muzen Cab
for Coba. Additional confusion is introduced by the strong Mexican influence,
particularly in the west.

432. The Chumayel adds these lines (Roys 1967: 166; the reference is apparently to the military orders):
    Destroyed are the plants
        Of the Ant people
    Who are to have plants later
        Because of the Skunk plants,
    The mother
        And father
    Of Rabbit plants,
        Ants,
    Cowbirds,
        Grackles,
    Blackbirds,
        And Mice.

THE SIXTEENTH CENTURY

2 Ahau

---

7. A Note from Tihosuco

2 Ahau was the twelfth in the Itza katun cycle. Tihosuco was its seat. It was halfway good in this katun. (442)

(18r) Cabil Ahau*
  U lah ca tz'it
Katun
  C u xocol
Maya Tzuc Pom*
  E hetz' katun*
Tan coch hom u uah
  Tan coch hom u y aal*
T u katunil
  Lah cabil Ahau ual e.*

Second Ahau
  Was the twelfth part
435 Of the *katun*
  To be counted.
Maya Tzuc Pom
  Was the seat of the *katun.*
Halfway clear was his food;
440 Halfway clear was his water
At the *katun* period
  Of this second Ahau's return.

---

433. 2 Ahau marks the first arrival of the Spanish on the coast of Yucatan, but this fact is ignored in the present text. The *katun* seat was Maya Tzuc Pom 'cycle grove of copal', which may be Tihosuco. The lord of the *katun* is nowhere named, but there is mention of a great fire and what may have been a smallpox epidemic.

437. Barrera 1948: 141 has Maya Uas Cuzamil 'place of the Maya swallow' and then Maya Tzuc Pom 'groves of Maya copal gum trees'.

438. The manuscript has *e* for *u*.

440. Many of the prophecies describe the "food and drink" of the *katun* as a metaphor for its general character.

442. According to Morley 1946: 241, the last *katun*-ending monument was erected at the end of this *katun*. He does not say where.

13 Ahau

---

8. A Time of Troubles

---

13 Ahau was the thirteenth in the Itza katun cycle. The seat was in Coba. It was usurped at the outset and there were rebellions throughout, amid war and pillage and suffering of all, living and dead, who rise to the bright heavens or descend to the evil center of the earth. The

(18r) Ox lahun Ahau*
  U y ox lahun tz'it
Katun
  C u xocol ti cabal
Ix Bach Can*
  U hetz' katun
Ek lahom
  U tz'ub
Nocpahom kin*
  Nocpahom u u ich u*
Emom u kikel che
  Y etel tunich
Elom caan
  Elom lum
Yuk xot
  Kin
Y okol cuxanob
  Y okol cimenob
Cuxlahom
  Cimenob
Uchlahom hom canal
  Naac-hom tibil beob canal
Emom lobol beob
  T u tz'u luum

13 Ahau
  Was the thirteenth part
445 Of the *katun*
  To be counted in the lands,
And Bach Can
  Was the seat of the *katun* again.
Darkened
450 Was its fold.
Rising was its sun;
  Rising was the face of its moon.
Descended were bloody sticks
  And stones.
455 Burned was the sky;
  Burned was the land.
General cutting
  And pain
Over the living;
460 Over the dead,
The resurrected
  And the dead:
Causing clear skies,
  Raising fear of the paths of heaven,
465 Descending the evil paths
  To the marrow of the earth.

---

443. 13 Ahau was the end of the *katun* cycle in the Itza count. However, eighty days before it ended (on November 4, 1539: 11.16.0.0.0 13 Ahau 7 Xul), a new calendar was introduced at Mayapan which thereafter counted the *katuns* by initial dates. There were further Spanish *entradas* on the west coast in the 1520s and 30s, but the present text doesn't mention them.

447. Bach Can 'chachalaca snake', another name for Coba 'chachalaca water'. The seating of the *katun* was disputed by Pot Xiu, a water priest (*pul ha*) of Merida (Barrera 1948: 48), and by Tihosuco and Tz'itz'om Tun.

451. Barrera 1948: 141 has *se volteará*.

452. That is, the beginning (sun) and ending (moon) of the *may* (or thirteen-*katun* cycle) were celebrated.

final ending katun *according to the Father of heaven and earth was 13 Ahau, at the end of the Itza cycle. (474)*

U xul
  U hitz'ibte katun
U than u yumil can
  Y etel lum
Lai y an t u cuch
  Ah ox lahun Ahau
T u kin
  U tz'oc katun ual e.

The end of—
  The termination of the *katun.*
The word of the Father of heaven
470 And earth
That was in the burden
  Of 13 Ahau
On the day
  This *katun* ended again.

9. The Council of Mayapan

The word and prophecy of the great sun priests, of the sages and prophets: the sun priest and Spokesman of the Jaguar was Xopan Nahuatl in 13 Ahau,

(10v) U tzol than*
  Ah kinob
U bobat than
  Noh ah kinob
Ah miatzob
  Profeta.
Lai
  U y ah kinilob la e
Chilam Balam*
  Ah *Xupan Nauat*

475 The account of the words
  Of the sun priests,
The prophetic words
  Of the great sun priests,
Sages
480 And prophets.
These
  Are the sun priesthoods then;
The Spokesman of the Jaguar
  Was Xopan Nahuatl.

475. The text alleges that Xupan Nauat (Nahuatl *xopan nahuatl* 'summer speaker') produced this prophecy in 1527, predicting the arrival of the Spanish in 1530. Perhaps he did, but certainly not in this form: it is very much influenced by knowledge of the Spanish invasion, even though it uses no Spanish words to describe it (except *profeta* in line 480). It was very likely written early in the following *katun,* though Xopan Nahuatl may have used some of the prescient expressions ascribed to him (e.g., line 489). From his Nahuatl name, one suspects Xopan Nahuatl of being a Xiu from Merida or Mani. Neither lineage name occurs elsewhere in the Tizimin. Tozzer 1941: 36 has further details.

483. *Chilam Balam* 'spokesman of the jaguar' was the speaker or "talking chief" under the lord of the *katun,* who was called the Jaguar because he wore a jaguar skin. Like other high officials—the Jaguar himself, the governors of the cities, the chiefs of the towns, and the occupants of all priesthoods—the Spokesman was always a trained sun priest (*ah kin*). He was also not only a prophet (*ah bobat*) but *the* official Prophet for a particular *katun.* Finally, he was expected to have the highest degree of training and expertise in religious and calendrical matters: he was supposed to be a sage (*ah miatz*). When disagreement arose over the prophecies, it was up to the Spokesman to resolve it. Failing that, a convocation of sages could be called. The authority of such a meeting appears to have exceeded that of the lord of the *katun* himself, and, though it was largely confined to the religious sphere, its ability to concert calendrical changes had a sweeping impact on political and economic affairs. A committee of sages was also responsible for the ritual examination of public officials, normally under the aegis of the Spokesman, acting as Great Sun Priest (*ah noh kin*). Most Spokesmen appear to

(note continued on following page)

and in 1527 he told the sun priests of the coming of the Spaniards. And they wrote it down and began to tell the truth of the coming of the Spanish. But it was not the katun prophecy that justified tribute; it was only a prediction of the sun priests and prophets from their books where the katun is recorded that told the nobles and captains it would be in three years. (514)

And so it was, and then spoke the devil, telling the captains that thirteen makes seven. So the devil said: the

$\doteq$ $\equiv$ ⬭ ⬭ ⬭

Ox lahun Ahau
   Ah *Xupan* u kaba
He uaxac ppel y abil
   Ox lahun Ahau
Y almah xicin ob ah kinob
   U natah ob
Ix u talel
   Y ulel tz'ulob
Ca ix u xocah ob
   Ti yunil
Ca ix hopp i
   Y alic ob
Hahil
   Binil ketailt ob

Ma ix u nah
   Katuntabalob y alah

Ix ca tz'ab
   Ca patan
Lai uchc u patcunah
   Thanil ob
Ah kinob
   Ah bobatob
Ti lic u xocic
   Ti yunob
T u catz' pop
   T u ppicul katun
Ta muk y alic ob al mehenob
   Y etel hol canob
Ox hab
   U kin y ulel*
C uch i
   Ca thanah i
Ku y okol ah bobat e
   Lai cisin
Ta muk y alic t u hol can ex e
   Ual ci tac y ahal cab
Ox lahun
   Ti uuc e
Ci
   U than cisin ti ob

485 In 13 Ahau
   Xopan was his name
   Who in the eighth year's time
   Of 13 Ahau
   Spoke to the ears of the sun priests
490   What they knew
   And the coming
   And arrival of the foreigners.
   They also recounted it then
   In the books,
495 And they began
   And spoke
   The truth
   Of the coming of their neighbors to them.
   But it was not the fulfillment
500   Of the spirit of their *katun* reckonings
   That they were also given
   Our tribute.
   That just made it expectable:
   The sayings
505 Of the sun priests
   And prophets
   Which were as told
   In the books.
   They rolled the mat
510   And totaled the *katun*
   While they told the nobles
   And captains
   That three years
   Would be the time of arrival.
515 It occurred.
   Then there spoke
   A god over the prophet:
   This was the devil,
   As he told your captains
520   To return just at dawn.
   Thirteen
   Makes seven then,
   Said
   The word of the devil to them,

(note continued from preceding page)
have been very good at ambiguous and oracular public statements that would preserve their reputation for profundity while sidestepping controversial issues. Their life expectancy may correspondingly have exceeded that of the Jaguars they served.

   514. That is, the priestly prophecies were misinterpreted to say that tribute was to begin in three years (1530). The misinterpretation was made by a "false prophet," 7 Sat Ay.

7 priest Sat Ay. That was the teaching of the 7 priest Sat Ay, who was unhappy with the Spaniards who were to end his rule. So the new count began and the tax for converts to God and the King, who ordered it in knowledge of their income and stacked and measured it. The nobles of the former Itza suffered extinction for salvation. (554)

Here they all are: Xopan Nahuatl the land reckoner and

T u men Uuc Sat Ai*
   U kaba cisin
Lai y an chun can e
   Ti bin c u ch'aal than ob

Te chun can e
   Ti cahana Uuc Sat Ay

T u men ya ti y ol
   U talel tz'ulob cach i
T u men bin hauac u tepal
   Cisin c uch i
Ca tun hopp u xocic ichil
   Ah ual kin
Te chil y ilabal
   U talel koch c uch i e
Y oklal
   T u y ol
Y an hun ahau canal
   Hun y ahau ti cab
T u than ob c uch i e
   U nat-h ob ix hi bal u cuchma e

Y etel bin u ppiculte
   U ppisante*
Y al
   U mehen
Ah Ytza
   Uchmal e
Num ya bin u cib e
   U pixan uil
Utz cuxlahebal
   Ychil u pitic num ya e
Lei y an
   Ichil t u lacal e
Xupan Nauat
   U kaba

525 Because the 7 priest Sat Ay
   Was the name of the devil
Who had the basic doctrine
   Which was going to prepare their
     word.
This is the basic doctrine
530   That was initiated by the 7 priest
     Sat Ay
Because his heart was sore
   That the foreigners had come
Because that was going to end his rule:
   The devil was finished.
535 For then began the count of the face
   Of the returned sun:
On the occasion of its appearance
   The tax came
Because
540   In essence
There was one lord on high,
   One lord on earth.
They had spoken
   And they also knew something of
     his burden.
545 And they will stack it up
   And measure it,
The born
   And engendered children
Of the Itza
550   That were.
Suffering goes its candle then,
   The soul of the moon.
Good may be resurrected
   In the avoidance of that suffering.
555 Here they are then
   In their completeness:
Xopan Nahuatl
   By name,

---

525. The 7 priest Sat Ay 'wait grease' was active in this and the following *katun* at Merida. If my surmise is correct, the number gods had corresponding priesthoods, but it may be that the first five number priests were the directional priests as well. The commonest number prefixes to personal names (if one includes the color prefixes) are 1 (red, east), 7, and 11, in that order. I believe 1 to be the commonest because it was the highest-ranking. Eleven is important because it symbolizes the inauguration of the second half of the *katun*. Seven is a problem. The contexts in which 7 priests are mentioned suggest to me that they early concluded that they could benefit from the ideological boost provided by the Christian week. If so, Sat Ay may have been the first to realize this. Compare the career of Cha Pat in 5 Ahau.

546. The removal and stacking of the burden were part of the *katun*-ending ceremonies. Compare lines 705–706.

the sun priests Kauil Ch'el,
Ahau Pech, and Puc Tun, the
Captains and Spokesmen of the
Jaguar. These are the sun priests
who knew the cycles and lands
exactly down to the end in
13 Ahau. Come to Mayapan in
13 Ahau, the 13 Gods told the
sun priest Spokesman: eat
and drink! On the days of one
and two, on the days of
three and four, on the days

La bin tzol e
   U tzolan cab
Y etel Ah Kin
   Ch'el
Na (A)hau Pech
   Na Puc Tun
Nacom Balam
   Chilam Balam
Lei
   Ah kinob
Ohel mailob
   U tzolan cab
Y etel katunob
   T u hum pis tun
Ti
   Ox lahun Ahau
Kuch *Mayapan*
   Ox lahun Ahau
(11r) He u thanob ox lahun ti ku*
   T u tzolah ti ah kin Chilam

Uien! Uien a man uah!*
   Uken! Uken a man haa!*
T u kin Puslum Pach*
   T u kin Thuchlum Ich*
T u kin Naclah Muyal*
   T u kin Naclah Uitz*

Who is going to count
560   The registered lands,
And the sun priests
   Kauil Ch'el,
Ahau Pech,
   And Puc Tun,
565 Captains of the Jaguar,
   And Spokesmen of the Jaguar.
These
   Are the sun priests
Who know the cycles
570   And the registered lands
And the *katuns*
   To the measured *tun*
Which is
   13 Ahau.
575 Come to Mayapan
   In 13 Ahau.
These are the words of the 13 Gods,
   Recounted to the sun priest and
   Spokesman:
Eat! Eat all your food!
580   Drink! Drink all your water!
On the day of Puslum Pach,
   On the day of Thuchlum Ich,
On the day of Naclah Muyal,
   On the day of Naclah Uitz,

577. There follows a valuable passage invoking the thirteen day numeral gods of the thirteen levels of heaven and giving their names, which are rarely cited (cf. lines 852 ff.).

579. Brinton 1882: 127 considers these lines a "strange song" and translates them as:

> Eat, eat, thou hast bread;
> Drink, drink, thou hast water;
> On that day, dust possesses the earth,
> On that day, a blight is on the face of the earth,
> On that day, a cloud rises,
> On that day, a mountain rises,
> On that day, a strong man seizes the land,
> On that day, things fall to ruin,
> On that day, the tender leaf is destroyed,
> On that day, the dying eyes are closed,
> On that day, three signs are on the tree,
> On that day, three generations hang there,
> On that day, the battle flag is raised,
> And they are scattered afar in the forests.

580. "Finishing the remainder" of food and water was an important part of the *katun*-ending ceremonies. Also see lines 2366 ff.

581. Puslum Pach 'hunchback', god of 1.

582. Thuchlum Ich 'squat face', god of 2.

583. Naclah Muyal 'rising storm', god of 3.

584. Naclah Uitz 'rising mountain', god of 4.

of five and six, on the days of
seven and eight, on the days
of nine and ten, on the days of
eleven, twelve, and thirteen. In
the countryside famine came.
The katun was celebrated
in the northwest, and the
Christian nobles were am-
bushed in the countryside. The
Itza were sacrificed in the port.
(608)

Ma Zuy was the captain in
the woods, and at the new year
Elom Tz'itz' took his final office
at Tz'itz'om Tun. He took it in
the woods because Lahun Chan

T u kin Chuclum Tz'iitz'*
  T u kin Hubul Hub*
T u kin Cotz' y Ol Ch'elem*
  T u kin Etz'el Etz'*
T u kin Ox Tz'alab u Nak Yax Che*
  T u kin Cuchlahom y Al Max*
T u kin Ox Ch'uilah Xotem*
  T u kin Pan Tzintzin y etel Ban
  Hob*
Y alan che
  Y alan haban
Emom
  Chac mitan uiih
Cam pat-hom u bel katun*
  Mis bon
Tali chikin
  Tali xaman
Manebal y al
  U mehen ku
Sat-hom y alan che
  Y alan haban
T u chac tun num ya y al

  U mehen Ah num Itza*

Elom u chi sus
  U chi kaknab
Nacom ti che
  Ah Ma Suy*
Elom Tz'iitz'
  T u yax tzol Pop
Ah Sitz'om Tun
  Ox lahun te u cuch
Ch'ab on u numteil cab
  U tzucteil cab*

585 On the day of Chuclum Tz'itz',
  On the day of Hubul Hub,
On the day of Cotz' y Ol Ch'elem,
  On the day of Etz'el Etz',
On the day of Ox Tz'alab u Nak Yax Che,
590   On the day of Cuchlahom y Al Max,
On the day of Ox Ch'uilah Xotem,
  On the days of Pan Tzintzin and
  Ban Hob,
Under the trees,
  Under the bushes.
595 Descended
  Is the great plague of hunger.
Much clarified is the road of the *katun*,
  Swept and painted.
Coming west:
600   Coming north:
The destined passage of the born
  And engendered of God,
Destroyed under the trees,
  Under the bushes,
605 At the red stone of the suffering of the
born children
  Of the engendered children of the
  poor Itza,
Who were burned at the edge of the sand,
  The edge of the sea.
The captain in the woods
610   Was Ma Zuy;
And Elom Tz'itz'
  At the new count of Pop;
And Tz'itz'om Tun
  Had its thirteenth burden,
615 Taken on in the thorntrees land,
  The grovetrees land,

---

585. Chuclum Tz'iitz' 'sooty hoof', god of 5.
586. Hubul Hub 'sinking snail', god of 6.
587. Cotz' y Ol Ch'elem 'rolling agave', god of 7.
588. Etz'el Etz' 'placing fakes', god of 8.
589. Ox Tz'alab u Nak Yax Che 'three squeezed inside the ceiba', god of 9.
590. Cuchlahom y Al Max 'carrying baby monkey', god of 10.
591. Ox Ch'uilah Xotem 'three hanging sentences', god of 11.
592. Pan Tzintzin 'old bugger', god of 12; Ban Hob 'many guts', god of 13.
597. *Cam pat-hom*: I read *can pathom* 'much cleared'.
606. The explicit identification of the Chan lineage of Emal as Itza is of interest. See also note 655.
610. Ma Zuy '?land rock' was apparently the *nacom* or military commander of the anti-Christian party.
616. Elom Tz'iitz' 'burned hoof' of Tz'itz'om Tun 'hoofed stone', north of Izamal, was installed as lord on 1 Pop in ceremonies in the wild, replacing the pro-Christian lord. His thirteenth office is his final and highest rank.

of Emal was killed by the priest of the east. It was a rain of fire over the Maya and the Christians alike. (624)

Then the sky calmed. The sacrificial priest of Emal was sacrificed by the eastern one. In 13 Ahau, it being the end of the Itza cycle, they decorated Chichen Itza and built a bonfire, and the priests assembled and conferred. And also on the day of baptism the unbaptized and the sun priests were told about Christianity—the God from the east and the Garden of Eden. And they destroyed Emal. (648)

T u men Lahun Chaan*
   Paaxnom Chac Tenel Ahau

Kaxbom kak
   T u tel chacil yooc
Ti tal i
   Chac kit-hom u kab yax che*

Chac-hom u kab nicte
   Chac-hom u xik mucuy*
T u kin
   Ix lelem caan
Auatnom Chac Tenel Ah Ya
   Paaxnom Sac Tenel Ahau*

T u kinil
   Ox lahun Ahau ual e
He Chi Ch'en Itza e
   Ox lahun te u cuch
Mis bom u petenil Chi Ch'en

   Hopom kak tan chumuc cah

Ti uchom u than tamba ah kinob

   Lai u ual ah bobatob e
Y etel y ubal
   Tut
He le ix u kin ha
   T u than ob e
Ah kinob e
   Ti ma ix kaxom ha i

Lay ubah ob u pec
   U xik mucuy
Ti te ku likin e
   Pec u cah u kab nicte

Pax u cah
   Sac Tenel Ahau

Because Lahun Chan
   Was destroyed by the East sacrificial priest.
It dropped fire
620   And poured down steam,
Which came
   And poured rain on the ceiba branches.
It rained on the flowering branches;
   It rained on the doves' wings;
625 And at that time
   The sky quieted.
Screamed the East sacrificial priest
   And destroyed the North sacrificial priest
At the time
630   Of 13 Ahau's return.
Then Chichen Itza,
   On the thirteenth of its burdens,
Swept and painted the country at Chichen,
   And burned the fire before the middle of the city.
635 Then the sun priests talked to each other.
   That was the return of the prophets.
And they listened
   And visited.
Likewise on the day of water
640   They spoke to
The sun priests
   And those who had not dropped water.
That was how they heard the message
   Of the dove wing:
645 That there was a God in the east:
   The awareness of the place of the flowering branch.
And they destroyed the city
   Of the North sacrificial priest,

---

617. 10 Chaan 'molar', the pro-Christian leader, was sacrificed by fire. See also line 607.

622. 'Ceiba branches' is a metaphor for the pagan Maya, faithful to the sacred ceiba tree.

624. 'Flowering branches' and 'doves' wings' are metaphors for the Christians, who brought war (flowers) and peace (doves). *Mucuy* is identified by Tozzer 1941: 20 as belonging to the genus *Columbina*.

628. Chac Tenel Ahau (*sic*) and Sac Tenel Ahau, the 'red and white death lords', were the sacrificial priests of the east (red) and the north (white). The former sacrificed the latter, 10 Chaan. The eastern priest may have been 7 Sat Ay. See also lines 525 ff.

Then they paced the katun *and performed the ceremonial circuit and held pig and rabbit rites, and Zulim Chan of Emal took his final office in Mayapan. Emal requested the office and the* katun *ended. Then came the sacrifices of the western priest at the pyramid, and plague and famine. All painted up to end the* katun, *the lord sacrificed and finished off the lords of the Snakes and Ants, Jaguars and Silent Leopards. At the end of the* katun *in the mid-*

T u kin
   Y an u chek be katun

Xoipahom t u chakanil
   Ix kan
Citam
   Thul*
Sulim Chan*
   Ti tal i
U katabal u cuch katun
   Ox lahun te u cuch Chakan
Ti kax i
   U pucsikal peten
Katal u cah
   U cuch Ah Emal

Ti tal i
   U cotz' pop katun
Ti tal i
   Num on t u cal ya
Auatnom Ek Tenel Ah Ya

   Ti uil uchom*
Mul tun tzek i
   Emom
Chac mitan kuch
   Chac mitan uiih
Hoi bon u u ich
   Ualac y ahaulil
T u kin ma ya cimlal
   Ti uil uchom
Ahau Canil
   Sinic
Balamil
   Y etel Hun Coyol*
Y ubil ti u hetz' katun

   Ti tal i
Auatnom
   Chum kin Uoo*

On the day
650   There was the pacing of the road of
     the *katun*,
Making the circuit of the fields,
   And the offices
Of pig
   And rabbit.
655 It was Zulim Chan
   Who came
And requested the burden of the *katun*,
   His thirteenth burden and field,
Which was tied
660   In the heart of the country,
Requesting the placement
   And the burden were the people of
     Emal.
Then came
   The rolling of the mat of the *katun*.
665 Then came
   Our suffering in severe pain:
The screaming of the West sacrificial
priest.
   At the moon it happened,
At the ruin
670   There descended
The great scab plague,
   The great famine.
Paint-spattered was his face
   To return the lordship
675 On the day of painless death,
   Which was the moon
Of the lords of Snakes,
   Ants,
Jaguars,
680   And Silent Leopards.
Hearing that it was the seating of the
katun,
   Then came
The screaming
   Of the middle day of Uo.

---

654. The implication may be that wild pigs and rabbits were sacrificed instead of people, out of deference to Christian sentiment.

655. Zulim Chaan 'yellow molar' of Emal 'descent' requested the lordship for the following *katun*, 11 Ahau. The Chan lineage of Emal appears to have been generally pro-Christian. See also line 617.

668. That is, the sacrificial priest of the west counterattacked. He is not identified by location or name. See also note 628.

680. Snakes, Ants, Jaguars, and Silent Leopards were military companies of the Christian persuasion. These orders continued to be a problem until 12 Ahau (the 1660s).

684. 11 Ahau 7 Uo; see also note 5275.

dle of Uo, Emal and Hol Tun Zuyua were enslaved, the north being beaten by the east. That is the curse of 13 Ahau. (690)

Lai u munal Ah Emal*

Bay ix Hol Tun *Suiua**
Auatnom Chac Tanal Ah Ya*
    Paxnom Sac Tenel Ahau

Lai u mut katun
    Ox lahun Ahau.

685   That was the enslavement of the people of Emal,
          And also of Hol Tun Zuyua.
      Screaming, the East sacrificial priest
          Destroyed the North sacrificial priest.
      That is the curse of *katun*
690   13 Ahau.

---

685. Emal 'descent', a coastal town to the north of Tizimin, alluded to frequently as "at the edge of the sand, at the edge of the sea." The site is still visible (Roys 1957: 102).
686. Hol Tun Zuyua 'wide stone bloody water', a town near Motul.
687. I read Chac Tenel Ahau. See also line 628. The red (east) sacrificial priest (?of Cozumel) defeats the white (north) (?of Emal).

---

10. The End of the Era

In 1539 Emal claimed the following katun, *then Hol Tun Zuyua and Tihosuco, and finally Zalam Koh Cheil. In the Tihosuco period the Xiu were*

⸪ ⸬ ◖ ◖ ◖

(11v) Ox lahun Ahau*
    U lubul
U cuch katun
    Ti Ah Emalob
Ba ix Hol Tun *Suiua*
    Ba ix Ho Tzuc Chakan*
Ti uil uchom
    Salam Koh Cheil*
T u cuch
    Ho Tzuc Chakan*

      13 Ahau
          Was the posting
      Of the burden of the *katun*
          To the people of Emal,
695   As well as Hol Tun Zuyua,
          As well as Tihosuco.
      In the moon it occurred
          At Zalam Koh Cheil.
      In the burden
700   Of Tihosuco

---

691. This text appears to belong to the very end of *katun* 13 Ahau, "posting the burden of the *katun* to the people of Emal," which was indeed the seat of the following *katun* (11 Ahau). "Posting" provides a rest stop for the burden of the *katun* and therefore symbolizes the transition from one time period to another, perhaps specifically referring to "requesting the burden." See also note 1702.
696. Ho Tzuc Chakan 'five grove meadow'; Barrera 1948: 144 says 'plain of the five fields': this is the modern Tihosuco. The "burden" of the *katun* seems to have been shifted there at some point during 13 Ahau.
698. But the "burden" of the *katun* ended up in Zalam Koh Cheil 'cross-eyed mask woods', apparently a dependency of Izamal and perhaps the modern Tecoh.
700. During the early part of the second decade of 11 Ahau (the 1550s).

painted and sacrificed on the plaza at the ending ceremonies in Mayapan in the dark of the moon. (710)

There were many duties to the seventh cycle and the final end of the katun. *Seven such ends occur in a cycle—seven such years—and, on the seventh, sacrifices end the* katun *with monuments. And custom-*

Uchc u num ya Ah Can Ul e

Uchc u ch'ohlam ch'oh

Uchc u num ya Ah Can Ul

Uay tam bitun Can Ul e*
Ti x u luksah
  U ppicil u cuch
Uai
  Sacl Ac Tun e*
Cum li cah ek uil a

  Ua ix kalah i*
Yabh i
  U cuch u ni uitz

Uuc te u picil u cuch
  Y an uay e
Uai u tz'ocol u than katun

  T u lacal e
Uuc te uil hab uay e
  Kin tun y abil
Uuc te ix ti hab
  Katun y ah uay e
Uuc te ti hab
  Ma ya cimlal
Uabal bin hetz'bal*
  Tz'ocebal u cuch katun

Uai
  Ca nanan

There occurred the suffering of the Can Uls.
  There occurred the painting with indigo.
There occurred the suffering of the Can Uls:
  There before the plaza of Can Ul,
705 Which was also the removal,
  The stacking of the burden
Here
  At Valladolid,
Just within the beginning of the dark of the moon,
710 Or else just at its completion.
For numerous
  Are the burdens of the mountaintop:
The seventh stacking of the burdens
  There has been here.
715 This is the ending of the word of the *katun*
  Altogether.
The seventh moon of the year here—
  And the calendar round;
And the seventh in the year
720 Of the *katun* of people here:
The seventh in the year
  Of painless death.
Pillars will be seated:
  The finishing of the burden of the *katun.*
725 Here then
  It is customary

---

704. Barrera 1948: 145 has *tam bi* 'plaster with paint' and (note 85) refers to the Nahua custom of painting the houses of rebels. He identifies the Ah Canul as the Nahua Guards of Mayapan who settled in Calkini, according to Landa. See also Roys 1967: 15, 63.

708. Sac(i)l Ac Tun 'white cave' is identified by Barrera 1948: 95 with Mayapan and translated as 'white carved stone'. I believe it to be Valladolid (*Zaci*), which is famous for its cave-cenote.

710. Or was this a lunar eclipse?

723. Up to a point this is good Itza doctrine: the end of *katun* 13 Ahau concludes the *katun* cycle. Here, however, we appear to confront Cozumel's justification for taking the half cycle away from Emal. *Katun* 1 Ahau ends the half cycle of the seven odd-numbered *katuns*, and Emal served as the seat of at least three of these (11 Ahau, 5 Ahau, and 1 Ahau). Counting the cycle from 13 to 1 Ahau instead of from 11 is not orthodox and implies a larger claim for Valladolid in the *katuns* to come. Valladolid was in fact the seat of the next two *katuns*, in 12 Ahau and 10 Ahau. The ingenuity of the Cozumel (or Valladolid) argument is that it tries to accommodate the Christian seven cycle within the Mayan system together with the Itza thirteen cycle and the Xiu nine cycle. Compare chapter 25.

arily, there are seven honey tamales at Valladolid and Cozumel. (730)

This is the whole word of the sun priest Uah, the pacer under the priest of Muzen Cab and Za Bac Na at the end of the thirteen katuns. *In seven more katuns the beginning will join the end for the dawn of all the Gods. (748)*

They were brought forth, and then came Itzam Cab Ain, at

Uuc ppel u cabil uah
    T u menel ix Sacl Ac Tun
Lai culan t u pucsikal peten

    Cusamil e*
Ti ulah
    Y etel u xul u than
Ah kin Uah*
    Ti ah lauac can chek i

Y oc Ah Musen Cab*
    Y etel Sa Bac Na*
T u lah y ahaulil
    Ah ox lahun Ahau*
Hun Ahau*
    U kin ti
Ca bin nupp tam ba
    Nac kin
Y etel u
    Y etel akab
Ti ca tal i
    U y ahal cab
Ti ox lahun ti ku
    T u men bolon ti ku
Ti ca sih i
    Ch'ab*
Ca sih i
    Ytzam Cab Ain*

To have seven honey tamales—
    Also on account of Valladolid
That is seated in the heart of the island
730   In Cozumel.
This is the arrival
    And the end of the word
Of the sun priest Uah,
    Who is the measurer of the four paces
735   Under the priest of Muzen Cab
    And Za Bac Na,
Which completes the lordship
    Of the thirteen lords.
1 Ahau
740   Is the day for it,
When they will join each other:
    The rising sun
And moon
    And night.
745   Then comes
    The dawn
From the 13 Gods
    For the 9 Gods,
Who are then born
750   And created.
Then is born
    Itzam Cab Ain

---

730. Cusamil 'chimney swifts', the modern Cozumel. See Tozzer 1941: 201.

733. Uah 'food', sun priest and "pacer" of the *katun*, seemingly at Izamal.

735. Ah Musen Cab 'damp lands', already an important lord in 13 Ahau, claimed the lordship of *katun* 11 Ahau by "tying (the mask) on his face" and going underground with the "nameless" 13 Gods. See also line 849. He was probably from Izamal. The name is sometimes written Muçen or Mucen.

736. Sabac Na 'soot house', another lord, also perhaps from Izamal. See also note 882. The name recalls the Quiche Zipak Na from the Nahuatl Cipactonal (Edmonson 1971: 927).

738. The sun priest "squares the *katun*" with reference to the four directions "in four paces."

739. It is quite possible that 13 Ahau is intended, as Barrera 1948: 146 believes. See, however, note 723.

750. The implication here may be that the twenty-*katun* cycle (the *baktun*) is even more important than the thirteen-*katun* cycle (the *may*). However, seven *katuns* after 13 Ahau is not an even *baktun* in Long Count dating: it would be 12.3.0.0.0. I nonetheless think that the idea is to emphasize the next seven *katun* endings in order to invoke a larger cycle as a protection against revisionism. It is also true that Merida ceased to seat the *katun* in the seventh *katun* from this date.

752. Ytzam Cab Ain 'lizard earth alligator' could be a god name, but I believe he was an Itza personage: Cab Ain of Izamal. He attempted to "fold the *katun*" but was sacrificed by the Xiu, despite the precaution of using a Xiu pseudonym, Uoh Puc 'glyph hill' (line 770).

the division ceremonies, raising the land and celebrating the 13 Gods and flooding the whole world. Then Itzam Cab Ain ended the katun with a flood. But the 9 Gods disagreed, and Itzam Cab Ain was sacrificed, the earth monster. Only he is given the name Uoh Puc, ending the lordship of the katun with the idol shrouded. (776)

Xot eb u kin
  Bal cah
Ca haulahom caan
  Ca nocpahi peten
Ca ix hopp i
  U hum ox lahun ti ku
Ca uch i
  Noh hai cabil*
Ca lik i
  Noh Ytzam Cab Ain
Tz'ocebal u than
  U uutz' katun
Lai hun yeciil
  Bin tz'oce(ce)bal u than katun*

Ma ix y oltah
  Bolon ti ku
Ca ix xot i
  U cal Ytzam Cab Ain
Ca u ch'aah u petenil
  U pach
Lai Ah Uoh Puc u kaba e
  Ma ix u toh pultah u kaba ti ob

Ti kaxan tun u ich
  Ualac y ahaulil la e.

Cutting the pyramid of the sun
  And the world.
755 Then the sky is divided;
  Then the land is raised,
And then there begins
  The Book of the 13 Gods.
Then occurs
760   The great flooding of the earth.
Then arises
  The great Itzam Cab Ain.
The ending of the word,
  The fold of the *katun*:
765 That is a flood
  Which will be the ending of the
  word of the *katun*.
But they did not agree—
  The 9 Gods;
And then will be cut
770   The throat of Itzam Cab Ain.
Who bears the country
  On his back.
That is Uoh Puc by name—
  For they didn't bear their right
  names—
775 To tie the stone face
  And return the lordship.

---

760. *Hay* 'flattening' but *hai(l)* 'flood'; see also line 765.
766. The manuscript has *tz'ocecebal*; I read *tz'ocebal*, as in line 763.

II Ahau

11. Divided Rule

Merida was the seat of the katun in 11 Ahau. Yax Chac

(13r) Ych Can Si Ho*
  U hetz' katun

Merida
  Was the seat of the *katun*

777. Ich Can Si Ho 'in heaven born five' is the modern Merida, seat of the Xiu cycle and *katun* from 1539 to 1638. The administrative organization reflected in the Tizimin vested a loose hegemony over the entire Mayan country in periodic councils of sages (*ah miatzob*). After 1539 there were two seats of the cycle, Mayapan and Merida, and consequently two councils, dividing the country along a north–south line running through Mayapan. The highest official in each area was the Jaguar or lord of the *katun*, sometimes also called the Rattlesnake (Ahau Can), who controlled public offices, land titles, and tribute rights within his half of the country. Theoretically the two Jaguars (Xiu and Itza) between them ruled over the modern territory of Yucatan, Campeche, and Quintana Roo. The Jaguar and his Spokesman were the only really general authorities, and the latter was ex officio the registrar of lands (*ah p'iz te*) and the Great Sun Priest (*ah noh kin*), in charge of the examination of public officials.

Each major city was the center of a province, ruled by a governor (*hal ach uinic*). There appear to have been eighteen provinces. I have tried to match the seventeen cities named in the Tizimin as seats of the cycle or the *katun* to the seventeen provinces identified by Roys 1957 from sixteenth-century tribute rolls, with the following results.

Seat	Province	Capital
Bacalar	*Uaymil*	Bacalar
Chab Le	(?Bahía de la Ascensión)	(?)
Champoton	*Chanputun*	Champoton
Chetumal	*Chetumal*	Chetumal
Chichen Itza	?*Sotuta*	Sotuta
Coba	Ecab	Ecab
Cozumel	*Cozumel*	Cozumel
Emal	Chikinchel	Chauaca
Izamal	Ahkinchel	Tecoh
Mayapan	?Hocaba	Hocaba
Merida	Chakan	Merida
Teabo	*Tutul Xiu*	Mani
Tihosuco	*Cochuah*	Tihosuco
Uxmal	?*Canpech*	Campeche
Valladolid	*Cupul*	Valladolid
Zotz'il	?Tases	Chancenote
Zuyua	?Cehpech	Motul
(?)	*Ahcanul*	?Calkini

(note continued on following page)

*was the lord, with ceremonies
and music, together with the 9
priest Oc Te, Yax Cutz, Zulim
Chan, and Champoton. Starving in the wilderness was the*

Ti buluc Ahau
   Katun
Yaxal Chac u u ich
   U y ahaulil t u canil*
Y et bal canal u al
   Canal utz'ub
Pecnom pax
   Pecnom soot
Ah Bolon y Oc Teil*
   T u kin y an Yax Cutz*
T u kin y an Sulim Chan
   T u kin y an Ah Chakan Putun*

Uilnom che
   Uilnom tunich
Ti tal i
   Y emel ychil buluc Ahau katun

In the 11 Ahau
780   *Katun.*
Yax Chac was the person
   In the lordship on high,
Including the sky water,
   The sky perfume.
785 Resounded the drum,
   Resounded the rattle
Of the 9 priest Oc Te
   At the time there was Yax Cutz;
At the time there was Zulim Chan;
790   At the time there was the lord of
   Champoton.
Starved trees,
   Starved rocks,
Which came
   To befall in *katun* 11 Ahau,

(note continued from preceding page)

It would appear that Chab Le was the eighteenth province, somewhere west of
Bahía de la Ascensión, which Roys leaves unassigned. Province names that occur
in the Tizimin are italicized. Province boundaries fluctuated over time, so I am
assuming that the boundaries were different when Chichen Itza ruled Sotuta,
Mayapan ruled Hocaba, Zotz'il ruled Tases, and Uxmal ruled Canpech. Roys does
not provide a capital for Ahcanul and doesn't identify Chab Le or Bahía de la
Ascensión as provinces. Tixchel and the Peten were not part of the Yucatecan
system.

   Smaller towns and villages were ruled by headmen or chiefs (*ba tabob*) and
their assistants (*ah kulelob*), and wards of the cities were ruled by counselors (*ah
cuch cabob*), according to Roys.

   All officials were supposed to be sun priests (*ah kin*), and they were presumably closely linked to the local levels of religious organization, headed by the
directional priesthoods of the Ba Cabs, who seem to have been ex officio captains
(*nacom*) for military and sacrificial purposes. The Ba Cabs of the *katun* seat thus
served as Captains of the Jaguar.

   The local organization imposed by the Spanish is nowhere mentioned in the
Tizimin either for the town (*cabildos, alcaldías, regidores*) or for the parish (*co-
fradías, maestros, sacristanes*).

   782. Both Zulim Chan of Emal and Yaxal Chac 'green rain' of Merida claimed
to seat *katun* 11 Ahau. The traditional opposition of east and west, Itza and Xiu,
was compounded by the Mayapan calendar reform in 1539 and by the arrival of
the Spaniards in Merida in 1541, as the texts of this period document. A new Itza
katun cycle began, scheduled to span the colonial period (1539 to 1796, but later
revised to run to 1824) and theoretically seated at Mayapan. The Xiu cycle was
already underway (1461 to 1718), and an effort was made to seat it at Merida,
which also claimed to seat the *katun* for the hundred years from 1539 to 1638.

   787. Bolon y Octeil 'nine footed', an unidentified lord. This may be a Mayan
day name, 9 Oc Te, possibly implying that he is a commoner, lacking one
surname.

   788. Yax Cutz 'green turkey', possibly a maternal kinsman of Yaxal Chac. The
Chacs were a leading lineage in Chichen Itza in the fifteenth century and Merida
in the sixteenth, and the Yaxals were prominent in Valladolid (line 4043) in the
seventeenth.

   790. Chakan Putun is the modern Champoton but may be a personal name
here.

fate of 11 Ahau, and poor food
was its food. (800)

Yax Chuen was killed, and
the news was spread by all and
sundry, telling children, old,
and young of the arrival of the
Spanish to change your clothes
to white: the bearded judges at
the capital in Merida and the
priests of the True God who is
to be worshiped everywhere
down here on earth: another

Okbaom
  Caan
Ox
  Koch
U uah
  Katun
Xotom u cal Yaxal Chuen*
  Uecom ix kay
U than ti bal cah
  Ti tal i
Ban ban ah kayil i*
  Ma mac ma ah kay
(. . . . .)
  Ah kainom pal
Ah kainom nu xib
  Ah kainom ix nuc
Ah kainom tan celem
  Ah kainom ix lok
Bay en t u y ulel au itz'in ex

  A sucun ex ti y ulel
U hel au ex
  U hel a nok
U sacil a buuc
  U sacil au ex
Xotob tz'ul*
  Ah mexob
Ich Can Si Ho
  U hetz' lumob
Hex
  Ah kin e
Cuxul ku
  Hahal ku*
La bin kultabac
  Ti hun yuklah
Ti cab
  Ti y emel
U chayan
  Tepal
T ix ma yum
  T ix ma na

795 Being sent out
  From heaven.
Breadnut
  And gourdroot
Were the food
800   Of the *katun*.
Cut was the throat of Yax Chuen,
  And scattered was the song
Of his word to the world.
  That came about.
805 Many, many were the singers
  And no one was not a singer:
(. . . . .)
  Sung to were children,
Sung to were men,
810   Sung to were wives,
Sung to were boys,
  Sung to were girls.
So be it: your younger brothers are
coming!
  Your older brothers are arriving
815 To change your pants,
  To change your clothes,
To whiten your dress,
  To whiten your pants—
The foreign judges,
820   The bearded men
Of Heaven Born Merida,
  The seat of the lands.
And they
  Are the sun priests
825 Of the living God,
  The True God.
He shall be worshiped
  In one communion
On earth
830   Below:
An additional
  Rule.
And for the fatherless,
  And for the motherless—

---

801. Yaxal Chuen 'green monkey', an unidentified lord, possibly a maternal kinsman of Yaxal Chac. A lord with the same name ruled Valladolid in the 1660s (line 4043). Barrera 1948: 95 pairs Yaxal Chuen with Ix Kan Yul Ta.

805. *Kay* 'sing' apparently implies 'blab, spread the word'.

819. Barrera 1948: 98 translates *xotob* as 'accursed'.

826. Hunab Ku 'sole god' is the Mayan creator, identified as a father. All the other gods are unified (*hunab*) in his person. He is distinguished to some degree from the Christian God, identified in these texts as *Dios* or the True God (Hahal Ku). Eventually the two concepts merged.

rule of the peasants. The Jaguar urged the people to become converted, and then began the tripartite government of Merida, in 11 Ahau. (846)

Balam u pol
   Cech u uinicil
Hoyan
   T u yam cah
Ti tal i
   U chun i
T ix u chun
   Ox kas tepal*
Ich Can Si Ho
   Lai u cuch
Buluc Ahau
   Katun a.*

835 Jaguar was the head
   And urged his people
To be sprinkled
   In the changed city.
So came about
840   Its founding,
And it was the founding
   Of the three-part rule
In Heaven Born Merida.
   That is the burden
845 Of 11 Ahau,
   The *katun* here.

842. Perhaps the tripartite government means Xiu, Itza, and Spanish.
846. Barrera 1948: 98 adds that *katun* 11 Ahau will end in 1848, which is correct in the Valladolid calendar. Similar dates are given in his texts for 9 Ahau (1872), 7 Ahau (1896), 5 Ahau (1920), 2 Ahau (1800), and 13 Ahau (1824), but 9 Ahau is incorrectly listed as 1822 and 5 Ahau as 1921.

12. The Flower *Katun* of the Xiu

In 11 Ahau the priest of Muzen Cab had finished off the 13 nameless Gods, who were just called Holy and Remote rather than by name, and who didn't show their faces either. Then at the new beginning the Gods who were exchanging places came and spoke, the 13

(11v) Ychil buluc Ahau*
   Ca lik i
Ah Musen Cab
   Kaax ix u u ich
Ox lahun ti ku
   Ma ix y oheltah ob u kaba
Cilich
   Citbil
Lai u kaba
   Y alah ob ti*
Ma ix chicanh i
   U u ich ti ob xan
Ca tz'oc i
   Y ahal cab
Ma ix y oheltah ob binil
   Ulebal ca ix cih i

In 11 Ahau
   Then arose
The priest of Muzen Cab
850   And tied the faces
Of the 13 Gods,
   But they didn't know their names.
"The Holy,"
   "The Remote,"
855 These are the names
   They called them.
And they also didn't show
   Their faces to them either.
At last
860   It dawned,
And they didn't know their going
   Or their coming, and then spoke

847. This is a particularly elliptical text, but it nonetheless has a great deal to say about the ideological struggles of this *katun*, which set Mayas against Spaniards, Xiu against Itza, prophets and priests against each other and against the warriors, and gods against gods.
856. See, however, lines 581 ff.

Itza Gods to the 9 Xiu Gods,
ordering war and punishment,
and there was war and punish-
ment. And the Itza Gods beat
them and abused them and
took away the four yearbearers
and the 5 priest Za Bac, Xiu
and Itza and the children of
both, for the first nine of the

Ox lahun ku
  Ti bolon ku*
Ca emi kak
  Ca emi tab
Ca emi tunich
  Y etel chee
Ca tal i
  U baxal
Che
  Y etel tunich*
Ca ix kuch i
  Ox lahun ti ku
Ca pax i
  U pol
Ca lah i
  U u ich
Ca tubab i
  Ca colpah i*
Can hel
  Y etel Ho Sabac*
Ca ch'abi ix kukil
  Ix yaxum
U ppuyem sicil
  U ppuyem topp
U teppah u y inah*
  Yax bolon tz'acab*

    The 13 Gods
      To the 9 Gods:
865 "Bring down fire.
      Bring down the rope.
    Bring down stones
      And trees."
    Then came
870   Pounding
    Of sticks
      And stones.
    And then appeared
      The 13 Gods
875 And beat
      Their heads
    And flattened
      Their faces,
    And they were spat on
880   And snatched away,
    The four yearbearers
      And the 5 priest Za Bac;
    And the quetzals were taken,
      And blue birds,
885 Crushing the Zic,
      Crushing the Top,
    And wrapping the seeds
      Of the first nine steps

---

864. Bolon ti Ku 'the nine who are gods' were the gods of the nine levels of the underworld. They are evoked here along with the 13 Gods as a symbol of the debate over the cycle. The ninth *katun* in the Itza cycle was the thirteenth in the Xiu count and vice versa. Each was thus in a position to claim identification with heaven and relegate the other to hell. Compare line 1094, in which the seven demons symbolize the Christian cycle.

An additional significance to the preoccupation with cycles of nine and thirteen is their relationship to the Venus year: $9 \times 65 = 13 \times 45 = 585$, just one day more than the approximate Venus cycle of 584 days. Hence, in either series, the coefficient of the day that ends the Venus year progresses backward by 1 each time it occurs. This kind of mathematics corresponds to other similar equations discovered by the Maya: $52 \times 365 = 73 \times 260$ (52 years equals 73 *tzol kins*), $72 \times 365 = 73 \times 360$ (72 years equals 73 *tuns*), and $8 \times 365 = 5 \times 584$ (8 years equals 5 Venus years). In such calculations the Maya were very close to the invention of an algebra.

872. "Fire and rope" and "sticks and stones" are frequent kennings for war.

880. That is, the Itza party won. The first five (i.e., the directional) priests of the Xiu were eliminated.

882. I read Hol Sabac 'head soot', apparently a Xiu lord, perhaps from Izamal. Compare Sabac Na (Nahuatl ?Cipactonal) in line 736 and *sabac* in line 1870. Landa 1929: 2: 88 discusses a ceremony called Zabacil Than, and the modern Lacandon have a god called Men Sabac. The word could also represent a lineage name: Za Bac. There follows a list of Xiu lineages: Kuk 'quetzal', Yax 'green', Sic 'squash seed', and Topp 'pumpkin seed'.

887. That is, the Itza carried off the heirs of the Xiu and sacrificed them.

888. Landa 1929: 2: 20 identifies *ah bolon zacab* as a god; Seler (ibid.) translates it as 'lord of the nine generations or of the nine doctors'.

thirteen levels. And they per-
formed the sacrifice of the
breast and then the heart, be-
cause the 13 Gods didn't know
that the heart is the end, and it
was 11 Ahau 7 Uo. (902)

And the wretches without
kin or spirits rot by the sea-
shore. There was a flood un-
leashed by the yearbearers to
clear the world for the next cy-
cle, killing youngest sons. The
katun ended in 1539 on 3 Oc 17

Ca bin i
   T u y ox lahun tas caan
Ca culh i
   U matz'il
Y etel u ni
   U baclil
Ca bin i
   U pucsikal
T u menel ox lahun ti ku
   Ma ix y oheltah binc i

U pucsikal
   U uil la e
Ca hut
   Lah i
Ix ma (12r) yumob
   Ah num yaob
Ix ma ichamob
   Cuxanob*
Ix ti manan u pucsikal
   Ca mucchahi ob
T u yam sus
   T u yam kaknab*
Hun uatz' hail
   Ti uch i
U col
   Can hel
To homocnac canal
   Homocnac ix cabal
T u katunil u nup
   U uutz'
Cimc i
   U thupil mehen
Lai u uutz' u katunil
   Oxil Oc u kinil ulc i uay e*

     Which went
890   To the thirteen levels of heaven.
    Then was cut
     The membrane
    And the nose
     Of the skeleton.
895 Then went
     The heart,
    On account of the 13 Gods.
     But they didn't know what was
      going.
    The heart
900   Of the moon there
    Is dropped
     Flat.
    And the fatherless,
     The miserable,
905 And those without spouses
     Or living relatives,
    And those that don't have hearts
     Then began to rot
    By the margin of the sand,
910   By the margin of the sea.
    One torrent of water
     Occurred,
    Which was released
     By the yearbearers.
915 That was the clearing of heaven
     And also the clearing of the lands
    For the period opposite
     The fold,
    Killing
920   Youngest sons.
    That is the fold of the *katun* cycle;
     3 Oc is the time it arrived here.

---

906. "Orphans" are peasants: nobles know their ancestry. The sense is that even widows and children of families of no account were carried off to be sacrificed at Emal. Doubtless it was difficult for the Itza to assault the Xiu strongholds at Merida and Mani after the Spanish were in residence there, so they turned their attention to the Xiu villages, consequently capturing few important nobles.

910. The reference is probably to Emal, which claimed to be the seat of *katun* 11 Ahau; see also lines 661–662. The counterclaimant was Merida (lines 778, 1171), but the present passage suggests the possibility that Izamal was also competing for the privilege.

922. The Xiu inaugurated the new *katun* in 1539 in their own way. The year began on 11 Ix 1 Pop (July 21). The Xiu ignored the Itza inauguration of the new *katun* on 11 Ahau 7 Uo (August 16) and initiated their own ceremonies on 3 Oc 17 Tzec (September 15), centering them on the terminal date of the old *katun*: 13 Ahau 7 Xul (November 4) and completing them on 1 Cimi 13 Ch'en (January 9, 1540). The seventy-six-day ceremonial program is described in the remainder of this chapter.

*Tzec; the katun prophecy ended
on 1 Cimi 13 Ch'en. And the
four Fathers of the Land subju-
gated the land, returning to the
east tree of fate, the senior one
of the four and symbol of its
subjugation. And they felled
the tree of the yearbearers and
seated the East priest Xib Yuy.
Then to the north tree of fate to
seat the North priest Hic, symbol of its subjugation. And then*

Hun Cimi u kinil tz'occ i
    U than katun ca ualh i
Can tul ku
    Can tul Ba Cab*
Lai hayes ob cab*
    Ca tz'oci hai cabil e
Ca ualh i
    Chac Imix che*
Lay y oc
    Mal can
Lay u chicul
    U hayal cab
Lay u coicinah che
    Ba Cab
U alic
    Kan Xib Yuy*
Ca ualh i
    Sac Imix che ti xaman
Lai u alic
    Sac Hic*
U chicul
    Hai cabil

1 Cimi is the time that ended
    The word of the returned *katun.*
925 The four gods—
    The four Fathers of the Land—
That is their flattening of the land.
    When the lands have been flattened
Then there returns
930 The red Imix tree
That is proceeding
    To pass the four.
That is the sign
    Of the flattening of the land.
935 That is the toppling of the tree
    Of the Fathers of the Land,
Called
    The East priest Xib Yuy.
Then there returns
940 The white Imix tree to the north.
He is called
    The North priest Hic,
The sign
    Of the flattening of the lands.

926. Ba Cab 'father of the land': the gods and priests of the four directions, identified also with the Chacs and the yearbearers.

927. What follows is one of many elliptical descriptions of ritual in the Tizimin. The ceremonial cycle was certainly both rich and varied, and like most of the rest of Mayan life it was calendrically organized. Some rituals were pegged to the life cycle, including naming, courtship, marriage, illness, induction into office, retirement, and burial. As time went on, much ritual was adjusted to the church calendar. At the outset, however, we may distinguish three primary ritual cycles: the *tzol kin,* the *tun,* and the *hab.* The *tzol kin* rituals emphasized in the Tizimin are the fire ceremonies of the Burners (*ah toc*), operating on a sixty-five-day cycle. The ceremonies governed by the *tun* are those that punctuate the lordship of the *katun,* mainly at five-year intervals: requesting office, taking the plate, making the ceremonial circuit, declaring the word of the *katun,* naming the remainder, suspending titles, and folding the mat (together with the ceremonial commemoration of ancestors). The rituals of the *hab* began with the new year and included at least one major ritual in each *uinal,* thus centering on a twenty-day cycle within the 365-day year. The most important ceremonies of all were the *katun* transitions every twenty *tuns* and the calendar round (*kin tun y abil*) transitions every fifty-two years. There is a continual play in the Tizimin between the Itza emphasis on *tun* and *katun* rituals and the Xiu emphasis on yearbearers and the calendar round.

930. There follows a counterclockwise ceremonial circuit to "flatten" (i.e., subdue) the land—by confirming titles (see also note 216). Each direction is identified by color and provided with an Imix tree, thought to symbolize cataclysm or destruction (Solís Alcalá 1949: 57), from the east (red) to the north (white) to the west (black) to the south (yellow) to the center (green blue).

938. Kan Xib Yuy 'yellow male matasano tree' appears to be a mistake for Chac Xib Yuy, presumptively the priest of the Ba Cab of the east. The matasano tree is the *Casimiroa.*

942. Zac Hic 'white ———?' is apparently the incomplete name of the Ba Cab priest of the north. Perhaps Ah Ic 'cane chile'.

the west tree of fate in the west country, the symbol of its subjugation. That is the west tree of fate, seating the West priest Tam Pic the Weak. Then the south tree of fate, the symbol of its subjugation, seating the South priest Oyal Mut. And then the middle tree of fate, the reminder of its subjugation, finishing the katun. (966)

By 11 Ahau there had been nine generations of sages seeking office, and the ninth term was 1538. That ended the cycle,

Ca ix ualh i
  Ek Imix che
T u chikin
  Peten
U chicul
  Hai cabil
Lai
  Ek Imix che
Culic Ek Tam Pic Tz'oy*

  Culic kanal Imix che
T u nohol
  Peten
U chicul
  U hayal cab
Culic Kan Oyal Mut*
  Ca culh i
Yax Imix che*
  T u chumuc cab
U kahlai
  Hai cabil
Cuntal u cah u lac
  U y anal katun la e
Buluc Ahau u kinil
  Y emel u than
Bolon tz'acab
  Miatz
Ti t u uutz'
  U katal u cuch katun

Bolon te*
  U cuch
Ca em i
  Ti canil Kan*
U kinil ual e
  Ca hau u cuch
Ca em i
  Tal i

945 Then also returns
  The black Imix tree
To the west
  Of the country,
The sign
950   Of the flattening of the lands:
That
  Is the black Imix tree,
Seating the West priest Tam Pic the Weak,
  Seating the yellow Imix tree
955 To the south
  Of the country,
The sign
  Of the flattening of the lands
Seating the South priest Oyal Mut.
960   Then is seated
The green Imix tree
  In the middle of the land,
The reminder
  Of the flattening of the lands.
965 Piled in its place is the whole
  Of the existence of this *katun*.
11 Ahau is the time
  Of the coming of the word
Of the nine steps
970   Of sages
Who folded
  And asked for the burden of the *katun*,
The ninth
  Of his burdens,
975 That came down
  On 4 Kan,
The time of the return
  That ended the burden.
Then it descended
980   And came

---

953. Ek Tam Pic Tz'oy 'black deep bedbug weak', the Ba Cab priest of the west.

959. Kan Oyal Mut 'yellow island pheasant', the Ba Cab priest of the south.

961. The inclusion of a fifth (center) stage in the circuit has a Mexican ring to it, presumably a Xiu rather than an Itza trait.

973. The symbolism by nines which follows may be an allusion to the lords of the night, gods of the underworld. See also note 864. It is thoroughly obscure but seems to involve a directional circuit of four (E-N-W-S) plus five (E-N-W-S-Center), which then repeats. Presumably there was a sage associated with each, and the rotation may have been by *uinals*, thus completing two cycles per *tun*.

976. 4 Kan was the yearbearer for 1545. It appears that the ceremonial circuit and the cycles of time enumerated in the preceding lines are those of the eighteen *uinals* of that year, each initiated on a day Kan.

which came to the center of the
sky to be reborn in the nine
bush houses and the nine cy-
cles with mouth and nose,
tongue and brain sacrifices.
(990)

Then came the feast of the
two Red Were Bats to suck the
flowers: the east and north and
west and south cups. And Hau
Nab, Hutz' Nab, Kuk Nab, Oyal
Nicte, Ninich Cacau, Chabi
Tok, 5 Xochitl, Hobon y Ol
Nicte, Kouol y Ol Nicte:
these are the Flowers, the sell-
ers of the cycles. These are the
Flower Houses, the Flower sun
priests and lords, the Flower
captains. Thus are the Flower

Tan y ol caan
   U ca put sihil
Bolon haban
   Y otoch
Y et emc i
   Bolon mayel
Ch'ahuc u chi
   Ch'ahuc u ni
Y ak
   Ch'ahuc ix u tz'amil
Ca em i
   Ca tul
Chac Uayab Sotz'*
   Lai tz'utz' e
U cabil ob nicte
   Ti ca hok i
Ix Chac Hoch' Kom
   Ix Sac Hoch' Kom
Ix Ek Hoch' Kom
   Ix Kan Hoch' Kom
Ix Hau Nab*
   Ix Hutz' Nab
Ix Kuk Nab
   Hokc i
Tun ix Oyal Nicte
   Ix Ninich Cacau
Ix Chabi Tok
   Ix *Mabil Xuchit*
Ix Hobon y Ol Nicte
   Ix Kouol y Ol Nicte
Lai
   Hokci ob nicte la e
Ah con
   Mayelob
Lai
   U na nicteob hokc i

Y utz'ub ah kin
   Y utz'ub ahau
Y utz'ub hol can
   Lai u cuch

Before the center of the sky,
   The second birth
Of the nine bush
   Houses.
985 There also descended
   The nine cycles,
Dripping at the mouth,
   Dripping at the nose,
The tongue,
990   And dripping its brains.
Then descended
   The two:
The Red Were Bats
   Who suck
995 The nectars of the Flowers.
   And then appeared
Also the red Hoch' Kom,
   And the white Hoch' Kom,
And the black Hoch' Kom,
1000   And the yellow Hoch' Kom,
And Hau Nab,
   And Hutz' Nab,
And Kuk Nab
   Appeared then,
1005 And Oyal Nicte,
   And Ninich Cacau,
And Chabi Tok,
   And Macuilxochitl,
And Hobon y Ol Nicte,
1010   And Kouol y Ol Nicte.
This
   Was the appearance of the Flowers,
The sellers
   Of the cycles.
1015 These
   Are the Flower Houses that
   appeared,
The blossom of the sun priest,
   The blossom of the lord,
The blossom of the captain.
1020 That is the burden

---

993. Chac Uayab Sotz' 'powerful were bat', the bat god, one of the more important of the Mayan divinities.

1001. These may be the lords of the night: (1) Hau Nab 'slice point', (2) Hutz'
Nab 'split point', (3) Kuk Nab 'quetzal point', (4) Oyal Nicte 'island flower',
(5) Ninich Cacau 'wormy cacao', (6) Chabi Tok 'digging knife', (7) Macuilxochitl
(Nahuatl) 'five flower' (the Nahuatl *xochitl* 'flower' corresponds to the day Ahau
'lord' in Maya), (8) Hobon y Ol Nicte 'colored heart flower' (this is the Hobnil in
Landa 1929: 2: 20), and (9) Kouol y Ol Nicte 'pouched heart flower'.

lords, bringing famine in 11
Ahau. It is the time not of the 9
Gods of hell, the nine lower lev-
els, but of the Flower survey of
the Xiu and the spirits, the
9 Flower Suckers. And, at
the center of the four Flower
priests, the sun priest sits
counting the tun. *(1044)*

And the thirteen Itza priests
appeared secretly for the proph-
ecy of the Flower and the
Flower rule. It was Za Uin who
was seated. Envy is his time;

Nicte ahau
  Ca em i
Ma ix uah
  U cuch nicte katun*
T u kinil
  Ma ix kuch i
U ch'abnac i
  Ku mitnal i
Bolon tz'acab
  Ca em i
U ch'ab nicte
  Ppis lim tee
Yax bac
  Tz'unun*
Ix u uay inah
  Ca em i
Ca u tz'utz'ah u kabil nicte

  Bolon y al nicte*
Ca tun hok i
  U puczikal nicte
Can hek
  Ix u lac nicteob e
Ti x culan ah kin
  Xocbil tun
Ti ca uch i
  U hokol ox lahun ti ku
Ma ix y oheltah ob
  Y emel u keban pop
Kuch i
  T u than
Cuch i
  Nicte
Ix u pop nicte
  Ix u kan che
Sa Uin
  Culic*
Sauin u luch
  Sauin u lac
Sauin u pucsikal
  Sauin u chi

Of the Flower lords
  When they descend.
And "there is no food"
  Is the burden of the Flower *katun*.
1025 In his time
  There also does not come
The creation
  Of the Gods of hell,
The nine steps
1030   That descend,
The creation of the Flowers,
  Of the measuring stick.
Blue bird
  And hummingbird
1035 Are also the spirits
  Who come down
When they suck the nectars of the
Flowers,
  The nine children of Flowers.
Then there appears
1040   The heart of the Flower:
Four branches
  And all the Flowers,
And there the sun priest is seated
  For the counting of the *tun*.
1045 When that is done
  There appear the 13 Gods,
But they don't know them,
  Descending to the unfolded mat,
And arriving
1050   At the word,
Bearing
  The Flower,
And the mat of the Flower,
  And the yellow throne.
1055 Za Uin
  Is seated:
Envy is his gourd;
  Envy is his plate;
Envy is his heart;
1060   Envy is his mouth.

1024. See note 1806.
1034. See note 119.
   1038. In the myth of the origin of the Xiu, the Hummingbird sipped the nectar of the 9 Flowers, producing little Flowers (Roys 1967: 105).
   1056. What follows is a pun on the name: *sauin* is 'envy'. It is a frequent expression for the contesting of the lordship, particularly by unqualified upstarts. Given the strongly hierarchical bent of Mayan society, envy is a particularly salient Mayan disease.

envy is his soul. Mad was the prophecy of the priest. Hungry and thirsty, he pretends to eat but faints, fasting and complaining. He takes the mask and throne and sits as lord, forgetting his parents, father and mother both, for truly he was misbegotten. He did not seek office properly from the 9 Gods or the 7 priest Sat Ay. He destroyed their spirit and murdered and strangled every one. (1100)

And the Itza prophet and sun priests were at fault, and partic-

Hach co u (12v) coil	Great is his madness,
U than	His word
Ti y ahaulil	In the lordship
T u kinil	At the time,
Auat uiil	1065 Crying food,
Auat ukul	Crying drink,
T u xai u chi	He opens his mouth
Lic u hanal	As though eating
T u pach	And afterward
U xau	1070 Gets dizzy,
C u uiil	Fasting
Auat ukul	And crying for drink.
Sip u than ti culic	Blame is the word of him who is seated,
	Blame is his teaching.
Sip u can	1075 Tied is the face
Kaxan u u ich*	Of him who is seated.
Ti culic	He takes his place,
Ch'a u cah tza*	Demands his mat place,
U cah pop	And sits
Culic	1080 As the lord,
T u y ahau	As if forgetting his father,
Lic tuban u yum	Forgetting his mother.
Tuban u naa	And he does not know the father
Ma ix y ohel u yum	Who engendered him,
Mehente	1085 And does not know the mother
Ma ix y ohel u na	Who bore him.
Sihese	For truly
Halil i	It was
Y an	By nose
T u ni	1090 And tongue he was born,
Y ak tz'etz'ec e*	Crier of the burden
U h auat cuch	He did not ask for.
Ma u matan	From the 9 Gods he descended,
Ti bolon ti ku em i	The 7 priest Sat Ay.
Ix Uuc Sat Ai*	1095 And then was destroyed their spirit;
Ca ix sati y ol	And then was destroyed their breath.
Ca ix sati y ik	Then their throats were cut;
	Their throats were tied,
Ca ch'aci u cal	By themselves,
U hich' u cal	1100 Alone.
T u ba	Blamed was the word of that prophet,
T u hunal	And blamed was that sun priest.
Sip u than ah bobat la e	
Sip ix ah kin la e	

1075. Tying the mask on his face.

1077. I read *tz'um*.

1090. Sexual insults are fairly common in the Tizimin, most often referring to sodomy or adultery.

1094. The allegation is that the usurping lord tried to justify himself in terms of the Christian calendar rather than the Itza cycle. Shocking! See also note 514.

ularly the lord and the captains, who just lay in their
hammocks and dropped their
shields and lances for the enemy and ran and didn't wait for
the end of the war. So they began hanging and taking prisoners but did not end the
katun. And they were sacrificed
by the Xiu. The priests and captains conferred during the war,
and at the end of 1548 the
chiefs were judged by the nobles of Kin Chil of Coba and
Miz Cit. (1142)

This is the word of the 13 Gods,

Sisip ahau
 Sipob ix hol can la e
Ti haulah i
 T u thubob
Ti noclah i
 Chimal
Ti noclah i
 Nab te
Lahun y al
 Y ah ual uincob
Ix ca ualh i
 Ma ix ti y oltah ob
U talel
 U tz'ocol u than
Katun
 Hol can i
Uil likci ob cuch i e
 U ch'uima ob
Ix tab t u kab
 Ma ix kaxan
U u ich katun
 U tz'ah ob ix u tan
Ti lomol nicte
 Ix cimc i
Ah kinob
 Ah miatzob
Ahauob
 Hol canob
Hokan ob
 Ix than
Ichil u y anal
 Katun e
T u bolon tun e
 Ti uil*
Uchom u xotom ba tabil*
 Ti y ahaulil
Y al
 U mehen
Ah Kin Chil Coba*
 Y etel Ah Mis Cit ual e*
U than
 Ox lahun ti ku

Twice blamed was the lord,
 And blamed were those captains—
1105 Who rested
 In the bottoms of the hammocks—
Who had dropped there
 The shields,
Who had dropped there
1110 The lances
Of the ten born children,
 The enemies,
And then turned back
 And didn't know
1115 About the coming
 Of the ending of the word
Of the war
 And soldiers.
They may have raised
1120 Their hangings,
And tying by the hands,
 And they did not tie
The face of the *katun*,
 And they gave up their fronts
1125 To the stabbing Flower
 And died.
The sun priests,
 The sages,
The lords,
1130 The captains
Entered
 And spoke
In the period
 Of the war,
1135 In the ninth *tun*,
 In the moon
Was the judging of the chiefs
 In the lordship,
The born
1140 And engendered children
Of Kin Chil of Coba
 And Miz Cit again.
This is the word
 Of the 13 Gods:

1136. That is, at the end of 1548 to 1549.
1137. Ba Tab 'fathers of the rope'; see also line 926, and compare the etymology of Ba Cab. *Bab* is 'father' in Ixil; compare Chol *pap*, Jicaque *bap*, Lenca *paab*, Sumo *pápa*, Ulua *papan*, Cuna *paba*, Cacopera *uapá*, and Huaxtec *pailom*.
1141. Kin Chil 'sun sailfish', lord of Coba 'chachalaca water' and of *katun* 13 Ahau in the early nineteenth century, and possibly also in the early sixteenth.
1142. Mis Cit 'sweep remove', another lord, presumably also of Coba. The reference is to the lord of 8 Ahau at the time of the fall of Mayapan.

not mine, for it happened
thrice on earth: thrice in this
katun: once on the day of
Naclah Uitz (1546), once on the
day of the sacrifice of the no-
bles of the poor Itza (1549), and
once at the end of the Xiu in
the Christianity of 11 Ahau
(1559). (1164)

Ma i
  T in than
Ca t uch i
  Ox uatz'*
T u uinicil ual e
  Y okol cab
Ca uch i
  Ox uatz' katun ual e
T u kin Naclah Uitz*
  Chuchul Chuch
T u kin chac tun
  Num ya
U y al
  U mehen
Ah num
  Ytza
Ma cetel bin tz'ocbal
  Nicte unicil
Nicte katun
  Ichil *Christianoil* ual e.

1145 It is not
  In my words.
For it happened
  On three occasions
To these people again
1150 On earth,
And it happened
  Three times in this *katun*'s return:
On the day of Naclah Uitz
  Bearing the load;
1155 And on the day of red stone
  Suffering
Of the born
  And engendered children
Of the sufferers,
1160 The Itza;
Otherwise will be the ending
  Of the Flower people,
The Flower *katun*
  On Christianity's return.

1148. That is, there were three prophecies in 11 Ahau, one at the beginning and others nine and eighteen years later.

1153. Naclah Uitz is the fourth of the 13 Gods; see also line 584. This may be a reference to a year with the numeral coefficient 4, perhaps 1545.

13.   The Mayapan Calendar of the Itza

Katun 11 Ahau was the start
of a new Itza katun *count. The*
Spaniards arrived at its begin-
ning. Merida was the katun
seat. The red-bearded gods

(16r) Buluc Ahau
  Katun
U yax chun
  U xocol katun*
U hun tz'it katun
  Ulic sac uinicob
Ich Can Si Ho
  U hetz' katun
Bee chac u mexob
  U mehen kin

1165 11 Ahau
  Was the *katun*.
It was the new base
  Of the counting of the *katun*.
The first part of the *katun*
1170 There arrived the white people.
Heaven Born Merida
  Was the seat of the *katun*.
So, red were the beards
  Of the sons of the sun,

1168. A direct reference to the Mayapan calendrical reform of 1539. See the appendix and Edmonson 1976. 11 Ahau began the Itza *may,* the *katun* cycle that ended in 1824.

*coming from the east were wel-
comed with tears. The bearded
foreigners displayed the white
God on the cross. Immediately
beforehand you expected them.
(1186)*

*They came to build, and
priests came with them, bringing the word of God to redeem
the world. So we wept over conversion, O peasants and nobles!
God's will be done, as He is the
Father of heaven and earth.
Welcome it when it comes to
Mani. (1206)*

Sac uinicob e
  Be okbac on ti tali ob
Ti likin u tal
  Ca uli ob uay e
Ah mexob
  Ah pulob*
Ti chicul ku sac
  Uaom che canal
Hun lub
  Hun auat u talel
Au ilc ex
  Mut y ahal cab t ex
Ulic ob hunac mol cheob
  Hunac mol tunichob
Y et ulc ob
  U yumil ca pixan*
Oclis u than hahal ku
  T au ol ex
Lei bin etz'kal
  A pac ti bal cah tusinil
U than ku likul canal

  Be okbac on ti tali ob
C ex u itz'in ex
  C ex sucun ex e
U than ku ma tusbil
  Be lic u talel u betabal i
U than u yumil caan
  Y etel luum
Kam ex
  Au ula ex
Talel u cah
  Ah tan tunob e.*

1175 Those white people;
  So we wept at their coming.
They came from the east;
  Then they arrived here,
The bearded men,
1180   The *guayaba* people,
And manifested the white God
  Standing on the tall pole.
One stop,
  One shout before they came,
1185 You saw them
  And awaited your dawn.
They came to assemble piles of trees,
  To assemble piles of stones,
And there came with them
1190   The fathers of our souls,
Bringing the word of the True God
  To your hearts.
That will be the setting of the roll,
  Your fold of the wicked world.
1195 The word of God will be raised on high.
  So we wept at their coming,
O younger brothers,
  O older brothers!
The word of God is no falsehood.
1200   Thus as it comes it will be done,
The word of the Father of heaven
  And earth.
Take it
  And welcome it,
1205 Coming to the town
  Of the front stone people.

1180. The Maya were impressed that the first thing the Spaniards ate was *guayaba*, so they nicknamed them "*guayaba* eaters," as well as "red beards," "foreigners," "white men," and "sons of the sun." See Tozzer 1941: 49. *Guayaba* is *Annona.*

1190. The first Franciscans reached Campeche in 1546 (Ancona 1878: 2: 36), Mani in 1548 (ibid.: 49), Merida, Conkal, and Izamal in 1549 (ibid.: 71), and Valladolid in 1552 (ibid.: 72).

1206. Barrera 1948: 126 associates Tan Tun with Cozumel. I speculate that it may refer to the façade of the church at Mani, first headquarters of the Franciscans in 1548.

14. The Death of the Gods

Tzin Yabun the Younger's prophecy: the announcement of the priestly succession in Yucatan at the request of the sun priests. If it is rejected, tell what you know to be true in no uncertain terms. You will make up your minds about the ruined Mayan gods, and forget the wretches and worship the True God and the world of the Father and Creator. (1238)

(10r) U *profesia*
    Na Tzin Yabun Chan*
U chi
    U than
U hel
    Ah kin
Te
    Peten
La u pak
    U hokol e
Yum
    Ah kinob
Ua bin putz'c ob
    Uchmal
Tz'a ex
    Ka a nat
T u than
    T u tzacil kak
A pixan ex
    Bin hahal kamic e
Xeth au ol
    T a kul Ah Ytza
Tubes a hauai
    A satai kul e
La a kult e
    U hahil ku lo e
T u lacal
    Y anil
Ah tepal e
    Yum
Y ah ch'ab
    U ti Tusinil e.

The prophecy
    Of Tzin Yabun the Younger,
The mouth,
1210   The word
Of the replacement
    To the sun priest
There
    In the country.
1215 That is the expectation,
    The request
Of the fathers,
    The sun priests.
If they should escape
1220   The occurrence,
Give out
    What you must know
In the word,
    In the purpose of fire,
1225 Only your souls
    Will accept the truth.
Your heart shattered
    At your Itza gods,
Forgetting your wretched,
1230   Your miserable deities,
Then you shall worship
    The True God the redeemer.
Everything
    In the existence
1235 Of the ruler,
    The Father,
Creator
    Even of the devil.

1208. The prophet Tzin Yabun 'manioc rattling' Chan 'the Younger' appears to belong to *katun* 11 Ahau and possibly to Merida. An alternative construal of his name might interpret -*tzin* as the Nahuatl honorific and his patronymic as Chan. His pro-Christian stance corresponds to that of the Itza Chans of Emal (see note 655). The use of a Nahuatlism would be more likely in a Xiu.

9 Ahau

15. A Plea for Unity

. . . let there finally be a prophet, a true one, to question in 9 Ahau the unity of the Maya. (1248)

(10r) . . . uil*
  Y anen mac
To ah kin
  Ah bobat
Bin toh alic
  U than uooh e
Ychil bolon Ahau ual e
  Max ca a nat e
Hunac
  Tzuc ti cab ual e.

. . . the moon
1240 Let there be someone
Who is a sun priest,
  A prophet,
Who will recite correctly
  The words of the glyphs
1245 In 9 Ahau again.
  Which of you knows
To unite
  And assemble in this land again?

1239. Roys 1967: 165–166 has a fuller text which identifies these lines as a fragment of the prophecy of Kauil Ch'el. The preceding part in Roys' translation is: "When the end of the katun shall come, lord, ye shall not understand when it comes. Who shall believe it shall come because of misery. It comes from the north, it comes from the west at that time when it shall be, lord."

Barrera 1948: 194 has: "The pictures of the katun are coming out, oh father, there will be no one who understands how they come nor even who put them on the wheel of the katuns, oh father. The rigor of misery shall come to the north and to the west . . ." This prophecy probably belongs to the beginning of 9 Ahau and is more likely Itza than Xiu. Unity was certainly a problem throughout the post-Classic and colonial periods.

16. Civil War

Teabo was the seat of katun 9 Ahau. The governors as-

(13v) Bolon Ahau
  Uuc i Ab Nal*

9 Ahau:
1250 7 Ab Nal

1250. Uuc y Ab Nal 'seven year corn-ear' I believe to be Teabo (*aliter* Ti Ab). The Kaua gives Uuccii Hab Nal. Barrera 1948: 98 translates this as '*aguas suyas*'

(note continued on following page)

sembled, but they were usurpers trying to be chiefs and sun priests and captains or lords in power but creating division and war. 9 Ahau was at fault: a bad katun *in its governance. It was a nine-day Xiu rule in a 7 priest Christian period, a time of war in the west. (1278)*

There was divided rule, with the North priest Uac Nal as

U hetz' katun
   Ti bolon Ahau
T u kin oclis t u ba
   Bi y alab hal ach uinicil
Ti ma lai
   Chen u u acunah u ba
Ti ba tabil*
   Ti ah kinil
Ba ix ti nacomal e
   Ti ualac y ahaulil*
T u pop
   T u tz'am
Hum pai y ol
   Ti y emel tab
Ti Ah Bolon Ahau la
   Sip u than
Sip u chi
   Sip u katun
(. . . . .)*
   Ti y ahaulilob
Ah bolon kin*
   Ah bolon tz'am
T u tepal Ah Uuc Cha Pat kin*

   U chamal katun*
Ca tal i
   Y emel tab e
Ek Imix uah*
   U uah katun
Ca kin
   Chicul*
Sac Uac Nal u u ich*

   Ti y ahaulil

Was the seat of the *katun*
   In 9 Ahau.
Then they assembled
   As told, the governors,
1255 But they weren't.
   They just elevated themselves
As chiefs,
   As sun priests,
And as captains
1260   Who were to rise to lordship
On the mat,
   On the throne—
A division of the heart
   Which was to bring down the rope
1265 In 9 Ahau's rule there.
   Blame was his word;
Blame his mouth,
   Blame his *katun*
(In the rules,)
1270   In the lordships
Of the nine-day,
   Nine-throne people,
In the rule of the 7 priest Cha Pat's days,
   Of the tobacco *katun*.
1275 Then came about
   The descent of the rope.
Black Imix food
   Was the food of the *katun*.
Two suns
1280   Appeared.
The North priest Zac Uac Nal was the person
   In the lordship.

(note continued from preceding page)
and equates it with Chichen Itza. Compare also Roys 1967: 133. Teabo contested the seating of this *katun* with Merida and claimed the privilege again from 1717 to 1757.

   1257. Barrera 1948: 98 translates this as 'those of the axe'.

   1260. The manuscript repeats *ti ualac*.

   1269. Line missing, perhaps *ti tepalob*.

   1271. I believe that the nines here refer to *katun* 9 Ahau. Barrera 1948: 99 has Ah Bolon Am.

   1273. Uuc Cha Pat 'seven lobster wait' appears to represent the Christian week. Barrera 1948: 99 omits Cha Pat.

   1274. See note 1806 on the nicknames of the *katuns*.

   1277. Barrera 1948: 99 translates this as 'comet of the *katun*'. See also note 930 on the Imix tree. Black is west.

   1280. Barrera 1948: 99 interprets this as a proper name.

   1281. Zac Uac Nal 'white six corn-ear' is identified in the Kaua as the ruling lord of Teabo (Uuccii Hab Nal).

lord: a beggar of a katun, starving and poor—famine and drunkenness—wandering and sacrificing and mean, with nine competing lords at the mercy of the military and grasping officials. It had its own character and stooped to honor sinners. (1306)

Ti okol uah
    Ti okal haa
U uah katun
    Ti uchom
Hak
    Otzil i
Katun u uiil
    Katun y ukul
Katun u ximbal
    Katun u pucsikal
Hach tz'etz'il i
    Than u kat i
Ah bolon tepal kin
    U col kab katun la
Bin u tz'a u ba
    Ti hol can thanil
U tz'oy y ahaulil
    Ti y an ban ban kulelil i
Y an u uah
    Y an u y aal
T u tz'oc hayan u pop
    T u tzic ti an
Ban cal pach i
    Lai than katun la e.

By stealing bread,
    By stealing water,
1285 Was the food of the *katun*
    That took place:
Choked
    And poor—
A *katun* of hunger,
1290   A *katun* of drinking,
A *katun* of walking,
    A *katun* of hearts.
Very small
    Was the word he wanted,
1295 The nine-rule time
    Of this grasping *katun*.
He will surrender himself
    To the captain's words—
The weakness of the lordship,
1300   Which had many, many officials
It had its food;
    It had its water.
He flattened his mat
    To honor those
1305 Of many adulteries.
    That was the word of this *katun*.

17. The Inquisition

9 Ahau was the second katun in the Itza count. Merida was its seat, and that was the beginning of Christianity in this area

(16r) Bolon Ahau
    U ca tz'it katun c u xocol*
Ich Can Si Ho
    U hetz' katun

T ix u hoppol
    U canal *xp̄tianoil* i
Yukchahom ti bal cah tusinil i
    Uai tac lum e

9 Ahau
    Was the second *katun*.
Heaven Born Merida
1310   Was the seat of the *katun* being counted;
And there was the beginning
    And rise of Christianity,
Which was spread to the wicked world
    In the adjacent lands.

1308. The second *katun* in the Itza count of the cycle. Merida, which was Xiu territory, claimed to seat the *katun* for the second time but was willing to make concessions to both the Itza and the Christians. While adopting the Itza cycle, Merida urged the Maya to come to the city of "our older brothers" to be converted. Merida claimed to be the seat of the *may* and the *katun* from 1539 to 1638. See also note 1168. The former claim was disputed by Mayapan, the latter one (in this *katun*) by Teabo.

and the beginning of the cathe-
dral in Merida. (1318)

It was a time of labor and
punishment by hanging, and
there was plague in the villages,
devastating the peasants with
lash and tribute. There was
great theft by the Christians,
but also the establishment of
the sacraments. Welcome it by
coming to the Spaniards' city.
(1340)

T ix u hoppol
  U pakal ku na

Y an chumuc cah
  Ti Ho
Ban meyah
  U cuch katun
T ix u hoppol
  Hich' cal i
Hopan ix kak tun i
  U kabob
U sac ib
  Teil cabob
Y et ulic u sabanob
  U taabob y okol bal cah
Ti tal i alam
  Ytz'inil
Ychil u cal tza
  U cal patan
T ix u noh ocol patan i
  T ix u noh ocol *xp̄tianoil* e

T ix u uatal uuc ppel *sacramento* i

  U than *Dios* noh
Kam ex
  A ula ex
Talel u cah
  Ca sucunob e.

1315   And there was the beginning
  And the construction of the god
  house
That is in the middle of the city
  Of Merida.
Piling on work
1320   Was the burden of the *katun*.
And there was the beginning
  Of the noose.
And started was the fever of the nose
  And limbs
1325 Of the white lima bean
  Grove lands,
Bringing with it their poison
  And their ropes over the world—
Affecting children
1330   And younger brothers
With the harsh lash,
  With the harsh tribute.
And there was great theft of tribute:
  There was the great theft of
  Christendom.
1335 There was the establishment of the
seven sacraments:
  The word of God is great.
Take it
  And welcome it,
Coming to the city
1340   Of our older brothers.

7 Ahau

---

18. Demoralization

In 7 Ahau Mayapan was the katun seat. The West priest was the lord officially, but Amayte Kauil was the lord who started the Flower sacrifices and the war, acting as governor of the world and priest and prophet. Nobody escaped the fate of the

(I3v) Uuc Ahau
  Katun
Mayapan
  U hetz' katun ti uuc Ahau
Ek Chu Uah u u ich

  Ti y ahaulil*
T u pop
  T u tz'am
Amayte Kauil u u ich
  T u canil ti y ahaulil
Hopic ci
  U tz'ocol u toppol
Ix bolon y ol nicte
  Tz'ibal y ol nicte
Nicteil uah
  Nicteil haa y aal
Tz'am lic u hal ach uinicil
  Bal cah
Tz'am lic ah kin
  Tz'am lic ah bobat
Ma mac bin u toc u ba
  T u halal can y ahaulil

Ti u u ich
  Y etel u pucsikal i

7 Ahau
  Was the *katun.*
Mayapan
  Was the seat of the *katun* in 7 Ahau.
1345 The West priest Chu Uah was the person
  In the lordship
Of mat
  And throne.
Amayte Kauil was the person
1350 On high in the lordship,
Who began
  And ended the sprouting
Of the nine-heart flower,
  The painted-heart flower.
1355 Flowery bread,
  Flowery water was its juice.
Acting like the governor
  Of the world—
Acting like a sun priest,
1360 Acting like a prophet.
Nobody will escape
  From the true teaching of the lordship,
Which is its face
  And its heart.

1346. Ek Chu Uah 'black gourd food' (Barrera 1948: 99 says 'black scorpion'; Landa 1929: 2: 82 considers it a god name) of Mayapan and Yaxal Chac 'green rain' of Merida claimed the lordship of *katun* 7 Ahau. A Yaxal Chac also ruled *katun* 11 Ahau, forty years earlier. Perhaps he was the same man, as he did not last out this *katun.* Neither did Chu Uah. Both seem to have been replaced by Amayte Kauil 'paper-tree deity' (Barrera 1948: 100 says 'square god') or Amayte Uitz 'paper-tree mountain', and the authors of both texts for this *katun* strongly disapprove. Merida was again Xiu and pro-Christian; Mayapan was Itza and pagan. The usurper had the support of the military orders and may also have been pro-Christian or Xiu or both.

time, with lust and sodomy ev-
erywhere day and night, con-
stant sin enslaving the hearts of
the rulers and blackening the
wilderness. The peasants lived
like animals in 7 Ahau. (1382)

People were crazy; Merida
went crazy completely, every-
where: drinking and feasting,
Xiu and Itza gorged themselves,
and the girls were shameless.
The lords did not even keep
their vigils. It was a time of
constant change of lords and
usurpations even by the mob,
ending the ceremonial calendar

Hunac tzuc ti cab
   Ppen cech cal pach y an i
Ti pulan
   Y oc t u lacal i
La u tucul t u kinil
   La u tucul ti akab
U keban kin
   U keban akab
U munal u pucsikal hal ach uinicob
   Ah bobatob
Ti u y ekabtic u che
   Y etel u tunich
Ix ma na
   Ix ma yum i
Chaan u ba
   Xaxak y oc
U uinicil
   Ah uuc Ahau katun
Hach coil than
   U than
Coil ximbal
   U ximbal Ich Can Si Ho

Uchom t u hoppol
   T u pach
Yuklahom bal cah
   T u lacal
Bolon tz'acab uah
   Bolon tz'acab haa
U y al ix kuk
   Y al ix yaxum
Uah uaan ti tz'atz'
   Uaan ti bulux e
Y utzil
   U cichpamil ch'uplal
Cichpamhom
   Ma cichpam
Bin ahac
   Ma ahan
Ti tal i
   U kinil
Uuc kin tepal i
   Ua sut tepal i
Homol tepal i
   Uuc kinil i
U tepal y an i
   U uinicilob e
Holil
   Och*

1365 He will gather lust in the land.
   There was lust and adultery,
Which was carried
   And sprouted everywhere.
That was the thought by day;
1370   That was the thought by night:
The sin of day;
   The sin of night,
Enslaving the hearts of the governors,
   The prophets,
1375 Which blackened the trees
   And the stones,
And the motherless
   And fatherless.
They demeaned themselves
1380   To crawling on all fours,
The people
   Of *katun* 7 Ahau.
Very mad words
   Were their words.
1385 Very mad behavior
   Was the behavior of Heaven Born
   Merida
From start
   To finish,
Covering the world
1390   Entirely.
Nine-step bread:
   Nine-step water
Of the quetzal born,
   The blue bird born.
1395 Food was raised to be sucked,
   Raised to be crammed down;
And goodness—
   The beauty of girls—
Being beautified
1400   Is not beauty.
Who should be awake
   Is not awake.
There came
   The time
1405 Of the seven-day rule,
   Of instant rule
And fallen rule.
   Seven-day
Rules took place
1410   By the people,
Ending
   The count.

1412. Barrera 1948: 104 translates Holil Och as 'possum rats', which is possible

(note continued on following page)

in peasant rule. The Strong Skunks, Jaguars, and Masked Deer and Rabbits were in the countryside and in power. Usurpers were in office and appointed the officials. Coveting power was the rule in 7 Ahau. (1434)

Ah paklen cab
   Bin tepalnac ob i
Bin u keulelte
   Hum Pai
Balam
   U Koh Ceeh
Thul uinicil
   (14r) Chehom u u ich*
T u cab
   T u peten
T u tepal
   T u y ahaulil
Ah mahan pop
   Ah mahan tz'am
Ah mahan tepal
   La u cah t u than
Bin u mul chek
   U hal ach uinicil cah
U sitz'il ahaulil
   Lai bin y ahaulil
Te
   Ah uuc Ahau la.

And the farmers
   Will rule over them.
1415 They will be robed
   As Strong Skunks,
Jaguars,
   Masked as Deer
And Rabbit people
1420   With wooden faces
In the land,
   In the country,
In the rule,
   In the lordship:
1425 Borrowers of the mat,
   Borrowers of the throne,
Borrowers of the rule.
   That is who was beginning to speak
And will pile up the pacing
1430   Of the governors of the towns.
The coveting of the lordship—
   That will be the lordship
There
   In this 7 Ahau.

(note continued from preceding page)
and could refer to the military orders. See also note 1459. Villa 1945: 103, 157 identifies it as a marsupial, which is an omen of death or illness.
   1420. That is, masked.

19. The Council of Merida

7 Ahau was the third katun in the Itza count. Merida was its seat. Yax Chac was its lord.

(16r) Uuc Ahau
   Katun
U y ox tz'it katun*
   C u xocol
Ich Can Si Ho
   U hetz' katun
Yaxal Chac u u ich
   Ti y ahaulil
T an u pax cabal
   T an u sot canal

1435 The 7 Ahau
   Katun
Was the third *katun*
   To be counted.
Heaven Born Merida
1440   Was the seat of the *katun*.
Yax Chac was the person
   In the lordship.
There was the breaking of the lands;
   There was the shaking of the heavens.

   1437. That is, the third *katun* in the Itza cycle.

Everything was torn up by war in this katun. *(1448)*

The sages began to confer over the crisis, foreseeing the end of the noble lineages, Itza and Xiu. Amayte Uitz was the usurper, and the military orders without authorization began the damned katun *and the Bech' Kab war. Welcome it when the missionaries come into our towns, and accept Christianity. (1474)*

Nicte uah
   Nicte ha
U cuch
   Katun
T ix u hoppol
   U tzuucil miatzob i
Cotz'bal u u ichob
   Yuklahom ti bal cah
Yum a
   U netzil uil
Kuk
   Yaxum
Amaite Uitz u u ich
   Bin u tus coil than

Balam Ochil*
   Balam Ch'amacil
Ma tub u tz'al e
   U than katun
T ix u hoppol
   U tzin tzin loc katun i
T ix u ho- (16v) -ppol
   U Bech' Kab nicte i*
Noh kam
   A u ula ex
Te
   U talel ichil
Ca cahal ex e
   Talel u cah
U kat *x͞ptianoil* ex
   T u tan kin ual e.

1445 Flower food,
     Flower water
  Were the burden
     Of the *katun*.
  And there was the beginning
1450   Of the gatherings of the sages,
  Rolling their eyes
     At what was spread in the world:
  These fathers
     Of the waning moon,
1455 Quetzal,
     And blue bird.
  Amayte Uitz was the leader,
     And lies and madness will be the word
  Of the Jaguar Possums,
1460   The Jaguar Foxes.
  Nowhere is given
     The word of the *katun*.
  And there is the beginning
     Of the asshole boils *katun*.
1465 And there was the beginning
     Of the Bech' Kab Flowers.
  The right is to be accepted:
     Welcome it!
  There
1470   Will come the pairs
  To your towns.
     Come to the towns
  To desire that you be Christian
     At midday again.

1459. Balam Ochil 'jaguar possums' and Balam Ch'amacil 'jaguar foxes': military orders.

1466. Bech' Kab 'quail branch'. See also lines 2141 and 2793, which appear to date this disturbance to the following *katun* (1604 or 1612).

THE SEVENTEENTH CENTURY

5 Ahau

20. Merida under the Dons

5 Ahau was the fourth in the Itza katun series. Merida was its seat and government. And there were hangings, and the people tried to kill the great lineages of the nobility. And usurpers went forth in the masks of the gods for the year-bearer ceremonies, exorcising the devil. (1500)

It was a time of rain and

(16v) Ho Ahau*
  U can tz'it
U xocol
  Katun
Ich Can Si Ho
  U hetz' katun
U tepal
  U maxil katunob
T ix y uchul
  Hich' cal i
T u nucul uinicob
  Ti u cimil
Noh ch'ibal i
  T ix u hoppol
Chibil al i
  Chibil mehen i
Co co al
  Co co mehen
Ti tal i
  U binel
U u ich ku
  U u ich kauil*
T u can helebil caan
  T u can helebil be i
T ix u hoppol
  U tza cisin i
T ix y ulel u kin chac

  Ix u esil i

1475 5 Ahau
  Was the fourth part
In the counting
  Of the *katun*.
Heaven Born Merida
1480   Was the seat of the *katun*,
The rule,
  The shield of the *katuns*.
And there occurred
  Hangings,
1485 Which people meant
  To be the death
Of the great lineages;
  And there was the beginning
Of descent by birth,
1490   Descent by engendering.
Crazy born,
  Crazy engendered children,
Came
  And went
1495 With the faces of the gods,
  The faces of the holy,
In the four changes of heaven,
  In the four changes of the road.
And that was the beginning
1500   Of the removing of the devil,
And that was the coming of the time of rain
  And witchcraft.

1475. The lordship of *katun* 5 Ahau was disputed by Merida, Uxmal, Zotz'il, and Emal, the first two Xiu, the last two Itza. The two brief texts on Merida and Zotz'il agree on the general character of the *katun*. The text on Emal is totally different and is by far the most detailed prophecy in any of the *Books of Chilam Balam*.

1496. This adds a further interesting detail to the ceremonial circuit of the *katun*: the priests were masked as yearbearer gods. Compare lines 938 ff.

witchcraft, and famine was everywhere, spelling the doom of the lineages and the rise of the East priest Ahau Can. This started the brief lordships of the military orders, who were sons of bitches. They were witches and miserable peasants from beginning to end—as God ordained. (1522)

Ti u hoppol uih i
　　Yukchahom ti bal cah i
Ti u likil u cal holil
　　Och ti chibal i
Ti u likil u cal Chac
　　Ahau Can ti chibal i*
Ti u hoppol ah ca kin tz'am

　　Ah ca kin pop i
Balam Och*
　　Balam Ch'amac
Pek
　　U mut machom
Ca u pucsikal
　　Pan u ca tz'ic unicil
Otzilhom
　　U u ich
T u kin
　　Uil
U cuch katun
　　U than ku canal uchom ual e.*

It was the beginning of famine,
　　Spread over the land,
1505 And raised the voice of the ending
　　Of the count of the lineages,
And raised the voice of the East priest
　　Ahau Can by descent.
There was the beginning of those of
the two-day throne,
1510 　　Those of the two-day mat:
Jaguar Possums
　　And Jaguar Foxes—
Dogs
　　By the reputation they got.
1515 Two were their hearts:
　　Many were the two-person people.
Impoverished were
　　Their faces
By sun
1520 　　And moon.
This was the burden of the *katun*,
　　The word of God on high that
occurred again.

1508. Ahau Can, a rain priest who lent himself to the leadership of the revolt of the military orders. A namesake figured in the politics of Chichen Itza and Izamal in the 1450s (see note 278).

1511. See note 680.

1522. *Ku canal* 'god of heaven', presumably the Christian god.

21. Zotz'il

Zotz'il was the seat of katun *5 Ahau. Puz Hom was lord, and*

(14r) Sotz'il*
　　U hetz'
Katun
　　Ti ho Ahau

Zotz'il
　　Was the seat
1525 Of the *katun*
　　In 5 Ahau.

1523. Zotz'il 'bats' is a city about six kilometers east of Tizimin. Its lord was Puz Hom 'dust dart', but he was not brave enough to assert his claim to the lordship, so he deputized Hun Tzol 'paper count' and Ben Palal 'spend child' of the military order of Foxes to make the ceremonial circuit of the villages. The lordship of the *katun* was disputed by Emal and Merida and perhaps also by Uxmal (line 2648).

Ma Zuy and Ben Pal were allies and besieged the city. The governor was afraid that the lords were hated and would be ambushed and have to hide from the vicious lords who were attacking each other to put down usurpers. A poor katun. (1548)

Pus Hom u u ich*
  Y ahaulilob cab i
Hun tzol Ma Sui
  Ben Palal
Bin y oces u ba
  Ti ch'amacil
Y oc mal ob
  U xolobal ob cah i
Bay lic u tucul
  U hal ach unicil*
Ma mac bin u yacun
  Y ahaulilob cab i
C u culnac
  T u ximbal
T u hunal
  Bin mucchahac
Ah tubul uah
  Ah tubul ha
Ti u chibil tam ba holil

  Ochi u sitz'il ob ahaulil
Ox koch*
  U uah katun a.

Puz Hom was the face
  Of the lords of the land.
For one count, Ma Zuy
1530 And Ben Pal
Will be brought together
  In alliance,
And proceed to bypass
  And surround the city.
1535 So it was the idea
  Of the governor
That nobody would like
  The lords of the land.
They would be followed
1540 If they walked
By themselves,
  And would have to start hiding.
Spitters of food,
  Spitters of water
1545 Who attack each other to end the count
  Of the coveters of the lordship.
Breadnut and gourdroot
  Were the food of this *katun.*

1527. Barrera 1948: 104 translates *pus hom* as 'cross-eyed'. The Kaua adds another lord named Kaua Hom.
1536. I read *uinicil.*
1547. *Ox* 'breadnut' (*Brosimum*) and *koch* 'gourdroot' were considered inadequate food, resorted to only in times of famine.

---

22. The Annals of Bacalar

13 KAN (1593)

In 1593 the priest of katun 5 Ahau was confirmed on Octo-

13 Kan (1593)

(1r) Ox hun Kan*
  T u hun te Pop*

13 Kan (1593)

On 13 Kan
1550 On the first of Pop

1549. This is the longest, most confusing, and most informative text in the Tizimin. It was finished by Kauil Ch'el 'god magpie' at Bak Halal 'four hundred change', the modern Bacalar, on 11 Chuen 18 Zac (February 8, 1596). The author thus claims to forecast the history of 5 Ahau two years before it was due to begin. He based his prophecy not on the history of the preceding 5 Ahau (which in any case we, at least, do not possess) but on the preceding cycle of the calendar round, fifty-two years earlier rather than 260 *tuns* earlier, as in all the other prophecies.

(rest of note 1549, and note 1550, on following page)

ber 23 to 24, 1593. This is its
history. It had the end at the
beginning, a new kind of katun

Ch'ab u lac katun*
  Ti ho Ahau*
Ti hab 1593 cuch i*
  T u holhun Seec y al kab a*
Heklai u cuch
  Lic u tal u alic la e
He uil
  T u kinil*

Was taken the plate of the *katun,*
  Which was 5 Ahau.
In the year 1593 it occurred,
  On 15 Tzec it dawned.
1555 The relation of the events
  Will be told as follows.
That was the moon
  At the sun:

(note continued from preceding page)

He was reading the earlier history (1541–1561), he says, from a hieroglyphic text
(which we also do not possess). Despite the eastern origin of the text and the
uniqueness of its inclusion in the Tizimin, Kauil Ch'el was a Xiu, identifying
himself with Xopan Nahuatl and Puc Tun as an adviser to the lord of Uxmal,
Hun Uitzil. He is simply borrowing the identity of an earlier prophet of 9 Ahau,
although we can't rule out the possibility that he moved to Bacalar in his old age.

Kauil Ch'el's calendrical and divinatory theory is, from the Itza point of view,
woefully primitive, and he doesn't understand the *katun* at all. He presents instead a year-by-year and calendar round (i.e., totally Nahua) view of the events he
chronicles, using *tun* (360 days) for *hab* (365 days) and misdating the *katun* by
five years. Nonetheless, his Mexican view of Mayan politics in this troubled
katun appears to be well informed, and his comprehension of the Mexican calendar is excellent. See Edmonson 1976.

1550. 13 Kan is a yearbearer in the Mayapan calendar in use in Yucatan from
1539 to 1752. The date 13 Kan 1 Pop (July 20, 1541, or July 7, 1593) is the date
intended. Without the particle *te*, a date of 13 Kan 0 Pop would be implied. This is
the twelfth year of a fifty-two-year cycle that began on 1 Kan 1 Pop in 1581. The
first thirteen of these years are associated with the east and the color red.

1551. 'Taking the plate of the *katun*' is the preliminary initiation of the priest
who will serve in the following *katun*, a ceremony normally to be expected five
years before the *katun* is to begin—in 1598.

1552. *Katun* 5 Ahau in the Tikal calendar ended on 12.0.0.0.0 5 Ahau 13 Zotz',
September 20, 1618. In the Mayapan calendar it would have been counted from
its beginning, eighty days before the end of the classical *katun* 7 Ahau on
11.19.0.0.0 7 Ahau 13 Ch'en, January 3, 1599. Thus the author expected that
katun 5 Ahau would begin on October 15, 1598, a correct five years after the
'taking of the plate'.

1553. The correlation is correct: 1593 indeed marks the initiation of a year 13
Kan and should have been the date for the anticipatory ceremony of the 'taking of
the plate'.

1554. This final dating assertion is complex. It refers to a date of 4 Cauac
15 Tzec, ninety-five days after the Mayan new year on 13 Kan 0 Pop. This was the
day of the "dawn" of the plate ceremony, that is, the eve of the ceremony itself,
which took place on 5 Ahau 16 Tzec. This is an anticipation of the calendar
reform of Valladolid: celebrating the eve was already customary.

Note that these dates do not make sense unless the writer is beginning the year
on 0 Pop. He is counting "old-style." The cue that he is doing so is the absence of
the particle *te* 'round' (cf. *hun te Pop* and line 2977). The classifier *p'iz* has the
same effect. The equivalent dates in the Mayapan calendar would be 4 Cauac
16 Tzec (*uac lahun te Tzec*) and 5 Ahau 17 Tzec. Having put both counts into play
the author proceeds to specify that he will use the Mayapan calendar (see note
1560).

1558. Sun time (*kinil*) and moon time (*uil*) are constantly paired poetically in
the Tizimin. In the present context, their normal order is inverted (see lines
1567–1568). In the other contexts the sun begins what the moon ends; hence
I believe the metaphoric assertion here is that the end (of the *katun*) was at the
beginning. Mathematical calculation demonstrates that such is precisely the case.
The colonial Mayapan calendar counts *katuns* by initial dates and begins the year

(note continued on following page)

invented in Mayapan, and was the beginning of the decline of the Itza and Xiu matrilineages, the beginning of the end of the legitimate nobility. (1570)

There used to be three pyramids at Akab P'ix, now in ruins near Yaxche. It was all moved

Hi u ch'abal
  Katun la e*
Mayapan u u ich
  U kex katun
T u kin*
  U y emel
Y al kuk
  Y al yaxum*
T u kin i
  Uil*
Chibil al
  Chibil mehen*
T u kin y an ox mul tun tzek*
  Pail Akab Ppix*
Ich ox hublah cot
  Ox tz'alab u nak Yax Che*

That was the creation
1560 Of this *katun.*
Mayapan was the face
  Of the change of the *katun,*
In the sun
  Of the decline
1565 Of the quetzal born,
  The blue bird born,
In the sun
  And moon
Of the born heirs
1570 And engendered heirs.
In the sun there were three ruins,
  The stone walls of Akab P'ix,
In the three collapsed walls,
  The three slabs near Yaxche.

(note continued from preceding page)

with 1 Pop rather than 0 Pop. This was the consequence of the calendar reform opportunely inaugurated at Mayapan in 1539, when the relevant Mayan cycles were in a conjunction almost uniquely favorable to such a change. See Edmonson 1976.

1560. That is, the inversion of the naming of the *katun* is responsible for the dating system now in use. The author is specifying which calendar he wants to use: that of Mayapan.

1563. In the sun: at the beginning.

1566. In a number of other passages the quetzal and the blue bird are paired, commonly as a poetic reference to the Itza and the Xiu. The allusion is to the Toltec traditions of Quetzalcoatl and Huitzilopochtli respectively. Other passages of the Tizimin make it clear that the eastern Maya objected to the western emphasis on the female line, presumably a consequence of the stronger survival of Mayan patriliny in the east. Accusing the westerners of matriliny, rather than merely of bilaterality, was an insult, but it was also a way of questioning their legitimacy. The Tizimin presents the eastern (Itza) viewpoint throughout.

1568. The normal sequence of sun and moon, like alpha and omega, implies eternity—all of time. Compare Quiche *u be q'ih, u be zaq* 'on the road of the sun, on the road of light'.

1570. The eastern lineages are claiming permanency because they are legitimate in both the maternal and paternal lines. Lines 1549 to 1572, translated by Makemson 1951: 3 as follows, will serve to illustrate the futility of any detailed comparison of her text with mine:

> Thirteen Kan on the first of Pop. Katun 5 Ahau follows along its path, the year being 1593, save that one year still remains to be checked off before the bearer of the future arrives.
>
> Now in those days when Mayapan was captured in battle, they confronted the katun of affliction. During the migration of the remnant of descendants, the remnant of the descendants of Yaxum, good fortune should have come to generation after generation of our sons; but instead there came all at once castigation, oppression, vigilance in the night. That was a long time ago.

1571. *Mul tun tzek* 'mounds of pebbled stone': ruined stone pyramids with the pebble fill showing.

1572. I am unable to locate Akab P'ix 'night vigil'. See, however, note 3234.

1574. Yax Che 'green tree, first tree, ceiba' is ubiquitous as a place-name in Yucatan, but, given that our documentation is from the east, the Yaxche about ten kilometers north of Chichen Itza seems a likely candidate. There is also a Yaxche near Tizimin.

north to Emal, beginning the
yearbearer ceremonies in the
Plaza by the Sea. And the
prophecy is accomplished of the
last half of katun *11 Ahau, for*
the new word will be done of
Jesus and the Ascension. That
is the word of this year. (1594)

T u kin
  Uil
Y an sac
  Pai hail*
T u kin thul
  Can Chacil*
Uaan ti tz'atz'
  Uaan t u xul ix tabeil haa*

Okom ix
  Tz'iban*
Tan y ol nicte kin i
  Uil t u katunil ual e*

Ti tal i
  U y anal than
Y okol ah chaan te
  Kin Ich Chaan*
Ca sih i
  Ual t u caanil e*
Lai bin u tha
  Ox lahun Kan ual e.*

1575 In the sun
  And moon
It was white
  At the seashore.
In the sun was the track
1580   Of the four rain gods,
Standing in the open,
  And standing at the edge of the salt
    water.
And done
  Is what was written
1585 In the middle of the Flower sun,
  The moon of the return of the
    katun cycle.
It is coming:
  The realization of the word
About Him of the Little Tree,
1590   The Sun Eye of the Little Tree,
Who was born
  And returned to heaven.
This will be his word;
  This is 13 Kan again.

1578. The implication seems to be that an important lineage abandoned Akab P'ix to move to the north coast for the next thirteen-year period, initiated by the year 1 Muluc, which has the associations of white and north. From Chichen Itza the most likely place to describe in this way would be Emal.

1580. The reference is to the establishment of a new ceremonial cycle. The rain gods and the yearbearers were more or less equated.

1582. *Uaan* 'erected' could be a reference to stelae.

1584. That is, what had been written is now accomplished.

1586. The Flower time or Flower *katun* is 11 Ahau (1539), the period of the founding of Merida, the arrival of the missionaries, and the war of the *katuns* (*u katun katunob*). It suggests the flower wars of central Mexico, and indeed the battles between the lords and the military orders in the sixteenth and seventeenth centuries have very much that flavor. It also refers to the Mexican lords, the Xiu, since this *katun* marked the final triumph of the Central Mexican calendar and its initial counting over the end-dated Mayan *katun*. From the "middle" to the "moon" of this *katun* is a chronological reference to the decade 1549 to 1559.

1590. The "word" of Christianity will be actualized. Such an expectation of the efficacy of the Word is Mayan as well as Greek and Hebrew (see Edmonson 1971: line 2277) and is entirely consonant with the intention of the present document, which is to prewrite history. I read this line as repeating the *chaan te* of the preceding line. The image of the cross as the little tree or the high tree is frequent in the Tizimin. The eye (or face) of the sun is a pre-Columbian expression for the high god.

1592. While there are Mayan antecedents, the reference to the resurrection of Christ seems clear. The conversion of Tutul Xiu of Mani took place in 1541 (Ancona 1878: 322–323).

1594. In other passages also 'word' and 'date' are poetically paired. Time is fate.

1 MULUC (1594)

In 1594 word came of the European calendar and seven-day week, recurring in two years. You will be dressed by the Spanish nobles, which is bitter. (1610)

1 Muluc (1594)

Lai ca bin culac*
  Hun Muluc ual*
T u kinil e
  Ti u than tam ba
Y okol u suyil cab
  Y okol ah uuc Cha Pat*
Uuc te u cuch
  Uuc te u ppic
Ti ual t u ca pis tun

  U*
Tal a u ex
  A nok*
T u men y al
  U mehen Sat Ai uinicil*

Tocan uah
  Tocan ha ti t u chij.

1 Muluc (1594)

1595 This is when there is to be seated
  1 Muluc again,
At the time
  That they told each other
About the swirling earth,
1600 About the 7 priest Cha Pat:
Sevenfold his burden,
  Sevenfold his pile,
Which returns on the second
measured *tun*—
  His time.
1605 Your loincloths
  And clothes will come
From the born
  And begotten children of the Sat Ay
people.
Burned is the bread
1610 And burned the water that is in his
mouth.

2 IX (1595)

In 1595 there was war, burning, and destruction every-

2 Ix (1595)

Caa Ix ual u kin tz'on*
  Bacal tza ual e
T u kin hopom kak
  Tan y ol peten
Elom ti cab
  Elom canal*

2 Ix (1595)

On 2 Ix returns the time of guns.
  The removal of bullets returns.
It is the time of flaming fires
  Before the heart of the country,
1615 Burning on earth,
  Burning in heaven.

1595. Seating was the ceremony initiating a priesthood, in this case for the yearbearer. It seems likely that in Classic times this meant seating one priest (and god) for the year, another for the four-year cycle, another for thirteen years (in years with the numeral prefix 1), and another for the *katun*.

1596. 1 Muluc 1 Pop (July 20, 1542, or July 7, 1594), the first of thirteen years associated with white and north.

1600. The implication is that the Maya were first told of the rotation of the earth and the seven-day week in 1542.

1604. The return of the weekday two *tuns* later is obscure but is consistent with the prophetic text. See also line 1668.

1606. Clothes are a recurrent reference to Spanish conquest, presumably alluding to later Spanish sumptuary laws dictating the white blouse and pants for Indian men.

1608. This couplet is of interest as defining Spanish bilateral descent with patrilineal emphasis in the same terms used for the apparently similar rules of the eastern Maya. There is an implication of the legitimacy of the Spanish nobility. Sa Tay 'atole drinkers' could be another of the many nicknames for the Spanish (but cf. Sat Ay). The Tizimin totally avoids *español* and *castellano*.

1611. 2 Ix 1 Pop (July 19, 1543, or July 6, 1595).

1616. The burning of milpas would normally occur about a month earlier. While the following phrase might suggest a fire ceremony, I believe fire is another metaphor for war, for the conquest of Uaymil in 1543 (Chamberlain 1948: 233) or the conquest of Bahía de la Ascensión in 1595 or both. The inversion of the

(note continued on following page)

where, and pillage in the name of religion, destroying the food supply and the native gods in heaven and on earth. (1624)

And the peasants were forced to move by the nine great lineages, destroying both fields and cities at the time of judgment, everywhere. By the half-way point, the son of 7 Eb was the lord by the sea with the East rain priests. There were

T u kin u ch'a och pak
   T u kin okot ba ti caan*
Satom uah
   Satom kauil
Okom cui
   Okom icim t u ho cam be*
Ti hun yuklah ti cab
   Hun yuklah canal
Bin pecnac xux
   Bin pecnac otzil*
T u than ah Bolon y Oc Te
   Y etel ah bolon kanan*
Luban u u ich chakan
   Luban u u ich paa*
T u kin
   (Iv) Bul u xotemal
Uaan ti cab
   Uaan ti peten*
Buluc Ch'ab Tan*
   U mehen Ah uuc Eb*
Lei tun
   T u kinil ual
Uchom
   T u chi kaknab*
He an u chi Chac Mumul Ain

   He an u chi Chac Uayab Xooc*

In the time of the seizure of food plants,
   In the time of dances on high,
Destroyed was the bread,
1620   Destroyed the gods.
Gone is the witch,
   Gone the owl at the four crossroads,
The one spread over the earth,
   The other over the sky.
1625 The bees will have been moved;
   The poor will have been moved
At the word of the nine trunks
   And the nine branches.
Fallen is the face of the field;
1630   Fallen is the face of the fort,
At the time
   Of the posting of the judgment.
Standing on the land,
   Standing in the country,
1635 The 11 priest Ch'ab Tan,
   The son of 7 Eb, was the one
That was the priest of the *tun*
   When the time returned,
Occurring
1640   At the edge of the sea—
Otherwise the port of the East priest Mumul Ain;
   Otherwise the port of the East priest Uayab Xoc.

(note continued from preceding page)

couplet 'heaven and earth' may continue to mean 'everywhere', but it also suggests that what was going on on earth was in imitation of heaven—a true battle of the gods.

1618. Seizure of crops as tribute was justified by the holding of the ceremonies. Did they dance on the pyramids or were the gods dancing?

1622. The witch and the owl are pagan idols, normally placed at the center of the city, the cosmic crossroads of the directions and the navel of the universe.

1626. The metaphor of the poor as bees is noteworthy. The Mayan peasants always migrated into the forests in times of trouble.

1628. The nine trunks and branches were the leading lineages of the west. *Bolon* 'nine' is also 'great', and the pun may be deliberate.

1630. The field is the countryside and the fort is Mayapan.

1634. Oppressing the tilled lands and the untilled alike.

1635. 11 Ch'ab Tan 'half taken' is the lord of the half *katun*. Compare note 3234.

1636. Though this appears to be a personal name, it could also be a date: 7 Eb 18 Pop (or 18 Kankin) in a year 2 Ix (1595–1596). I believe 7 Eb was the lord in the year 2 Ix, but at the halfway point of the *katun*, in 9 Muluc, Ol Zip succeeded him. This is the only use of a Mayan personal day name in the Tizimin. 7 Eb may have been a nobody, or this may be another name for somebody else whom we know only by surnames.

1640. Presumptively Emal.

1642. Mumul Ain 'clay alligator' and Uayab Xooc 'were shark' were both East priests.

_forced migrations in the second
half of the_ katun. _This was the
third year of_ katun _5 Ahau.
(1650)_

T u kin	At the time
U mol ba xux	Of the swarming of bees,
Ti yala haa	1645 Which is the remainder of water,
Ti yala y och*	Which is the remainder of food,
Ualac hi	The measure of the occasions
Ox uutz' katun ual e*	Was three folds of that _katun_ again
T u kin hi ix y ahaulil	From the time which was also the lordship
Ah ho Ahau katun.	1650 Of the 5 Ahau _katun._

3 CAUAC (1596)

_In 1596 were the return to the
towns and the beginning of the
ceremonies for the final half,
the time of the end of the cycle.
(1658)_

_And there was missionizing
by the Europeans at the end of
this_ katun. _And there was fighting over the control of the villages, and war began again at_

3 Cauac (1596)

Oxil Cauac*
  Ual u kin
U pec t u ch'enil*
  T u y ac tunil
Binel u cah u tzacle kauil

  Binel u than u ximbalte akab*

U tzotz ha
  Tux ual y ukic haa*
T u chi
  Ual
U uiic
  Yala uah*
Ti ch'ab i
  U pucsikal*
T u men Ah Uuc Te Cui
  Ah Uuc Cha Pat
Ti to t u kinil
  T u katunil ual e
U uiil che
  U uiil tunich*

3 Cauac (1596)

On third Cauac
  There returned the time
Of the move to the wells,
  To the springs,
1655 The coming of the start of cursing the gods,
  The coming of the word of the approach of night,
Finishing off the water
  Where one returned to drink water.
On that occasion
1660   Was the return
Of the moon
  Of remaining bread,
Which was the seizure
  Of hearts
1665 By the 7 priest Te Cuy,
  The 7 priest Cha Pat.
It was at the time
  Of this _katun_'s return,
The moon of wood,
1670   The moon of stone

1646. The remainder (_yal_) was an installment of tribute due at the end of the _katun_, which comes two years after the present date. The priest of the second half of the _katun_ was the 'father of the remainder'.

1648. That is, this is the third year of the "_katun_" being chronicled, atypically beginning with the taking of the plate. That's the Xiu for you. The author is ambiguous throughout over whether to trace the real _katun_ (1598–1618) or a pseudo-_katun_ that fits better with calendar round divination (1593–1613). He switches back and forth.

1651. 3 Cauac 1 Pop (July 19, 1544, or July 6, 1596).

1653. The people came back to the towns (wells) and villages (springs) from the wild.

1656. This initiated the open rejection of the Mayan gods and the darkening of the religion of light.

1658. Vitiating the water sacrifices and hence the sacredness of the wells and springs—the towns and villages.

1662. That is, the last installment of the _katun_ tax is due this year.

1664. That is, conversion.

1670. Beginning in conversion, the _katun_ ends in warfare: sticks and stones.

that point. This was the third year. On 13 Ahau, at the halfway mark between 11 Ahau and 9 Ahau, was the end of the reign, ending the cycle with five months to go with the removal of the ruler. That was the significance of 1596. (1692)

Y okol culan t u ch'enil
　Ti y ac tunil*
Nicte ual c u tuch'ub
　Nicte ual u uah*
Ti y ahaulil
　Lai u uah la e
T u kin u ch'a cuch
　T u y ox pis tun ual e
Ti to
　Uil
Ah ox hun Ahau ual e
　Buluc Ch'ab Tan
Buluc Ahau
　Bolon Ahau
Lai u lukul u cuch
　La ix lic u tz'ocol
Cabal kol
　Hoo te u cuch
Ca ti luk i
　Ti y ahaulil*
Lai u kinil
　Oxil Cauac la e.

Over the seating at the well,
　At the spring.
The Flowers headed up again;
　Flowers were again the food
1675 In that lordship.
　That was its food.
At that time he took the burden.
　It was the third measured *tun* again.
Which was soon
1680　The moon
Of 13 Ahau then,
　11 Ch'ab Tan,
11 Ahau,
　9 Ahau.
1685 This was the removal of his burden,
　And that was also like the end,
The doubling of the cycle.
　Five rounds were his burden,
When he was removed
1690　Who was in the lordship.
That was the time
　Of 3 Cauac then.

4 KAN (1597)

1597 was a quarter of katun 5 Ahau. At the beginning of the katun, ancestral ceremonies were held in the central plaza.

4 Kan (1597)

Canil Kan*
　Ual u kin i
T u tzelep katun*
　Ti hoo Ahau
T u kin
　T u katunil*
Ox kokol tzek
　Auatnom yax cach*
T u ho cam be
　T u ho can luub*

4 Kan (1597)

Fourth Kan
　Was the return of the day
1695 At the side of the *katun*,
　Which was 5 Ahau
In the sun
　In the *katun* count.
Three stone rattles:
1700　The green fly screeched
At the entry of the four crossroads,
　At the entry of the four rests,

1672. Disputing the seating of the priests in the towns and villages.
1674. And bringing on another "flower war."
1690. We appear to be dealing here not with the lordship of the *katun* but with some more restricted term of office. The lord in question took office in 1595. He was due to leave it on 9 Ahau 2 Muan of the following year. However, on 13 Ahau 2 Yax, halfway between 11 Ahau 2 Xul and the end of his term, he left office five *uinals* early. He was probably forced out because of pro-Christian tendencies.
1693. 4 Kan 1 Pop (July 19, 1545, or July 6, 1597).
1695. The confusion continues with the identification of this fifth year as the side of the *katun*. The side of the classical *katun* would have come five years later and would have been counted by *tuns*, not by years.
1698. A pseudohieroglyph marks this as the beginning of *katun* 5 Ahau, but it is still a year early.
1700. Ceremonies for the ancestors, who are commonly identified with flies.
1702. The image of the road is central to Yucatecan cosmology. Life is a road. Fulfilling one's road is achieving one's destiny. One form of doing so is marriage:

(note continued on following page)

Then spoke the lesser priests. And the East priest Uayab Xoc won in hard fighting, and Christianity was defeated in the countryside in the middle of Uo, 1597. And he announced

T u than
  Ca t u likil
Auatnom cui
  Auatnom icim
Auatnom ah ya
  Ulom u kat Chac Uayab Xooc*

Hom che
  Hom tunich*
T u kin y an Ah Uuc Chu Uah*
  Elom u u ich
T u cab
  T u ch'enil
Auatnom chum kin Uoo
  T u kin ti canil Kan*
U chabalhal u than

  Ulom u y anal than*

Y okol sac boc*
  Y okol chac bob
Y okol may çu i
  Ti ual
T u ho pis tun e
  Ah ho Ahau
U pec Ah Buluc Ch'ab Tan*
  Talic cah y alic u than kin

U than uooh
  U tichpahal ual

It said
  When it arose.
1705 The screeching of the owl,
  The screeching of the witch,
The screeching of the sorcerer.
  Come is the desire of the East priest Uayab Xoc:
The wooden arrow,
1710   The stone arrow.
In the time of the 7 priest Chu Uah
  Burned was his face
On the ground
  At the wellside,
1715 Lamenting the middle day of Uo
  At that time, which was fourth Kan.
It was the bringing into being of his word,
  The coming of the existence of the word
Over the white stalks,
1720   Over the red stalks,
Over the cycle sign,
  Which is the return
To this fifth measured *tun*
  Of 5 Ahau,
1725 The Mover of the 11 priest Ch'ab Tan,
  Come to begin to say the word of the time,
The word of the glyph,
  The fulfillment of the return

(note continued from preceding page)

c in tz'oocl in bel 'I finish my road' is 'I marry'. The sun and the gods also follow their roads, which intersect in the center of the community, which is the center of the universe. Because one is always carrying a burden—of duty, office, and fate—the roads are provided with rest stops, platforms on which one may temporarily deposit one's burden by backing up to them and slipping off the tumpline of duty. The image here is of ceremonial platforms of this sort at the entry to a central plaza, though nonceremonial ones occur on real trails.

1708. This identifies Uayab Xoc with the nativist Mayan cause.

1710. Compare line 1670. Adding arrows seems to strengthen the image.

1711. 7 Chu Uah 'atole gourds' also seems to be a symbol for the Christian week. Gourds were used ritually in the counting of time. Chu Uah is also a southeastern lineage name and, according to Landa 1929: 2: 82, a god name. The Spanish invasion of Cochuah took place in 1544 (Chamberlain 1948: 233).

1716. The date implied would be (in the year 4 Kan) that of 4 Ix 11 Uo, thirty days after the new year. As August 18, 1545, this could very well refer to the beginning of the Great Mayan Revolt, which probably started in the northeast.

1718. In fulfillment of the prophecy, possibly that of Uayab Xoc.

1719. I read *bob* for *boc*. Stalks are lineages.

1725. My supposition is that the Mover of 11 Ch'ab Tan is due in the fifth year of the *katun*. He is thus on time if we start the *katun* five years early, as the author seems to want to do. The function of the Mover was to initiate the prophecy of the midpoint of the *katun*.

his prophecy for the northeast at the time of the quarter katun, the halfway point of the prediction of the defeat of the Itza. And he preached Christianity. (1734)

And the traditionalists fought back, ending the cycle, and the East priest Bol Ay prophesied that it was time in 1597 to change everything. And the priests and peasants fought over cutting out the existing katun. (1748)

(3r) Uchom y okol ah num Ytza*
  Lai u than u kat u cuchil

Ca ti lik i
  Y alic u than
U mehen kin
  U mehen akab*
Ualac ti uchom u kin

  U chibil tam ba
Holil och
  Y etel Chac Bol Ai
T ix y ulel
  U y anal than xan i*
Ti canil Kan ual e
  U kin
U pec caan
  U pec luum*
Nac tam ba nom ah kin

  Nac tam ba u luum ychil peten

Ut uch katun
  Cat cul.

Which occurred over the suffering Itza.
1730 This was the word he wanted to bear,
And which he raised,
  Speaking the word
Of the young day,
  Of the young night.
1735 In order to return him who had had his day,
  They were biting each other,
Ending the cycle.
  And the East priest Bol Ay,
Who was also the arrival,
1740 The existence of the word as well
On this fourth Kan,
  The day
Of the movement of heaven,
  The movement of earth,
1745 Knocking together the stubborn sun priests,
  Knocking together the lands in the country,
The pruning of the *katun*
  When it is seated.

5 MULUC (1598)

This may be the fulfillment of the katun in 1598. At the new year a good harvest was predicted for 1598, but first

5 Muluc (1598)

Hi ix lai ual*
  Bin u nahin
T u kinil ual e
  T u katunil ual e
Ti ho Muluc
  U kin u ch'aic u bel
T u kin u hoch' ich
  Ti tun
Y alic u xeic
  U lukah u chi e.
Ti hoo Ahau ual u kin
  Ychil ho Muluc

5 Muluc (1598)

Perhaps this may also be the return
1750 Which will be fulfilled
In this time,
  This *katun*,
Which is 5 Muluc,
  The time of his taking his road—
1755 At the time of his decorating his face
  For the *tun*,
Which is said to be his vomit,
  The flow of his mouth there.
In 5 Ahau was the return of the day
1760 On 5 Muluc.

1729. Page 2 is misnumbered in the manuscript. We thus go from 1v to 3r to 3v to 2r to 2v to 4r.

1734. The defeat of the Itza was the prophecy of the Mover, who had become Christian. But the Mayan party fought back.

1740. They were also prophets.

1744. It sounds like an earthquake, but I believe the sense to be figurative. Yucatan is outside the earthquake zone. The implication appears to be that the battle was between traditionalist priests and Christianized peasants.

1749. 5 Muluc 1 Pop (July 19, 1546, or July 6, 1598). This "may also be the return" because the true date of 5 Ahau in the colonial *tun* count falls in this year, namely on 5 Ahau 12 Zip (August 25, 1598)—at harvesttime, as the following lines note.

there was famine and then later
drought, and that did it. The
sun priest attacked Christianity all by himself in public.
Mayan drinking and Christian
baptizing were everywhere as
the end of the katun got closer.
Maybe it was time to move to
the towns and villages, as it
had been when the Itza were

U kin
  Y anhom uil uah*

Hum pach tzucubil
  Y anhom uil haa
T u tepal
  T u hunal
Y oklal
  Patal u than
T u sipic u cuch
  T u tatah than
T u bel
  T u hunal.
Uaan ti tz'atz'
  Uaan ti bulux . . . te*
Y ukul ti kin
  Ti akab*
T ix tam beil
  . . . haa*
Hun yukla
  Ti cab
T u kin tepal
  Ualac
Hun uatz'
  Hun tz'on*
Hi va le
  T u kinil hi u pec
T u ch'enil
  Ti y ac tunil
T u men bai uchc i
  Ti Ah Ytza ca lik i*
T u cal ya
  Ca u p'atah
U ch'enil
  U y ac tunil
T u kin
  U hokol

In the sun
  Was the occurrence of food
    shortage,
And in the last part
  The occurrence of water shortage.
1765 That was enough
  All by itself,
Because
  Awaiting his word,
He blamed the burden
1770 On the declared word,
On the road
  By himself,
Standing in the clear,
  Standing at the full . . . tree,
1775 Drinking by day
  And night,
And renewing
  . . . with water
All over
1780 In the land
At the time the rule
  Was to return.
One bend,
  One shot
1785 Perhaps it was,
  That it was time maybe to move
To the wellsides,
  To the springs.
Because thus it had happened
1790 To the Itza when they arose
At the hole of pain,
  When they abandoned
The wellsides
  And springs
1795 At the time
  Of their appearing

1762. There may be an intentional pun here, contrasting sun-beginning with
moon-ending. Uil means both 'moon time' and 'shortage'. The following couplet
makes it clear that the latter meaning is primary.
1774. Letters missing.
1776. A traditionalist Mayan priest blamed the famine and drought on Christianity, even standing before the cross as he did so and holding traditional Mayan
ceremonies requiring drinking.
1778. Letters missing.
1784. This expression is frequent and implies both a short distance and a short
time.
1790. The Itza had abandoned the towns and villages but were now considering
reoccupying them. Abandonment of villages took place in the Great Mayan Revolt of 1545 to 1546 (Chamberlain 1948: 246).

exiled from them and came to the wilderness, and that was the outcome. (1802)

Ich lumil che
   Ich lumil tunich
Y al
   U than
U xotemal kin
   U xotemal katun ual e.

In the lands of wood,
   In the lands of stone.
So says
1800   The word
Of the judgment of the time,
   The judgment of the *katun*'s return.

6 IX (1599)

In 1599 5 Ahau began. There was a Mayan revival on the feast of the 4 Gods. After a year of the East priest Bol Ay, Tzay Can came and was established as the legitimate ruler in prosperity. (1818)

But it didn't last, being betrayed by the son of the late Max Can in fulfillment of what had happened in 12 Ahau (1421).

6 Ix (1599)

Uac Hix*
   U kinil
U lubul
   U tzol ch'ich' katun*
Ti ual u colal ex
   U colal nok*
Ch'ab t u kin
   T u kin Uh Ahau Can

T u pachil tun
   Ti Chac Bol Ai*

Lai ul
   T u kin Tzai Can
U pacte Ah Tem Pop
   Ah Ten Tz'am ti tal i*
U xeic t u chi
   U lukah e
Lai het man t u cal
   Ti ma t u pan i
T u men u tzotz
   T u men u conic
U mehen
   Ah Max Can bin i*
Ua u haulic u choch
   U y ex
U max kin
   (3v) U max katun e*

6 Ix (1599)

6 Ix
   Is the time
1805 Of the posting
   Of the order of the bird *katun*.
It is the return of loose pants,
   Of loose clothes,
Created on the day,
1810   Created on the day of the Lords
      Four,
After the *tun*
   Which belonged to the East priest
      Bol Ay.
That was the arrival
   At the day of Tzay Can,
1815 The sight of the lord step mat,
   The lord step throne who has come
Vomiting from his mouth
   And flowing forth.
That splits and passes to the throat
1820 Without quenching
Because it was wasted,
   Because it was sold
By the son
   Of Max Can who is gone.
1825 Then he finishes the guts,
   The pants
Of the monkey time,
   The monkey *katun*.

1803. 6 Ix 1 Pop (July 18, 1547, or July 5, 1599).

1806. Posting the *katun* means initiating it and ending its predecessor. This is an explicit adoption of the classical *katun* ideology. *Katun* 5 Ahau is nicknamed the bird *katun*, for reasons unknown. It is likely that all thirteen of the *katuns* had nicknames, though only a few can be securely identified: 13 Ahau, deer (line 5272); 11 Ahau, flower (line 1024); 9 Ahau, wax? tobacco? (lines 1274, 1913); 7 Ahau, deer? (line 2123, but line 5272); 5 Ahau, bird (lines 1843, 2124); 3 Ahau, black? (line 2776); 1 Ahau, flint? (line 2386, but see line 4348); 12 Ahau, monkey (line 4094); 8 Ahau, flint? (line 4348); and 4 Ahau, turtle (line 4720).

1808. Loose or red clothes are Mayan; white clothes are Spanish.

1812. Bol Ay 'roll grease' seems always to be involved in war.

1816. The mat and the throne are symbols of legitimate authority.

1824. Max Can 'monkey snake' is a personal name.

1828. The passage refers to events in the monkey *katun*, 12 Ahau (1421).

The city traitor, the pretended easterner, came from the northwest on the beginning of the katun *and betrayed the legitimate heir of Zuhuy Zip. It was all his fault that everything was finally disrupted at the ka-tun sacrifices. Break chickens, break eggs: everything was torn up from start to finish all at once. (1852)*

So there was no sacrifice, you peasants, because you disrupted the rites and destroyed tradition. So go into servitude rather than living as Mayas.

U manab
  Cabal
Hebal u than
  Chac u u ex
Tali ti xaman
  Tali ti chikin
T u kin
  T u katunil
U conic y al
  U mehen Uuc Suhui Sip*

T u kin y an sip u than
  Sip u chi
Ti uil uchom pax ti cab

  Uchom soot canal

T u tzol ch'ich' katun
  T u lom uatz' katun*

T u kin ha tab ak
  Bai ch'ich' heeb*
Heb tan ba nom caan
  Heb tan ba nom muyal
T u u ich kin
  T u u ich u
Ualac hun uatz'
  Hun tz'on
Hii ual e
  Ma mac bin atz'ab*
C ech ah mab na e
  C ech ah mab yum e
T ech u uatz'
  T ech u tz'oi katun e

Sati u canil
  Sati ual t u pach e
T u kin y an u mol ba
  Sohol a u okol
Ma a u ex
  Ma a nok

The ghost
1830 Of the town
With the split word
  And the red pants
Coming from the north,
  Coming from the west
1835 In the sun
  Of the *katun* period,
Selling the born
  And engendered son of the 7 priest
  Zuhuy Zip.
On that day his word is blame,
1840 His mouth is blame.
In the moon was the occurrence of breaking on earth,
  The occurrence of shaking in heaven,
On the count of the bird *katun*,
  On the stabbing of the bend of the *katun*.
1845 At the time of torn chickens
  Thus are the birds' eggs.
The stubborn skies revolving,
  The stubborn storms revolving
In the face of the sun,
1850 In the face of the moon,
To return one bend,
  One shot.
Perhaps that's it:
  No one is going to be bent,
1855 Ye motherless,
  Ye fatherless.
You who are the bend,
  You who are the weakness of this *katun*,
Destroying its sprouting,
1860 Destroying the return afterward.
At that time there will be gathered
  Cotton around you:
Not your pants,
  Not your clothes.

1838. Zuhuy Zip 'virgin deer' was the traditionalist ruler at Emal and probably the father of Ol Zip. What follows is a pun on his patronymic. Landa 1929: 2: 54 considers Zuhuy Zip a god. Villa 1945: 103 identifies Zip as a deer spirit among the modern Maya.

1844. Counting the *katun* and stabbing the bend of the *katun* are presumably ceremonies appropriate to this year, the second in the traditional count.

1846. This sounds like an aphorism, perhaps implying that, if one generation is disrupted, so is the other.

1854. Bent over the sacrificial stone.

This is no time for usurpers.
(1866)

7 CAUAC (1600)

In 1600 at the new year cere-
monies there was still rebellion
of the peasants, destroying
buildings throughout the pe-
riod, capturing the eastern lin-
eages and breaking the power of
the military orders, taking cap-
tives and dragging them away
because of hunger and thirst.
The ruler was crazy, treating the
half katun all over again as
though it were Uayeb for the
Itza—three years before the
half katun. (1896)

Ma t u kin u ti al a mahan koh*

Ix mahan nail e.

7 Cauac (1600)

Uucul Cauac u kin*
  T u uuc pis tun
T u hunte Pop
  T u kin u ch'a sabac*
U max kin
  U max katun*
Mul tun
  Tzek
T u kin
  U lach lam
Pach
  Chac bob*
T u kin u paic u coo
  T u kin u hotz'ic y ich'ac Cab
  Coh*
Bin olal
  U kan chek u piix
Bin ual u taninte y oc
  U tan u kab
T u men u sitz'bic uah
  U sitz'bic haa
Hach co u u ich
  Ti y ahaulil
Ca ti lik i
  T u men Buluc Ch'ab Tan*
Ualac hi
  Ual
U tupul u kak
  U xotemal Ah Ytza
Ox uutz' katun i
  Uil e.

1865 It is not the time for those of borrowed
masks
    And borrowed houses.

7 Cauac (1600)

Seventh Cauac is the day
  Of the seventh measured *tun*
On the first of Pop,
1870 At the time of getting soot,
The monkey day,
  The monkey *katun;*
Piled stone,
  Masonry
1875 At the time
  Of the period sinking.
Seizing
  The red stalk:
It was the time of breaking the beak—
1880 It was the time of pulling the claws
  of the Earth Lion.
There came the desire
  For many paces on one's knees.
Then will be the redirecting of feet,
  The directing of hands
1885 Toward the desire for food,
  The desire for water.
Very mad was his face
  In the lordship
When he arose,
1890 Because of the 11 priest Ch'ab Tan:
The return perhaps,
  The return
Of the quenching of the fire,
  The judgment of the Itza—
1895 Three turns of the *katun,*
  Its moon.

1865. To be maskless is to be without religious authority; to be without a
house or motherless is to be totally illegitimate.

1867. 7 Cauac 1 Pop (July 18, 1548, or July 5, 1600).

1870. Soot (*sabac*) was used ceremonially for body paint in the new year ceremonies. Cauac is a west year (black).

1872. Peasants are monkeys.

1878. *Chac bob* 'red stalk' is another of the metaphors for war. See also lines
2555 and 3757.

1880. Cab Coh 'earth lion' is the potto or kinkajou (*Potos*). It was also the
name of a pro-Christian military order.

1890. As noted in line 2068, the mid *katun* ceremonies were due three years
later. This is another of the bits of evidence that different priests were calculating
katuns differently, causing bitter religious disputes.

8 KAN (1601)

In 1601 in 5 Ahau there was a drought, burning up plants high and low, starting fires to the north right down to the sea-shore, burning up the crops and plants as in Merida in 9 Ahau (1559). There was civil war among the Itza, weakening them with hauling water. There were brigands in the fields, thieves in the fields, affronting the half-cycle god at the katun ceremonies and destroying order by the Christianized

8 Kan (1601)

Ti uaxacil Kan*
  T u hun te Pop
T u uaxac pis tun ual e
  Ti hoo Ahau
Uil u kin
  Ti thuchan ti y ac tunil
Elom uil uitz
  Elom uil calap*
Hopom kak
  Ti noh suc te
Elom uil kaknab
  U chi sus
Elom sicil
  Elom kum e
Elom macal
  Tz'amal
Ual u cib katun
  Si Hoo uchom*
Ual u nap tam ba
  U cuch Ah Itza
U kamic u chich
  Y etel u cuch
Ua kom
  Chal tun
Bin xobnac nom
  Xobnac ceeh*
Tan sacil
  Chakan
Kitz nom
  Ix kan itzam thul
T u chakanil
  Ti uil
U u ich ah at ol
  (2r) Ah Mai Cuc*
T u kin
  T u katunil
Satanil
  T u cuch hab
Sac u y ex
  Sac u nok

8 Kan (1601)

On the eighth Kan
  On the first of Pop,
On the eighth measured *tun* again
1900 In 5 Ahau
The sun returned
  And sank low in the springs.
Burned were the plants of the hills;
  Burned were the plants of the flats.
1905 There were flaming fires
  On the southern grassland.
Burned were the plants of the sea
  At the edge of the sand.
Burned were the squash shoots;
1910 Burned were the squashes,
Burned were the yams
  And poppies.
A return of the wax *katun*
  Of Merida.
1915 A return to biting each other:
  The burden of the Itza.
The taking of their strength
  And burden,
Either of the pit
1920 Or of the cistern.
Then came the whistling partridge,
  The whistling deer
Before the squash vines
  In the fields,
1925 The drumming partridge
  And yellow lizard hawk
In the fields,
  In the plants,
In the face of the remainder spirit,
1930 The spirit of the cycle round
At the time,
  At the *katun* period
Of the destruction
  Of the burden of the year.
1935 White are his pants,
  White his clothes.

1897. 8 Kan 1 Pop (July 18, 1549, or July 5, 1601).

1904. I read *tzalab*.

1914. Probably a reference to *katun* 9 Ahau (1559), when Merida was the seat of the *katun*. See also note 1806.

1922. Skulking people pretending to be animals: the military orders.

1930. Another reference to the approach of the half-cycle ceremonies. The priest of the second decade of a *katun* is identified with the remainder. Also see note 1729 on the pagination of the manuscript.

peasants. Then there was a hurricane, announcing the half katun three years later. (1942)

9 MULUC (1602)

In 1602 at the midpoint of 5
Ahau, Ol Zip took charge as
during the captivity, and the
heirs of the nobility renewed
the purification movement of
the Itza peasants of 12 Ahau
(1421). The bastards! Laughing
and playing music! And in the
northwest! (1964)

The time came to change the
Fathers of the Land, erecting

T u kin y an u y iklil ha*

   Bin u kat u cuchil
Yala kin Buluc Ch'ab Tan

   T u buluc pis tun.
T u uaxac pis tun
   Bin uchom ual e.

9 Muluc (1602)

Ti bolon Muluc*
   T u hun te Pop
Talom tun
   Y al kaba ho Ahau*
U y alic
   U than Ah Uuc y Ol Sip*
Ualac t u kin num on chu

   Num on celem
T u kin u tal u mehenancil no xib

   U y alancil ix nuc
Ch'ab t u kin tan
   Ch'abom u than u suyil cab

U max kin
   U max Ah Ytza e*
T u kin y an *tzintzin* coc xul
   T u kin y an *tzintzin* bac toc

Cheeh
   U u ich
Kit hom be
   Kit hom heleb
Tab ua xaman
   Tab ua chikin
Canal
   Ual u u ich
Haom can
   Ti Ahau Can

At that time there was a water
tempest
   Which came to desire its burden,
The remaining time of the 11 priest
Ch'ab Tan
1940   In the eleventh measured *tun*.
In the eighth measured *tun*
   That will have returned there.

9 Muluc (1602)

On 9 Muluc
   On the first of Pop
1945 Came the *tun*
   Of the dawn of 5 Ahau
To speak
   The word of the 7 priest Ol Zip,
To return to the time of our suffering
breasts,
1950   Our suffering shoulders,
To the time of the coming of the
generation of men,
   Of the bearing of women,
Creating at that time the appearance,
   The creation of the word of the
virgin earth,
1955 The monkey sun,
   The monkeys of the Itza
In that sun there were asshole buggers;
   In that sun there were asshole
pederasts
With laughing
1960   Faces.
The fired clay trumpet,
   The fire-changed trumpet
Where it may be north,
   Where it may be west.
1965 The sky
   Changed its face.
Removed are the four
   Who are the Lords Four.

1937. The hurricane is apparently regarded as a portent of the half *katun*, here
predicted for three years later. According to line 1603, it should be two years later.

1943. 9 Muluc 1 Pop (July 18, 1550, or July 5, 1602).

1946. According to the initial chronology of this chapter, this is the tenth *tun*
of the *katun*. It is thus the "dawn" (i.e., the eve) of the second half cycle.

1948. Ol Zip 'heart deer' may well have been the son of and legitimate successor to Zuhuy Zip. He was prominent throughout 5 Ahau and again in 1 Ahau
as a leading lord of Emal.

1956. A kind of pun on the monkey *katun*, 12 Ahau, and monkeys as peasants.

the monuments for the ances-
tors. Ol Zip and the rebels held
the ceremony of changing the
katun *for the* katun *that was*
ending, surrendering his office
before the public at the right
time in 1602. (1990)

Likan u che
   Likan u tunich
Y okol u na
   Y okol u yum*
T u men Ah Uuc y Ol Sip
   (. . . . .)*
T u men Uuc Tz'ac Sitz'il
   Uuc Tz'ac Tzotz*
T u kinil
   Ti ualac
Hom
   Ahal katun
Ca koch u u ich
   Ti y ahaulil
Bin tz'oces u than*
   Ix chaante u u ich
Emom u luk
   Y okol u u ich paal
Ualac bin u ximbalte akab
   Bin u ximbalte kin
Ti u u ich caan
   T u bolon tun.

Erected was the tree,
1970   Erected was the stone
Over the mother,
   Over the father
Because of the 7 priest Ol Zip,
   (. . . . .)
1975 Because of the 7 priest Tz'ac Tzitz',
   Because of the 7 priest Tz'ac Tzotz,
At the time
   Which was to return,
The descent
1980   And waking of the *katun,*
When his face was taxed
   In the lordship.
His word was to be ended
   And his face would be seen,
1985 His removal descending
   Over the face of the children,
To return to the bringing of night
   And the bringing of day
Which is the face of heaven
1990   On the ninth *tun.*

10 IX (1603)

In 1603 were the katun *cere-*
monies for the half katun, *an-*
nouncing the folding of the
tuns. *They marked the end and*

10 Ix (1603)

Ti lahun Hix
   T u hun te Pop*
T u kin
   T u katunil
T u kin u tepal
   Ho Ahau
Emom canil
   Ual canil
Utz'ub
   Y utz'ub tun*
Ah tepal
   T u ch'ub uil

10 Ix (1603)

On 10 Ix
   On the first of Pop
On the day
   Of the *katun* period,
1995 On the day of the rule
   Of 5 Ahau,
Descended the news,
   Returned the news
Of the fold,
2000   The folding of the *tuns,*
The divider
   That designates the moon,

1972. The implication of ancestor monuments is of interest.

1974. Line missing.

1976. Another reference to the seven-day week, perhaps. Ol Zip plays an ambiguous role in the political struggle of this period and eventually turns Christian. See line 2684. The implication of several 7 priests (of different towns?) getting together is of interest.

1983. It was actually the half *katun* that was ending, but it was time to retire definitively the active priest of 7 Ahau, who had served honorifically in the first half of 5 Ahau.

1992. 10 Ix 1 Pop (July 17, 1551, or July 4, 1603).

2000. The folding of the *tuns* marks the halfway point in the *katun,* the ceremonies for which are described colorfully and circumstantially in the following passage.

designated the ceremony, preparing the town that would rule the priesthood and government for the inauguration of Amayte Kauil in authority and office and the priesthood. For the half katun was to be retired, and the rulership changed throughout the wilderness. (2028)

The announcement was made and the preparations started for fasting and penance and self-denial. And the Center priest Bol Ay returned for the ceremony of beginning rather than ending amid general re-

U cah	The town
T u kin	At the time
U ch'aic	2005 Of taking
U tepal	The rule—
Patal u cah	Shaping the town
U acunah u ca	To prepare his town
T u uaante	That it should be raised,
Accunah u cah	2010 And preparing the town
T u than	For his word,
T u luch	For his gourd,
T u tz'aam	For his throne,
T u pop	For his mat,
T u kan che	2015 For the yellow throne
Amayte Ku ual*	Of Amayte Ku's return.
Lic u cutal	Like his seating,
Ca bin culac	When he is to be seated
T u hanal	In his office,
Tocol u than	2020 Seizing his word,
Tocol u cah u luch	He seizes the town of his gourd,
Toocol u cah u laac	Seizing the town of his plate
T u men patal u cah	To prepare the town
T u kin t u tz'ap tun	For the day to pack the tuns,
T u kin u hel pop	2025 For the day to change the mat,
U hel tz'am	To change the throne.
Hokom ich lumil che	He appears in the lands of wood,
Ich lumil tunich	In the lands of stone;
Y alab than	Spoken is his word
Y etel u caan	2030 And his teaching.
Sihil u can (2v) u luch	Born are the sprouts for his gourd,
U chebal y ukul	The shoots for his drink
T u kin	On the day
Choch ich	Of bright fruit.
Ch'och' t u luch	2035 Salty is his gourd,
Ch'och'	And salty
U al	The liquid
Y ukul	He was to drink.
T u kin u tzol pop	On the day of counting mats
Yax Bol Ai ual*	2040 The Center priest Bol Ay returns.
Ma t u chi chucan yaal	Not on the occasion of completing his trust:
T u kin u ch'a matan	On the day of taking requests.
Ppitil ppit	Jumping over and over
Tzayal tzai	And seeking and seeking:
U ne can	2045 The snakes' tails
Tzai ne ba ob	Seek their own tails—

2016. Amayte Ku 'paper-tree god' is mentioned also in line 2811. Compare note 3890.

2040. The implication is that, at the midpoint of the katun, people filed applications for the positions they wished to occupy ten years later.

joicing of the rebels, as Ol Zip
held the fire ceremonies, fasting. And the mats were folded,
marking the new decade and
the old one, by the priest of the
Center, who sorrowfully con-
fronted the new ruler and gave
the power into his custody,
marking the half katun with his
confession to the rain god. And
immediately Ol Zip did penance on his body. Then the
dance was held for the two
gods, the old and the new, and
he destroyed the idol commem-
orating the plague and punish-

Ti ual uchom
   T u kin u ch'a kak Ah Uuc y Ol
Sip
T u kin toc sitz'il satai hail

   T u kin u lukul
Yala pop
   Yala u lac
Uatal
   U cah tun
U nup
   Ix ah kin
Yax u pix
   Coc
Tun num ya
   Amaite u u ich
T u yum yala
   Ah tz'am
C u tz'abal ti
   U yalomal
Ah pop
   T u canil
Lai u pacat
   Buluc Ch'ab Tan
La chi
   T u y autic u pixan
Si y ah tun
   Chac
Ua la chi hun auat
   Hun tz'on hi e
Lai u kinil
   Ua sak
Pach
   Nahc i e
Lai u kinil
   Y okot ba
Ah Ua Tun
   Ah Nij Pop*
Ah Ma Suy
   U kin y Ahal Cab
Ca ix emec tun Kin Chil

   Ah Chac Chibal
La chi ix t u kuchul
   T u kinil u chac mitan

At the return that has occurred,
   On the day that the 7 priest Ol Zip
   seizes fire,
On the day of seizure of the pangs of
thirst,
2050   On the day of the removal
Of the remainder of the mats,
   The remainder of the plates,
Erecting
   The beginning of the *tun*
2055 And its opposite also,
   And the sun priest.
Green are his clothes,
   Ragged,
A miserable *tun*.
2060   Amayte was the person
Who was father of the remainder,
   The man on the throne,
And it is given to him,
   The remaining time—
2065 To the ruler
   To keep.
That was the appearance
   Of the 11 priest Ch'ab Tan.
That was the occasion
2070   When he bared his soul
To the idol
   Of the rain god,
Or that was the occasion, one shout,
   One shot.
2075 That was the time
   Of the itch either
On the back
   Or the belly.
That was the time
2080   For dancing,
For Ua Tun,
   Niy Pop,
Ma Zuy,
   The time of Ahal Cab,
2085 And when he shall have felled the
stone of Kin Chil
   Of Chac Chib.
That was the occasion of the arrival
   Of the time of the red plague,

2082. The old dispensation required the erection of monuments, the new one
the inspection of mats. There may be more sense here than I can find in the
dictionaries.

ment of the Itza nobles in the grove at Mayapan. (2094)

So ended 1603, which ended the oppression of the peasants at Yaxche, which was destroyed. So Ol Zip took his oath immediately and eagerly—a nobody, but he took his oath in the center, ending the barbarian control of Mayapan that began in 7 Ahau and ended in 5 Ahau. It now ended with an eastern celebration outside the city, an-

Num ya Ah Itza
  U xotemal
Y al
  U mehen
Uai ti tzucub te
  Mayapan
Ti u tupic
  U tz'ocol
T u kinil
  Lahun Hix ual e
Ti u tz'oc
  T u u ex hool
T u kin
  Ox cuchlahom
(Itz'in)*
  Y al max
Ox tz'alab
  U nak Yax Che
Ox ch'uilah
  Xuthen
T u kin u ch'a matan
  P'il tec
T u kin u ch'a ah tzotz
  U ch'a matan
Oy
  Otz*
T u kin
  U ch'aic u matan
Hol can be
  Hol can lub
Ti emom
  U cuch uitz
Y okol may cu i*
  Uai uchom *Mayapan*
T u may ceeh
  T u xau cutz man i*

Uai u man
  Uay y uchul
U y okot chac tz'itz'ib
  Chac tum pilix*

The suffering of the Itza,
2090   The judgment
Of the born
  And engendered children.
That was in the grove of trees
  At *Mayapan*
2095 Which was the extinction,
  The ending
Of the period
  Of 10 Ix again.
It was the end
2100   Which more or less finished
The period
  Of the thrice burdened,
Of the younger brothers,
  The monkey born
2105 At the three pyramids
  Near Yaxche.
The three were removed
  And reduced
On the day he got the request.
2110   He just snatched it in a wink
On the day the Grabber got it,
  Got his request.
He was weak
  And poor
2115 On the day
  He took his request
At the gate of four roads,
  The gate of four rests,
Which lowered
2120   The burden of the mountain
Over the cycle seat.
  That occurred at Mayapan
In the cycle of Ceh.
  In the claw of the Curassow it
  passed then.
2125 There it passed so
  There it was to occur.
There was the dance of the Red Cardinal
  The New Red Parrot

2103. *Itz'in* is crossed out in the manuscript.

2114. The derogatory statements about Ol Zip may well relate to his being a 7 priest but he appears to have inherited that position legitimately, and his fasts and ceremonial behavior were exemplary.

2121. Ending the control of Mayapan by the hill tribes of the west.

2124. It began in the deer *katun* and ended in the bird one. See note 1806. *Cutz* 'curassow' has been identified as *Agriocharis* and as *Crax* (Tozzer 1941: 202). It may be a constellation, however.

2128. The eastern (red) dance for 5 Ahau (bird).

ticipating by ten years what
was coming in the next katun,
the alliance of the northeastern
lineages with baptism and the
rule of Cab Bech' at Yaxche. Ol
Zip ended the disorder of 5
Ahau when he took the office
and the priesthood, succeeding
as a Maya, legitimately in his
seventeenth year, as the towns
and villages will learn. (2160)

T u may ac tun
  Lai uaan tan chakan

Uchom ti to
  T u katunil
Bin i
  Ual uchom
T u men lai u katunil
  Ca uch i*
Hapai Canil*
  T u kin u ch'a tam ba
Mumul
  Aal
Auatnom Bech'*
  T u kab yax che
U tz'oc tzotz
  U tz'oc zitz'il
Y ahaulil
  Ah ho Ahau ual e
T u kin u u acunic u luch

  Y etz'cunic u pop
Ch'a u cah
  Ti y ah kin
U kex ah kin e
  T u hol u pop
He ix t a u ex
  Y etel a nok
U buc
  T u than
Lai u koch
  T u uuc lahun ual e*
Ca bin hokoc t u ch'enil
  Ti y ac tunil.

In the cycle of the spring of water,
2130   Standing there in the middle of the field.
That was early
  In the katun period
And is going
  To occur again,
2135 Because that is the katun period
  When it occurred.
The Hapay Cans
  Then seized each other,
Splashing
2140   Water,
While the Bech' screamed
  In the branches of the ceiba.
The end of lust;
  The end of desire:
2145 The lordship
  Of 5 Ahau was that again.
On the day of the placement of his gourd,
  The setting out of his mat,
He got his place
2150   As the sun priest,
The successor to that sun priest
  At the head of the mat.
He is also in your pants
  And your clothes,
2155 Clothed
  In his word.
That is the tax
  In the seventeenth tun again
When it shall appear in the wells
2160   And springs.

11 CAUAC (1604)

1604 was the designation of
the successor priest, who was

11 Cauac (1604)

(4r) Bulucil Cauac*
  T u hun te Pop
T u buluc pis tun
  Ti to t u tepal

11 Cauac (1604)

Eleventh Cauac
  On the first of Pop
On the eleventh measured tun,
  Which is the one ruled by

2136. That is, in 3 Ahau.

2137. The Cans appear somewhat consistently on the rebel (Christian) side of the struggle. See also lines 677, 1814, and 2045.

2141. Cab Bech' 'land quail' became lord in 6 Cauac: 1560 or 1612. See also line 2795. Compare Bech' Kab.

2158. Ol Zip could have been born in 1586, in which case he was only thirteen when he was passed over as a successor to his father (see line 1838).

2161. 11 Cauac 1 Pop (July 17, 1552, or July 4, 1604). See also note 1729 on the pagination of the manuscript.

installed in office and set up
with the Fathers of the Land.
He was seated in 1604. The four
stars of the Fathers of the Land
and the moon appeared at the
katun festival. The Fathers of
the Land took office, taking of-
fice with ceremony and drink
on November 3, 1604. (2192)

Then came a missionary be-
fore whom they danced for God
for a Christian festival, being

Ah ca kin pop
  Ah ca kin tz'am
Etz'tal
  U cah
U luch
  Ah okol koh*
U atal
  U cah
Ah koh Ba Cab
  Ah Can Tzicnal*
Ti cutal ti tun
  Ua t u buluc pis tun katun e

Hokan Ah Can Tzicnal

  Hokan Ah Can Ek*
Ah sac
  Tzi u*
T u kin
  T u katunil*
T u ch'aic u bal
  Ah Can Tzicnal
Ch'a u cah
  T u bel
Ix tol och*
  T u kin
U tz'amic
  U ci katun*
(Ox Lamat)*
  T u buluc te Xul ual e*
U hokol u y anal than

  U y anal caan
Ti uil tun
  Okot ba ti ku canal
T u kin
  Tzayal can

2165 Him of the two-day mat,
  Him of the two-day throne,
Setting
  The place
Of the gourd
2170   Of those of the weeping masks,
Standing
  In the place
Of the masked Fathers of the Land,
  The four Honored Ones,
2175 Who come in this *tun,*
  Or in the eleventh measured *tun* of
  the *katun.*
The four Honored Ones having
appeared,
  The four Stars having appeared,
And the Light,
2180   The sacred Moon,
On the day
  Of the *katun* period.
They take office,
  The four Honored Ones,
2185 Taking their place
  On the road
As the impersonators
  Of the day
For soaking
2190   The wine of the *katun,*
  (3 Lamat)
  On the ninth of Xul again.
There appearing the existence of the
word,
  The existence of heaven
2195 In the moon of the *tun,*
  They dance to God on high.
On the day
  Of seeking heaven,

2170. It is of interest that the masks of the Ba Cabs weep. Compare line 2348.

2174. Landa 1929: 2: 26 gives *canzicnal* as a god.

2178. The star or planetary associations of the Ba Cabs are not known.

2180. The Ba Cabs may be associated with the moon as a sign of termination (the second half of the *katun*): the first half of the *katun* would then be the sun half. Contrast in the prophecies for the two halves is common.

2182. On the day 5 Ahau.

2187. *Ix tol och* 'actor': the impersonators of the Ba Cabs for the ceremonies.

2190. *Ci* 'wine, sweet', probably honey mead or balche, which is not specifically mentioned in the Tizimin, though wine and drinking are frequent.

2191. Ox Lamat may have been omitted.

2192. 3 Lamat 10 Xul (November 3, 1552, or October 21, 1604). It may be significant that the earlier date falls on the day after All Souls'.

converted to Christian dress as
the ruler decreed (as a Christian Maya) for the rest of the
katun. (2208)

Then came the East priest Bol
Ay and Bol Ay the Younger, producing civil war among the Itza
throughout the countryside,
which lined up with the native
gods on the very day of the katun ceremonies. That brought
back the suffering and tribula-
tions of the nobility. There was
continuous punishment from
beginning to end from am-
bushes in the countryside, like
a great wind of the rain god,
sweeping everything before it—
the scourge of the land. (2244)

U ch'aic
  U y anal
U y ex
  U nok
U y anal ah tem pop
  Ah ten tz'am
Te u u ich ti caan
  Ti y ahaulil
Lic u talel
  T u ppat be katun e

T u ch'aic u bel
  Chac Bol Ay
Y etel Bol Ai Can
  Chac Bol Ai ul
Ualac hi u ch'a tam ba
  Ah Ytza
Tan y ol che
  Tan y ol haban
Ti y alic
  U pixan siyah
Tun
  Chac
T u kin
  U katunil
Num ya uay i
  Ual u num ya
T u cal ya
  U manes
Y al
  U mehen
U xotemal ob kin
  U xotemal ob akab
T u kin
  U
Mul
  At xux*
T u hool che
  T u hool haban
T u kin u mol tam ba
  Y ikil cab
Chac
  Ba yab
Cat
  Cex
Ah num
  Ah sas mil e.*

Of taking on
2200 The nature of
His pants,
  His clothes,
The nature of the step mat lord,
  The step throne lord—
2205 There with his eye on heaven
  In the lordship
As he comes
  To the remainder of the road of the
    katun,
Then take office
2210 The East priest Bol Ay
And Bol Ay the Younger.
  The East priest Bol Ay arrives,
Whereupon they seize each other,
  The Itza,
2215 Amongst the trees,
  Amongst the bushes.
He declared
  His soul born
To the idol
2220 Of the rain god
On the day
  Of the katun period.
Suffering it is,
  The return of suffering,
2225 Filled with pain
  To be endured
By the born
  And engendered child,
The judgments of their day,
2230 The judgments of their night
In the sun
  And moon
Of the wasp,
  The short wasp
2235 In the hole in the tree,
  The hole in the bush.
On that day they collect each other
  The winds of the earth,
The rain god
2240 Spirit,
Clear
  And smooth,
Punisher
  And brightener of the lands.

2234. I read u xux. 'Ambush' for 'wasp' is a guess: it seems to fit the following
couplet.
2244. I read sas luumil e.

12 KAN (1605)

On the twelfth year in 1605 came the message of the Son of God and eternity. Again in the twelfth year there was a universal drought. Penance was imposed of fifty-two years of dancing with tears of joy for God, in the seventh of which katun 5 Ahau ends and there may be war in the west. (2272)

And this year we went back to the towns and villages to get food. The two sun priests officiated, and the new one, Amayte, had thirteen knots counted in

12 Kan (1605)

T u lahum pis tun
  T u kinil
Lah ca ual Kan
  T u hun te Pop*
U kinil y alic u than kin
  U than tam ba u kuchil
U mehen kin
  U mehen akab
Ualac uil cabal
  Ualac uil canal
Ti ual
  T u lah ca pis tun
Elom caan
  Elom luum
U tz'oc sitz'il
  Ba la ua ma uchom e
Kin tun y abil
  Lai bin uchebal
Okot ba ti Hunab Ku
  U y oksah ah tepal cochom

Uuc te hab
  Kin tun y abil*
Bin uakac chal tun
  Bin elec u ku ch'ich'*
Bin hopoc
  U kab suc te
T u cal chakan
  T u hem uitz
Ti tun
  Sutnom
T u ch'enil
  Ti y ac tunil
U ch'a pak
  Och
T u y okot ba ah kin
  T u nup ix e*
Yax buc e*
  Ox lahun pis u ppic

12 Kan (1605)

2245 On the twelfth measured *tun*,
        At the time
      Of twelfth Kan
        On the first of Pop,
      The time speaks the word of the day,
2250   Telling each other of the arrival
      Of the son of day,
        The son of night
      To return the moons of earth,
        To return the moons of heaven,
2255 Which return
        On the twelfth measured *tun*.
      Burned the sky,
        Burned the earth.
      The end of desire,
2260   And nothing may be done then
      But a calendar round.
        What may be done
      Is dancing to the Sole God,
        Eyes streaming for the distributor of
        pleasure,
2265 The seventh year
        Of the calendar round.
      The cisterns may burst;
        The bird god may be burned.
      Then may flame
2270   The grass tree branch
      At the pass to the fields
        Between the hills
      On the *tun*
        That is returned
2275 To the wells,
        To the springs
      To get the plants
        And food.
      The sun priest danced
2280   With his mate then.
      New are his clothes.
        And thirteen measures

2248. 12 Kan 1 Pop (July 17, 1553, or July 4, 1605).
2266. Actually the seventh *tun* of the Itza *katun*.
2268. The bursting of cisterns is a characteristically apocalyptic Mayan image for the end of a cycle. Burning the bird god ends *katun* 5 Ahau. See also note 1806.
2280. With his opposite number.
2281. New perhaps because of the completion of the first thirteen years of the *katun* and the fact that he is the symbol of the new cycle to come.

*his sash. Solemnly they made
the circuit of the villages again
to claim the allegiance of the
land, to be sacrificed as rulers
and end the disorders. So that
was done again in the villages.
(2298)*

*Then came the command of
heaven from the Spokesman
of God, the one to examine
closely the nobility of the Itza.
And the sacrifice was performed everywhere, from Zac-
nicteil to Cozumel, in the*

Mocol
  U kax nak*
Amayte u u ich ah kin e*
  Lai bin ocbal
T u ch'enil
  (4v) T u y ac tunil t u ca ten
Bin kamac u payal chi
  Bin t u y ac tunil
Bin u cimes u ba

  T u kokolil
Ah Tem Pop
  Ah Tem Tz'am
Ti ual u tz'ocol sitz'il

  Ti ual u tz'ocol cotz i e

Ca tun sutnac ti y ac tunil
  T u ch'enil t u ca ten e

T ix tal tun u y anal than

  U y anal caan
T u than ah noh kin

  Chilam
H ix binac
  H ix maac
Lai
  Bin ilic
Tac pach
  Tac tan
U y alomal
  U mehen Ah Ytza

T u chac tun
  Num ya ual e
Ti uchom ual e
  Ti hetz'om
T u lumil Sak Nicteil
  T u petenil Cusamil*

Are the piles,
  The knottings of his sash.
2285 Amayte was the sun priest;
  There will be the progression
To the wells,
  To the springs for the second time.
He goes to take the edge of the shore;
2290   He goes to the springs;
He goes that he may have himself
killed
  At the flaying
Of the step mat lord,
  The step throne lord,
2295 Which is the return of the ending of
desire,
  Which is the return of the ending of
  plucking.
So then it is repeated at the springs,
  At the wells for the second time
  there.
And then also there came the nature
of the word,
2300   The nature of the sky
In the word of the priest of the great
sun,
  The Spokesman.
He is also to go;
  He is also the person,
2305 The one
  Coming to see
Close behind,
  Close before
The matrilineal
2310   And patrilineal descendants of the
Itza,
At the red stone
  Of sacrifice that is.
That is what occurred then;
  He has been seated
2315 In the lands of white flowers,
  In the country of Cozumel.

2284. The successor priest seemingly counts the days by piles (of corn?) and
knots in his sash.

2285. Amayte Ku was the priest of the second half of the *katun* (see line 2060).
His return to traditionalism matches a resurgence of idolatry at Chancenote in
1605 (Sánchez 1892: 310).

2316. Sacnicteil 'field of white flowers' is located a few kilometers west of
Sotuta. Cusamil 'flock of swallows' is the modern Cozumel. The *zac nicte* is
Plumeria alba, called in Spanish *flor de mayo blanco*. The *cusam* has been
identified as *Chaetura* and as *Stelgidopteryx*. Tozzer 1941 calls it a chimney swift.

villages and the fields and be-
fore the Fort. And it went on
that summer quickly. The Itza
commoners again swore loyalty,
and the peasants, to the katun
prophecy and judgment of the
Itza. For it was time in 1605 for
the ceremonies establishing the
priest and rule of katun 5 Ahau
in 1605. (2354)

Mayapan
  Uchom ual e
T u cal ch'en
  T u cal y ac tun
Tan sacil
  Chakan
T u kin tz'am coot
  T u kin y an paa
Ti ual uchom
  Y okol
U chanil cab

  U bucchanil uitz

(. . . . .)*
  T u sesebil
U max kin
  U max Ah Itza
Ti ual y alic
  U than
Ix ma yum t u kinil
  T u kinil
T u katunil ual e
  Ti tun u kinil
Y alic
  U than
U xotemal
  U mehen Ah Ytza
Bin i
  Ua t u kinil
Ah ho Ahau
  T u lah ca pis tun uchom

U kulil sum ci
  U chan katun u cheeh koh che*

Can etz'lic u luch
  Can etz'lic u lac
Can etz'lic u xeec
  T u katunil
Ah ho Ahau
  T u lah ca pis ual e.

Mayapan:
  It happened there again
In the pass of the well,
2320 In the pass of the spring
Before the whitening
  Fields.
At the sun given the ditch,
  At the sun there was a wall,
2325 Which has returned
  And is departing,
The beginning of the clothing of the
earth,
  The beginning of the clothing of the
hills
(. . . . .)
2330 As quickly as possible,
The monkeys of the sun,
  The monkeys of the Itza,
Who again spoke,
  His word
2335 And the fatherless of the time too,
  At the time
Of this *katun* period again,
  Which was then the time
He spoke
2340 His word,
His judgment
  Of the sons of the Itza.
It is to be
  If it is in the time
2345 When 5 Ahau
  And the twelfth measured *tun*
    occurred:
The arranging of the maguey rope,
  The little *katun* of the laughing
    wooden mask.
He is placing his gourd;
2350 He is placing his bowl;
He is placing his seat
  In the *katun* period
Of 5 Ahau
  On the twelfth measured *tun* again.

13 MULUC (1606)

In the thirteenth year 1606

13 Muluc (1606)

T u y ox lahun pis tun
  U kinil

13 Muluc (1606)

2355 On the thirteenth measured *tun*
  Was the time

2329. Line missing.
2348. Compare the weeping masks of the Ba Cabs, line 2170.

*began, and the next day was
the overthrow of the ruler. In
the thirteenth year of the katun
they divided in four the remainder of the katun to the
end. Both drink and food were
collected at the katun ceremonies of 5 Ahau. (2379)*

*Like Mumul Ain, who took
charge in the year 1445, they
will bring back the East priest
Cul Tun of Merida to Valladolid
and throughout the country.
And the katun ceremonies will
be held throughout the Itza*

Ti ox hun Muluc*
    Ti hun te Pop
Ti hunil Oc*
    U kin u tepal
Ca bin emom pop e
    Emom tz'am e
Y ox lahun pis
    Katun ual e
T u kinil mul tepal
    T u yala tepal canil
Hunacil u luch
    Hunacil u lac
Uchebal
    U mumul chitic
U tzotz haa*
    U ppuyul
U xelel
    Yala uah
Yala u tzotz
    Bin u mumul chit e
T u kinil
    T u katunil
Ho Ahau ual e
    Ti hokan
Chac
    Mumul Ain
Ca culhi
    Ti y ahaulil
Ti ho habnal
    Tok katun*
Uay i
    Ual uchom
Chac
    Na Cul Tun*
Ich Can Si Ho
    Ti Sacl Ac Tun
Tan chakan
    T u pucsikal peten
T u kin
    U tuch'ub katun
Y okol u petenil Ah Ytza
    Uchom te

Of 13 Muluc
    On the first of Pop.
The first Oc
2360   Is the day of his rule.
Then the mat will be lowered,
    And the throne will be lowered.
The thirteenth measure
    Of this *katun,*
2365 At the time of pile division,
    The remainder of the rule was four,
The completion of his gourd,
    The completion of his plate
For the fulfillment
2370   Of the piling up and filling
Of tots of water,
    Of fragments
And crumbs
    Of remaining food,
2375 Of remaining tots,
    Which will all be piled up and filled
At the time
    In the *katun* period
Of 5 Ahau's return,
2380   On the appearance
Of the East priest
    Mumul Ain
When he was seated
    In the lordship
2385 In the fifth year period
    Of the flint *katun.*
That's it:
    There returned
The East priest
2390   Cul Tun
Of Heaven Born Merida,
    To Valladolid
In the middle of the fields,
    In the heart of the country
2395 On the day
    Of the gourds of the *katun*
Over the country of the Itza
    Which occurred there,

2357. 13 Muluc 1 Pop (July 17, 1554, or July 4, 1606).
2359. 1 Oc 2 Pop is the next day.
2371. *Tzotz* is unknown to me in this context. Barrera 1948: 180 has '*sobras de agua*', which makes sense.
2386. See note 1806. The year would be 1445.
2390. Cul Tun 'shrub stone', the East priest at Merida in 1554.

land, cursing Christianity. That
may or may not happen. That is
the word for you peasants.
(2408)

Tan chakan
    Bin u tzacl e
U mehen kin
    U mehen akab
H ix uchac
    H ix ma uchac
Lei
    A than
C ech ah mab na e
    C ech ah mab yum e.

In the middle of those fields,
2400   Which will be the cursing
Of the son of day,
    The son of night.
That also may occur;
    That also may not occur.
2405 That then
    Is the word for you
Ye motherless
    And ye fatherless.

1 IX (1607)

In 1607, the fourteenth year,
the civil war resumed with
Uayab Xoc. There was fire and
shark divining of the mysteries,
and prediction by storms, as-
tronomy, second sight, and
eclipses during 1607. It was a

1 Ix (1607)

(5r) T u can lahun pis
    U hun te Pop*
T u can lahun tun u kinil
    T u katunil
Ual ci u xixtic u ba

    Ah xixteel ul Chac Uayab Xoc

T u kin u ti tzay kak*
    U tzai ne xoc
Lai ual tzailic
    Ca tzay i
Ti caan
    Ti muyal
T u kinil
    Yuklah chaan
T u kinil u macal u u ich kin

    U macal u u ich u
(Ti ual uchom)*
    T u can lahun tun ual e

1 Ix (1607)

On the fourteenth measure
2410   On the first of Pop,
On the fourteenth *tun* is the time
    In the *katun* period.
There remains being made to fight
oneself.
    The fighters arrive with the East
    priest Uayab Xoc
2415 At the time of seeking fire,
    Of seeking shark tails.
That is the return of seeking things,
    When one seeks then
In the sky,
2420   In storms,
Sun phases,
    Far seeing,
At the time of covering of the face of
the sun,
    Of covering of the face of the moon,
2425 (Which recurred)
    On the fourteenth *tun* again.

2410. 1 Ix 1 Pop (July 16, 1555, or July 3, 1607). This is the reference date for the
correlation of the Mayan and Christian calendars from 1539 to 1555. The leap year
correction is ignored, and one always looks ahead to the next year 1 Ix, which is a
day that began on July 16. Thus Landa was told correctly that the Mayan new year
fell on Sunday, July 16, 1553. And Thompson 1958 was correct in giving July 17 as
the date because he was counting days completed, like a Classic Maya; Landa's
informants were colonial. After 1555 the reference date shifts to fifty-two years
later—1607—and is again pegged to July 16. But the Maya would have added (or
subtracted from the Christian date) an additional correction of thirteen days (the
number of Ix or leap years in the fifty-two-year cycle). See, however, line 2980,
which uses a different reference year, 1 Kan (see Edmonson 1976). The year 1 Ix
also marks the shift of the ceremonial cycle to the west and to the color black.

2415. There follows a series of references to forms of divination: by fire, by
sharks' tails, by the stars, by the sun, by storms, by clairvoyance, and by eclipses.
A resurgence of idolatry at Tizimin is reported for 1607 (Sánchez 1892: 270, 311),
as well as a rain of blood at Cupul and Valladolid.

2425. Text for missing line suggested by Roys n.d.

*year of dissipation, adults and
children suffering alike. (2432)*

*The governor was overthrown
and put out of office, and the
town was destroyed by Uayab
Xoc at the pyramids, and no
one attended the ceremonies at
the right time. Even the commemoration of the Itza was
skipped. The northwest united
the hill lineages again in 1607—
a time of suffering, a time of
peasant revolt in the towns and
villages. According to the prediction in the glyphs, either the*

Satan *xiuit**
  T u men u coch e
Num chi t u na
  Num ch t u yum
Numen chu
  Numen celem
Satan yala
  Hal ach uinic
Mananhom u hel
  Mananhom u hel kan
Satal u cah
  T u ch'aah
Chac
  Uayab Xooc
T u kin mul tun ya
  Mul tun tzek
Ma mac bin
  Ca tz'ab
T u kin chaan
  T u katunil ual e
Mananhom uil yala

  U xotemal Ah Ytza
Ualac xaman
  Ualac uil chikin
U nupp tam ba chibalnom tun

  U bobil uitz*
Ti ual uchom
  T u can lahun tun ual e
U num ya kin
  U num ya katun
Emom xulab
  Emom chac uay ah cab
Paic t u ch'enel
  Ti y ac tunil
Uchom
  Bai c u y alic kulen

Tz'ib
  Y etel uooh
Ualac t u can lahun tun
  Y uchul uac satai ba tabil*

Destroyed is the year
  By pleasure:
Suffering mouth for the mother,
2430 Suffering mouth for the father;
Suffer girls,
  Suffer boys.
Destroyed is the residue
  Of the governor.
2435 Already past is his change;
  Already past is his change of office,
Destroying the town
  He had seized,
The East priest
2440 Uayab Xoc
On the day of the pyramid of pain,
  Of the stone pyramid.
No one goes
  When it is given
2445 On the seen day,
  On the return of the *katun* period.
Already past is the moon of the
remainder
  Of the judgment of the Itza
To return to the north,
2450 To return to the west.
They join together the descendants of
the *tun*,
  The stalks of the hills,
Which recurred
  In this fourteenth *tun* again,
2455 The day of suffering,
  The *katun* of suffering.
Descended are the stingers
  Descended are red were bees,
Attracted to the wells,
2460 To the springs,
Occurring
  According to what is in the
arrangement
Of the writing
  And glyphs.
2465 It was to return in this fourteenth *tun*
  Or was to occur at the need of the
chiefs,

2427. *Xihuitl* 'year', a rare Nahuatlism in Yucatec, is particularly rare in calendrical matters.

2452. The stalks of the hills are the Xiu lineages of the Puuc, the only hills in
Yucatan.

2466. The ambiguity suggested in line 2426 is repeated here. The governor was
replaced either because the priests certified that the fourteenth year was the

(note continued on following page)

priests or the captains replaced the governors. (2468)

2 CAUAC (1608)

In the fifteenth year, 1608, the last quarter of 5 Ahau petered out and was wrapped up with the vigil of the successor, the custodian of offices. On his last day, Sun Eye of the Cross appeared and spoke, and the half-katun priest departed to settle in the west. (2496)

But the new priest was afraid to take office because of the violence in the countryside and

U mumuk hal ach uinic
   T u can lahun tun ual e.

2 Cauac (1608)

T u ho hun te
   U kinil
Ah cabil Cauac
   T u hun te Pop*
U chek tam ba katun
   T u lah u than Ah ho Ahau
Emom u taa
   Emom u toon*
Hokan tab
   Hokan halal
T u hoo lhun tun ual e*
   U kin u pacat cot
Ich ah tzai kan che
   Ah hai kin bak
Ah toc
   Ah tz'utz'lah i
U kinil u muxul tun
   U muxul kan
T u kin u tuctal
   Halal
Hokan Kin Ich Chaan Te

   Kin Ich t u than
Buluc Ch'ab Tan
   Bin i
Uil letz'nac
   U ch'ibal
Y okol u tz'ulil cab
   U bucchanil uitz e
Ma u ch'a u matan
   Ix ti ti be
T u kin che
   Tun cimil
Hatz'cab u cah
   Hatz'cabnah i
Ix cahcunab
   Xe kik

The renewal of the governors
   In this fourteenth *tun* again.

2 Cauac (1608)

In the fifteenth *tun*
2470   At the time of
Second Cauac
   On the first of Pop,
The *katuns* pace each other.
   Completed is the word of 5 Ahau;
2475 Descended is his word;
   Descended is his secret.
There appeared the tying up;
   There appeared the edging
On this return of the fifteenth *tun*,
2480   The day of the eagle-eyed watch
Of the seeker of the throne,
   The coiler of four hundred days,
The Burner,
   The Sucking of the time
2485 Of the total of the days,
   The total of the offices.
On the day of the fulfillment
   Of the truth
There appeared Sun Eye of the Little Tree.
2490   Sun Eye spoke.
The 11 priest Ch'ab Tan
   Departed then,
Settled his moon,
   His perch
2495 Over the budding land,
   Beginning to clothe those hills.
He did not take his request,
   And shook with fear then
On the day of wood
2500   And stone death,
Pounding on his place
   And then having pounded,
Also beginning to initiate
   Blood vomit.

(note continued from preceding page)
correct time or because the village headmen (*ba tabil*) decided upon it. The author of the prophecy isn't sure which.

   2472. 2 Cauac 1 Pop (July 16, 1556, or July 3, 1608).

   2476. The text implies 'descended is his shit; descended are his balls'. This must have surprised the copyist but he wrote it anyway—repeatedly. In another passage (line 3885) he did get it right: *ox kax u than* 'three divisions are their word'. *Toon* means both 'testicles' and 'secret'.

   2479. I read *hoo lahun*.

the attacks and plague that af-
flicted the end of 5 Ahau. At
the beginning of 1608 Itzas were
being tortured. The next day
the cycle was announced, and
the prophecy of the repetition of
the katun cycle of the yearbearers, the Fathers of the
Land: the definitive announcement for 1608. And there was a
ceremony of renewal for the
last quarter katun, and the
priest did penance and accepted punishment to see if he
deserved the priesthood. (2540)

Lai u munal
    U kax cuch katun
Ti ho Ahau katun
    U habil ual e
T u hun te uil katun
    Hun te uil ti hab
U pac ob Ah Itza
    (5v) Kaxan ti che
U ca kin
    U co katun
May
    Ual y ohel
U ximbalt kin
    U ximbalte akab
Sutnac
    Ual u pucsikal
T u men u co katun
    Ti u col can gel*
Ah Can Tzicnal
    Ba Cab
Talel u cah
    U tz'ocol than
T u kin
    Ua cabil Cauac
Ti y uchul yuk ba
    Nom Cab*
Ti tal i
    U pacax
Emel katun
    U katun ix tol och
U munal
    U tzacil
U baxal katun
    Bin u nat e
Ua y an ah kin
    Ua tz'acan u pixan la e.*

2505 That was the slavery,
    The tying of the burden of the katun,
Which was the 5 Ahau katun,
    That year again
At the first moon of the katun,
2510   The first moon of the year
Of the beating of the Itzas
    Tied to trees.
The second day
    Of the cycling katun
2515 The cycle
    And return are known.
The probable course of the days,
    The probable course of the nights,
Having returned
2520   The repetition of its heart
By the cycling katun
    By the turning of the four changers
The four Honored Ones,
    Fathers of the Land
2525 Coming to begin
    And end the word
On the day—
    Or second Cauac—
That was to occur the drinking of mole
2530   And partridge honey—
Who came
    To reseed
The declining katun
    And the katun of the impersonators,
2535 The slavery,
    The cursing,
The beating of the katun.
    It will be known then
Whether there is a sun priest,
2540   Whether this has cured his soul.

3 KAN (1609)

The sixteenth year was the
beginning of the end: 1609.

3 Kan (1609)

T u uac lahun tun
    T u kinil i uil

3 Kan (1609)

In the sixteenth tun,
    In the sun of the moon,

2522. *Cangel* is a curious but frequent aberration. As far as I can recall, it
represents the only use of the letter *g* in Maya. I read it as *can hel* 'four changers'
(as it is often written), but note that it may also be seen as *c angel* 'our angels',
and I suspect the later colonial Maya thought about it that way too. Either way,
these are the yearbearers, Burners, Chacs, Ba Cabs, and presumably the preconquest Pauah Tuns as well, though the latter are not mentioned in the Tizimin.
    2530. See note 2856.
    2540. Penance and vigils were standard measures of the legitimacy and worth
of priests, along with knowledge of the esoteric lore.

Land titles ended, and the new ruler was designated and punished secretly in 1609, because the rule was rotating to the west from the east and north lineages. (2556)

Subdued were the Itza warriors at the time of the feast for the installation of the ruler. He wept as he started into the wilderness to demonstrate his authority, initiating his priestly and secular power as priest of 3 Ahau. And he changed the pol-

Ti Ah oxil Kan
   T u hun te Pop*
U kax cuch katun*
   He x y ahaulil cabob

Kaxan u u ich
   Ti ualac y ahaulil

Ma mac bin thanic
   U baxal katun*
T u kinil
   Oxil Kan*
Colbom
   Y ekel
Chac bob
   Sac bob
Hotz'om y ich'ac
   Hotz'om u co
U balmil
   Ah Ytza
Manac
   T u kin
Chac bul hail
   Chac bul ik
Hokan
   U u ich ku
T ah pop
   T ah tz'am
Y oklal tal
   U cah u binel
T u che
   T u tunich
U pacte
   U kohbal*
Binel u cah u luch
   U kan che
Binel u cah u pop
   T u ch'ab e
Be Ah ox Ahau ual e
   Ti tal i

That was third Kan
   On the first of Pop,
2545 The tying of the burden of the *katun*
   That was also the lordship of the lands.
Tied was the face
   Of him who was to return the lordship.
No one will tell
2550   Of the beating of the *katun*
At the time
   Of third Kan,
It having been turned
   To blackness.
2555 Red stalk,
   White stalk.
Pulled were the claws,
   Pulled the madness
Of the Jaguars
2560   Of the Itza,
This having occurred
   On the day
Of red bean soup,
   Red bean chile,
2565 And there having appeared
   The face of god
In him of the mat,
   In him of the throne.
Because he came
2570   To begin his journey
In the trees,
   In the rocks,
That he may manifest
   His being endowed with the mask,
2575 Going along to begin his gourd,
   His yellow throne,
Going along to begin his mat,
   Which has been taken.
So 3 Ahau it is again
2580   Who comes.

2544. 3 Kan 1 Pop (July 16, 1557, or July 3, 1609).

2545. Tying the burden is a ritual symbol of termination of office for gods and men. In this sixteenth year of the *katun*, land titles were suspended, and the struggle over who had the right to renew them dominates the rest of the *katun*.

2550. The penance of the *katun* priest was particularly severe, presumably as a consequence of the dissension.

2552. Here finally the ceremonial cycle usually associated with the thirteen numbers is shifted to the west (black) from the east (red) and north (white) lineages (stalks). The shift is two years late, which may be due to additional calendrical disagreements. See also note 2410.

2574. The Jaguar priest made his ceremonial circuit masked.

icy and priesthood of the katun, *shifting the priesthood and the lordship to the northwest. So in 1609 the lands reverted to the lord of the* katun, *and the lordship of 5 Ahau was suspended around 1609. (2598)*

U y anal ahaulil
  U hel than
U hel ah kin
  T u hel tam ba katun
Talel u cah u helic u luch
  U helic u laac
U hel
  Y ahaulil
Ualac xaman
  Ualac chikin*
Ti to
  T u uac lahun tun
U sut u petenil
  Ti y ahaulil katun
Ti to ualac y ahaulil
  Ah ho Ahau ual e
Tac pach
  Tac tan ual e.*

The nature of the lordship
  Is the change of the word,
The change of the sun priest.
  The *katuns* exchange each other,
2585 Coming to begin to change his gourd,
  To change his plate.
The change
  Of the lordship
To return to the north,
2590 To return to the west.
At that,
  In the sixteenth *tun*
He returns his country
  To the lordship of the *katun*.
2595 At that he is to return to the lordship
  Of 5 Ahau again:
Shortly after
  Or shortly before, that is.

4 MULUC (1610)

1610 was the application deadline for public office. They marked the end and awaited the end of the katun *with drinking and sacrifices at the*

4 Muluc (1610)

T u uuc lahun tun
  Ti ca Muluc*
U kuchul u kinil
  U tzai katun
T u kin mumul
  Uil katun
U ti al u mucul
  Uiil katun
U kuchul u kinil
  Sac hail*
Ah baac
  Balam habil
Mul tun tzek
  (Mul tun ya)*
Ah ox kokol tzek*
  Ah mis peten
Kin tun y abil*
  Ma ya cimlal*

4 Muluc (1610)

In the seventeenth *tun*
2600 On 4 Muluc
Was the arrival of the time
  Of the seeking of the *katun*
At the time of piling up
  The moon of the *katun*,
2605 So as to await
  The moon of the *katun*,
The arrival of the time
  Of white water,
A bone
2610 And jaguar year.
The ruin
  (. . . . .)
Three stone rattles
  Sweepers of the country
2615 The calendar round
  Painless death

2590. Further evidence that the struggle of the period was between the northwest (Merida and Uxmal) and the northeast (Emal and perhaps Zotz'il).
2598. That is, shortly after 1609 and shortly before the end of *katun* 5 Ahau in 1618.
2600. 4 Muluc 1 Pop (July 16, 1558, or July 3, 1610). The manuscript has *ca* for *can*.
2608. *Sac hail* 'white liquid' I assume to be a holy (white) drink.
2612. Line missing, possibly *mul tun ya* 'pyramid of pain'.
2613. *Ox kokol tzek* recurs every thirteen years. See 4 Kan, line 1699.
2615. *Kin tun y abil* 'day-*tun*-year period' is the time when the 260-day, 360-day, and 365-day counts come out even. Thus it may refer either to 52 years (*hab*) and 72 *tzol kins* or to 72 years and 73 *tuns*. The three cycles coincide only once in 3,744 years, and the expression appears to be used in the Tizimin to mean "maximal cycle," hence the 52-year calendar round.
2616. *Ma ya cimlal* 'no pain killing' could be etymologized as 'Maya death' and

(note continued on following page)

pyramid, scouring the forest for
human sacrifices with fasting
and ceremony. They decimated
the villages to the south and
the people on the roads. There
was mourning everywhere, end-
ing the half katun *on January 2,*
1611, precisely. The period
ended with the ancestor rites.
Three years of death and de-
struction is the ceremonial
duty, fate, and fulfillment of the
seventeenth year. (2642)

These are the sevenfold glyph

T u kinil ukah	In the time of thirst,
T u kinil uiih	In the time of fasting
Bin manac ha	The water will be gone
Bi ticinac sayab ob	2620 The springs will be dissipated
U noholil	In the southern
Luum	Lands
Bin kiknac be	The roads will be bloody,
Bin kiknac heleb	The stops will be bloody
Auatnom bul	2625 Mourning bowls
Cum t u hol cah*	And gourds at the entrance to the
	towns.
Buluc Ch'ab Tan	The 11 priest Ch'ab Tan,
Buluc te ti Chuen*	The eleventh of Chuen
U u ich	Is its face
T u tepal	2630 Exactly.
Okom ku	Gone is the god
Okom bal cah	Gone is the world
Ti tun u kahsic u na	In the *tun* of remembering one's mother,
(6r) U yum*	One's father.
Ox uutz' katun u cimi e	2635 Three folds of *katuns* of this death,
Sati e	This destruction
Bin y alan che	Will be under the trees,
Y alan haban e*	Under the bushes,
T u men u than kin	Because the word of the day,
U kahlai	2640 The word of history
Bin uchebal	Will be accomplished
Ti uuc lahun tun	In the seventeenth *tun*.
Bay i li ichil uuc tz'acab uooh*	Thus only in seven steps of glyphs
Tz'ab u xoc ob	Are given the counts

(note continued from preceding page)

has been so interpreted. It is relevant to note that the preceding expression *kin tun y abil* could be rendered 'sun stone sickness', a pun which cannot be ruled out. I believe in any case that 'painless death' means sacrifice and have so interpreted it throughout (see line 5269). It is very frequently, but not always, associated with the year or the calendar round. Aside from this expression, the word "Maya" does not occur in the Tizimin until the eighteenth century.

2626. I have no ethnographic warrant for mourning bowls at the entrances to towns. Votive mounds of stones were found at the entrances to Quiche towns in Guatemala.

2628. 11 Chuen 3 Zac (February 3, 1559, or January 21, 1611) would be the only occurrence of this date within a year 4 Muluc. In 1559 this was the day after Candlemas. The real date of the mid *katun* was 4 Ahau 2 Zip in 1608, Mayapan-style.

2634. Commemoration of ancestors. See also note 1700.

2638. The tree and the arbor are attributes of the direction gods in the *Ritual of the Bacabs*. See Roys 1965.

2643. The word *tz'acab* is not a classifier. It follows that there is more than one glyph to a 'step', but there is no way of knowing how many more. Nor is it clear how much of the preceding text is covered by seven 'steps' of glyphs: the forty-four lines of the 4 Muluc prophecy? the seventeen years from 1593 to 1610? It is not even clear that 'steps' are standard units. I am inclined to guess that one 'step' may be a "fold" in a codex-style book, and from the length of the exegesis on glyphs that follows I would suppose that the reference is to the whole of the preceding chapter. Also see lines 5435 ff.

accounts of Puc Tun, the Spokesman of Hun Uitzil of Uxmal,
the translation of the glyphs of
the earlier priest Kauil Ch'el,
who saw it as an obligation of
the Spokesmen of the Jaguar
from the gods and as a sign of
class warfare. Penance is the
advice of the glyph. There is
also a personage depicted as a
Christian warning of poverty
and starvation. So the glyphs
say. (2676)

Ah kin Chilam
  Y etel ah kin Na Puc Tun*
U h ah kin Hun *Uitzil**
  Chac Uxmal
Lai u hoksay
  T u uooh *anahte*
T u than ah kin Ch'el*

  Yax nat e
Ti y ilah
  Licil u lubul koch
Lai alab ti ob
  Chilam Balam
T u men Hunab Ku
  Ox lahun ti ku
Lai bin
  Lub bal
Sinic
  Balam Habil
Hun
  Coyol
Y ubil ual e
  T u than uoh
Ix binac h ix maac
  Xan uai
Y okol chapat che
  Ua ix ma uchac t oon e
Uchom ix y okol uah
  Ua ix y okol haa
Y oklal ox koch*
  U than katun la e
Bai chican ichil uooh katun

  Ychil *anahte.**

2645 Of the sun priest Spokesman
  And the sun priest Puc Tun
Sun priest of Hun Uitzil,
  The rain priest of Uxmal.
This is the explanation
2650 To the glyphs of the paper
In the words of the sun priest Kauil
Ch'el,
  The first to know it,
Who saw it
  As a signal of the debt.
2655 This was told to them,
  The Spokesmen of the Jaguar,
By the Sole God,
  The 13 Gods.
That then
2660 Will be the sign of something:
An ant
  And jaguar year period.
Silence
  And abstention
2665 Is the news again:
  The glyph has spoken.
Also to go on there is also a person
  There too
Over the centipede tree,
2670 And if it is not to happen to us too
There did occur also begging bread
  Or also begging water,
Lamenting the breadnut and gourdroot
  Is the word of this *katun.*
2675 Thus it is shown in the glyph of the
katun
  In the paper.

5 IX (1611)

Then occurred the return to
the center at Mayapan and the

5 Ix (1611)

Uai ual t u xaman cab

  T u nohol cab
Uai tan cah
  Mayapan

5 Ix (1611)

This is the return from the north
country
  To the south country
That is the capital,
2680 Mayapan

2646. Puc Tun 'hill stone' was a Xiu prophet of 5 Ahau (1598) at Uxmal.
  2647. Hun Uitzil 'one hummingbird', East priest and governor of Uxmal in 5
Ahau (1598). I read *u y ah kin.*
  2651. Kauil Ch'el was a notable prophet of 9 Ahau (1559). We appear to have a
namesake here, especially if, as I suppose, the present text was written in 3 Ahau.
  2673. The Maya had a recurrent theory that they were destined to pay tribute
to the Spanish only for a limited time. See also note 5290.
  2676. The allusion to postconquest glyphic writing seems quite clear. *Anahte*
'book' from Nahuatl *amatl* 'paper' and Maya *te* 'tree'.

conversion of Cha Pat and the
conversion of Ol Zip, at the be-
ginning of 1611, toward the end
of 5 Ahau. (2692)

   Then was the enslavement of
Cap Uah of Tayasal, causing
dissension, and the priests
ended the ceremony by inaugu-
rating Uuc Het in 1611. Back in
exile with a Spanish saint to
protect the lake; abandoned by

Ti uil manabtic u ba
  Ah Uuc Cha Pat*
T ix uil u manabtic u ba

  Ah Uuc y Ol Sip ual e.*
T u kuchul
  U cuch kinil
Ah ho Hix*
  T u uaxac lahun tun
U hitz'il katun ual e
  T u kin u kaxal
U cuch
  Ah ho Ahau
Ti tun u munal
  (Ti tun u munal)*
Ah Cap Uah*
  Tun holom t u cal ya

Auatnom pax che
  Thannom tan y ol ha*
Hach u kin
  U ch'eeh tam ba
U cah ix tol och
  Ti tal i
U hel ep than i
  U cumtal ti ahaulil
Ah Uuc Het
  Lai u than
T u uaxac lahun pis
  Ti ual
U sutup peten
  U pacahtal Ah Itza
Bin ual ximbalnac koh

  Cib uinlis
He uac hitz'hal u than
  Tan chumuc haa

In the moon of the self-transformation
  Of the 7 priest Cha Pat
That was also the moon of the self-
transformation
  Of the 7 priest Ol Zip again,
2685 On the arrival
  Of the burden of the time
Of 5 Ix
  In the eighteenth *tun*,
The ending of the *katun* again
2690   On the day of the tying
Of the burden
  Of 5 Ahau,
In the *tun* of his slavery,
  In the *tun* of the slavery
2695 Of the stuffer of tamales,
  Tun of completion of the filling of
pain,
Lamented by the wooden drum
  Spoken in the middle of the water.
Greatly they hurt
2700   And beat each other,
And the impersonators started
  And came
And finally closed the word,
  The inauguration into the lordship
2705 Of Uuc Het.
  That is the word
On the eighteenth measure
  Which is the return
Back to the country:
2710   The chastisement of the Itza.
There will have been the parading of
the mask,
  The human figure of wax
That may be worshiped
  In the middle of the water

2682. Initially I thought this might refer to the Gregorian reform of the Christian calendar, promulgated by the pope in 1582, but the chronology of the Tizimin remains Julian at least down to Corpus Christi of 1629. Indeed, the only Gregorian dates in the Tizimin belong to the middle nineteenth century. Also see line 3116 and the notes to chapter 24.

2684. Ol Zip had attempted to play a conciliatory role in the religious struggle. He now became Christian.

2687. 5 Ix 1 Pop (July 15, 1559, or July 2, 1611).

2694. Line crossed out in the manuscript.

2695. Cap Uah 'stuff tamales,' possibly a personal name.

2698. It is almost impossible to find a place "in the middle of the water" on the Yucatan Peninsula. The reference is quite likely to Lake Peten. See also line 2714. But Lake Bacalar cannot be ruled out. Tan Xuluc Mul is mentioned by name in other *Books of Chilam Balam*. See Bricker 1981 for a discussion of the Peten Itza embassy to Merida in 1614.

the Maya lords, Cap Uah spread the new religion and worship and new calendar and customs, destroying the wooden idols of 11 Ahau and destroying even the metal idols, because of two days' drinking and a riot. And when they got back to the towns and villages the respected nobles were seized and beaten. The return of the Itza was a disaster. They suffered penance in fulfillment of the oath of office but also at the desire of the villages. (2750)

And heaven and earth were moved by the rumors of the eastern lineages in the towns and villages. And the lord of the katun *just sat there because*

Ppatbe u cah
   Satai ahaulil
Ch'ehel u than
   Ti tal i
Y utzil ahaulil
   Uatal u cah
U hel u luch
   U hel u nok
Ti uchac hatz'hal
   Bom koh che
He tun
   Buluc Ahau e*
T u kin u salam pop
   U paclam pacat
Koh che cheehnom
   Koh che mascab

T u menel ti ca kin cii
   Ox kin chanal
T u kin
   U sutup
T u ch'enil
   Ti y ac tunil
Uchom u ch'a tam ba
   Mehentzil*
He boh t u tzelec
   U pacax ha
U than y oklal kuch i

   T u kinil u sutup Ah Itza
Likul t u cal ya
   T u cal ukah
Bai ual
   Bin ualak nahbal
U kat
   (6v) U cuchil
U y anal
   Ix y ac tunil
Ti uchom u pec can
   Ti uchom u pec luum
Humnon ix Chac
   Ix Chu Ah*
T u ch'enil
   Ti y ac tunil
Tan u cucul it
   Koh che

2715 Or whose place may be abandoned,
   Needing the lordship,
Broadcasting the word
   That is coming,
The goodness of the lordship
2720   Standing in the place
Of the change of the gourd,
   The change of the clothes,
Where may occur the beating,
   The end of the wooden mask,
2725 Which is then
   On 11 Ahau,
On the day of the dried mat,
   The pounded flat look
At the wooden mask,
2730   The hammered wooden mask of metal,
Because it is the second day of wine,
   The third day of rioting.
At the time
   Of the return
2735 To the wells
   To the springs
Occurred the seizing each other
   Of the honored sons,
That is beating on the legs,
2740   The reseeding of water,
The speaking of lamentation for the arrival
   Of the time of the return of the Itza,
Arising at the pass of pain,
   The pass of thirst.
2745 Thus is the return
   Or else the fulfillment
Of the desire
   Of the burden
Of his existence—
2750   Also of the springs
Which occurred moving heaven,
   Which occurred moving earth.
Hummed both Chacs
   And Chu Uahs
2755 At the wells,
   At the springs,
And he just sat on his ass,
   The wooden mask,

2726. A day rather than a *katun*: 11 Ahau 7 Pop (July 21, 1559, or July 8, 1611).
2738. The noble factions attacked each other.
2754. I believe Chac to be a Xiu and Chu and Uah to be Itza lineage names.

of the northeast war, the true sacrificer of the katun. (2762)

6 CAUAC (1612)

In 1612 they broke off and went back to sacrificing the priests over the lordship of 3 Ahau by the sea. Various lords in the female line caused the destruction of Quetzalcoatl in the plague of the final year. (2788)

The priesthood being open, it was seized by Cab Bech' in the last year of the katun. *Cab*

T u men chac uen co
    Sac uen co
Ah maben tok
    U chan katun.

6 Cauac (1612)

Uacil Cauac*
    Ti bolon hun tun
U kuchul u kinil
    Pailam kab
Ti ual
    T u kin
T u yabil ual e
    Ma ya cimlal
Y etel u hach
    Pik tam ba
Ah Uuc Te Cuy
    Y etel Ah Chac Mitan Ch'oc*
T u kokol
    Box katun
Ti uchom
    T u chi kaknab
Lai Ah Ma Suy
    Sitz'om Tun*
Chac Hubil Ahau*
    Sihom al
Lai
    U kin uch
C u sin
    Choch Kukul Can
T u katunil
    U cucul it
Ah chichic sot ti tun

    U chichic sot katun i*
Ti hokan
    U ch'a u matan
Ca bin u Bech' Kab
    Ti
T u bolon hun tun
    U kin u chichic sot katun

Because of red sleep madness,
2760   White sleep madness,
Chest knife
    And tooth of the *katun*.

6 Cauac (1612)

Sixth Cauac
    In the nineteenth *tun*
2765 Was the arrival of the time
    Of separated hands,
Which is the return
    To the day
Of this year again,
2770   Painless death.
And they propose
    To remove each other,
The 7 priest Te Cuy
    And the East priest Mitan Ch'oc
2775 In the smear
    Of the black *katun*.
Which occurred
    At the edge of the sea:
Ma Zuy,
2780   Zitz'om Tun,
And the East priest Hub Ahau,
    The born children.
That then
    Is the day occurring
2785 That flattens
    And levels Kukul Can
In the *katun* period
    Of runny asses,
The priest of the full swelling in the *tun*,
2790   Of the full swollen *katun*,
Who appeared
    To take his request.
Then Bech' is going
    For it
2795 In the nineteenth *tun*,
    The time of the full swollen *katun*,

2763. 6 Cauac 1 Pop (July 15, 1560, or July 2, 1612).

2774. These sound like pejorative names for the two factions, Christian and Maya respectively: 7 Te Cuy 'tree hex' and Chac Mitan Ch'oc 'red plague rot'. They could also be personal names with titles.

2780. Ma Zuy is also associated with Tz'itz'om Tun in 13 Ahau (1539).

2781. Chac Hubil Ahau 'red snail lord' is not otherwise mentioned in the Tizimin.

2790. The nearly completed *katun*.

*Bech' came to the lake and
caused chaos among the nobility. Sodomites and liars
exhausted 1612. Copal was
collected for the god for the ceremony of the end of the katun.
The insignia were taken by
Uayab Xoc of Emal and P'iz Te*

Nak tam ba u than Cabil Bech'

   Y etel ix tan y ol haa*
U ch'ab u matan coil
   Ch'ab coil
U coil mehen
   Y al
U mehen *tzintzin*
   Coc xul
Ma ix tan y al u than
   Ua bin laac t u kinil
Ti y abil
   Uacil Cauac
U uatal chic che
   Numen y ol
Amaite Ku u u ich
   Ca sutz'
Y okol yax che
   Yaxum pul
Y okol uil
   U xotemal katun
Paibehom ppus
   Paibchom koh
Pachalhom Chac Uayab Xoc

   Hokom ah ppis te*

Approaching each other the words of
Cab Bech'
   And the middle of the water,
Creating the reign of madness,
2800   Creating madness,
The madness of the engendered
   And born children,
The sons of sodomy,
   Ass buggers.
2805 For there is no weight to his word
   If that is all of his time
In the year
   Of sixth Cauac,
The collection of graceful trees
2810   To inform the spirit
Of Amayte Ku
   When he is stopped
Over the ceiba,
   The dove *guayaba,*
2815 Over the moon
   And judgment of the *katun.*
The humps having been separated,
   The masks having been separated,
Having backed up the East priest
Uayab Xoc;
2820   There having appeared P'iz Te

2798. Possibly a personal name but more likely a place-name personification of the leader of the Peten Itza, Can Ek, who is not mentioned by name in the Tizimin.

2803. *Tzintzin* from Nahuatl *tzintli* 'anus'. "Sodomist" is a frequent colonial insult. The modern Maya lean toward insulting mothers.

2820. *Ah p'is te* 'measuring stick', a personage, but the designation may be a title rather than a name. The town of P'is Te is a few kilometers west of Chichen Itza.

Mayan ideas of measurement are closely linked to the use of numeral classifiers, of which the language provides an almost indefinite number. The generic units are a measure (*p'iz*) or a count (*och, tzol, xoc*).

Linear distance is measured by the knuckle (*p'uc, pic*), palm (*nab*), span from thumb to forefinger (*mab*), foot (*oc*), forearm (*kok*), waist (*xoc*), pace (*chek*), arm span (*zap*), and man's length (*ualah*). Larger units are the *mac* of about 24 meters, blowgun shot (*tz'on*), shout (*auat*), post or rest (*lub*), and sleep (*uay*). Horizontal distances are conceived of in length (*uat, uac*) and width (*hat*); vertical distance, conceived of as a matter of levels (*kaz, xay*), is measured by the rise or step (*eb, tem*) or fall (*hom*).

Area concepts include the square (*am*) and circle (*pet*). Agricultural land is measured by the rope or *cuerda* (about 437 square meters) or by the day's labor (*kin*).

Volume measures are the pinch of two fingers (*nip'*) and three fingers (*thuth*), fistful (*lap'*), handful (*kab*), fold (*uutz'*) of about seven liters, armload (*kal*), and backload (*cuch, patan*). Particular substances are counted by the containers in which they were typically carried, but these do not appear to be standardized. Weight and force are only vaguely specified.

Time measures of less than a day are not precise: an instant (*zut*), an instance (*chi, put, ten, uatz'*), or an interval (*yam*). Hours of the day are indicated by a

(note continued on following page)

*to impose authority in the west,
but they fell out over the passing of the* katun *and came to
blows over the office and disrupted the* katun. *(2832)*

7 KAN (1613)

*By the time of 1613 someone
had to settle it and take over as
ruler. The priesthood would
have to wait on the fasting of
the end of the* katun. *(2845)*

*Ol Kauil then arrived at the
katun ceremony to take the office held for him. It was agreed*

U ch'ab u matan
   Ualac uil chikin
U napp tam ba
   U chibal tam bail
U tz'ocol u than ho Ahau
   U uatal ox *toscum**
T u bolon tun
   Y uchul chuc tam ba
Ualac y ahaulil
   Ti ualac u than
Talan ti cib
   Lai y an t u ppicul katun la e.

7 Kan (1613)

Ti uil uucil Kan*
   U kinil u hitz'il
Talel u cah
   U ch'a be katun
Ah pop
   Ah tz'am
Bin u patab
   U luch
T u cal yaa
   T u cal num ya
T u hitz' katun
   Cal pul uiih
Bin u acunte
   Ah Uaxac y Ol Kauil*
Ca bin
   Kuchuc
U kinil
   U katunil ual e
Cam pat-hom be
   Tal i
Ti caan
   Heb tam ba

To create the mandate
   And return the moon to the west.
They pinch each other;
   They bite each other,
2825 Ending the word of 5 Ahau,
   Voicing the three "voices"
On the nineteenth *tun.*
   Occurring socking each other
To bear the lordship,
2830   To bear its word,
Having come to the desire for that;
   That was the tearing up of the
   katun then.

7 Kan (1613)

At the moon of seventh Kan,
   The time of the ending,
2835 One may come to settle
   And take the road of the *katun,*
The man of the mat,
   The man of the throne.
He then will be awaited;
2840   His gourd
Filled the pain,
   Filled the suffering
At the end of the *katun.*
   Throat-bearing hunger
2845 May be made to arise.
   The 8 priest Ol Kauil
Will then
   Be due to arrive
At the time
2850   Of that *katun.*
The road having been kept waiting,
   He comes then.
In heaven
   They divide each other,

(note continued from preceding page)

gesture representing the angle of the sun, those of the night by the angle of the
Big Dipper, and noon (*tan kin*), rest stops (*lub*), and dawn (*al kab*) are specified.
The measurement of larger intervals of time is incredibly sophisticated and pre-
cise (see "calendar" in the index).

Value is expressed in a count of specific goods, particularly the cacao bean
(*cacau*) and the quetzal feather (*kuk*). Colonial tribute is paid largely in agricultural produce, textiles, and wax, and colonial punishment is measured by the
lash stroke (*p'uc*).

2826. *Toscum* from Nahuatl *tozcome* 'voices': the "voices" of the *katun* were
three pseudoprophets, Nahuas at that!

2833. 7 Kan 1 Pop (July 15, 1561, or July 2, 1613).

2846. 8 Ol Kauil 'heart god', the priest designate for 3 Ahau.

to divide the land, weakening it, east and west. Then the lord was able to unite people to end the katun and be installed and take command. He claimed the katun in 1613. (2874)

Normalcy returned with the lineages of Tok, Uah, and Kauil as usual in 1613. On July 8, 1613, they started to survey the land and by August 31, 1613,

Nom cab
　Sutup nom*
Ualac oy
　Och caan
Ti chikin
　Ti lakin
U cuch
　Ti y ahaulil
Talel
　U cah u mol ba
T u cuch
　T u tepal
Ti tun u tz'ocol u cuch katun

　Kaxan u u ich
Binel u cah u tz'am
　Binel u cah u pop y it
Binel u than
　T u sitz'il katun

Ti uucil Kan
　U kin
U pa sa . . .*
　(7r) . . . he uac y an u uah
　katun
T u kin
　U pai Tok*
U pai Uah
　U pai Kauil
Ti uchom
　T u sitz'il katun
Uucil Kan
　U kin.
Ox hun Oc*
　Uil u kin
U chek
　Oc katun
Y etel canil Cauac*
　Uil

2855　The partridge lands,
　　　The moonflower partridge,
　　To return to a weak
　　　Shadow of heaven
　　In the west,
2860　　In the east.
　　The burden
　　　Of him who is in the lordship
　　May be coming
　　　To begin to collect itself,
2865　To carry it
　　　To its completion,
　　Which is then the end of the burden of
　　the *katun.*
　　　His face tied up.
　　He may be coming to begin his throne,
2870　　Coming to begin his mat,
　　Coming to say
　　　That he has been wanting the
　　　katun.
　　Seventh Kan
　　　Was the time
2875　His bread atole . . .
　　　. . . that may be the food of the
　　　katun
　　On the day
　　　Of the division of the Tok,
　　Of the division of the Uah,
2880　　Of the division of the Kauil,
　　Which occurred
　　　For the desire of the *katun,*
　　Seventh Kan
　　　Being its day.
2885　13 Oc
　　　Was the moon of the sun
　　Of pacing
　　　The steps of the *katun,*
　　And fourth Cauac
2890　　The moon

2856. Zutup Nom 'moonflower partridge', a diviner who disagreed with Nom Cab about the fate of *katun* 3 Ahau? They could have been cousins. See also line 2530.

2875. There may be a word missing here.

2878. Tok 'knives', Uah 'bread', and Kauil 'god' were lineages, scrapping over the lordship. Apparently they all lost.

2885. 13 Oc 7 Pop (July 21, 1561, or July 8, 1613).

2889. 4 Cauac 16 Zotz' (September 13, 1561, or August 31, 1613). It may be significant that the next day is 5 Ahau. The new *katun* would have begun on 3 Ahau 17 Mac (March 15, 1614) but would still be five years early by the traditional (Mayapan) count.

they finished it and changed rulers and started to change priests. The change of rulers ended 5 Ahau, who had done his duty and surrendered his office. His Spokesman was re-placed at the shrine and the cy-cle was ended at Mayapan, his seat and origin, and in the vil-lages with sacrifices. A new one started immediately as the ka-tun was folded. (2926)

U ualak u uutz' katun
  U kin u ppatic
U pop
  U tz'am
Talel
  U cah
U hel u luch
  U hel u pop
U hel u tz'am
  U hel y ahaulil
U lubul u cuch
  Ah ho Ahau
U pacat pach ual e
  T u ch'a matan
Binan u luch
  Binan u pop
Binan y ah pulil u than
  Uatal t u cah u heel cab

T u yax cheil
  T u tzuc teil cab
Ha li li uchan
  T u tz'oc u cuch katun
Ti to uil y okol *Mayapan*
  Ti uchom may cu
U y etz'
  U ch'ibal
T u ch'enil
  Ti y ac tunil
Ti x uchom cim cehil
  Ma ya cimlal
Ti uchom
  Yax cahil
Sibis
  Sibisil
T u kin u tz'oc katunob
  U uutz' hun tz'it katun.

To erect the fold of the *katun*,
  The day he abandons
His mat,
  His throne.
2895 There may be coming
  The beginning
Of the change of his gourd,
  The change of his mat,
The change of his throne,
2900 The change of his lordship,
The fall of the burden
  Of 5 Ahau.
Looking back at it
  He has taken the request.
2905 Gone is his gourd,
  Gone is his mat,
Gone is the bearer of his word.
  Standing in his place is the change of the land
In the ceiba grove,
2910 In the copse land.
Truly then it is done;
  The burden of the *katun* is finished.
Which is one moon over Mayapan,
  The cycle seat,
2915 His setting,
  His lineage,
At the wells,
  At the welling fountains.
And there occurred deer death
2920 And painless death.
There occurred
  The first settlement
As fact,
  As possible
2925 On the day they finished the *katuns*,
  The fold of one *katun*.

8 MULUC (1614)

In 1614 came the new tun cycle. (2930)

8 Muluc (1614)

Uaxac Muluc
  T u hun te Pop*
U la may tun
  Ti ul i.

8 Muluc (1614)

8 Muluc
  On the first of Pop
Arrived the cycle of the *tun*,
2930 Which arrived then.

2 IX (1596)

So I, Kauil Ch'el, and Puc

2 Ix (1596)

On c en
  Ah Kauil Ch'el

2 Ix (1596)

Then I,
  Kauil Ch'el

2928. 8 Muluc 1 Pop (July 15, 1562, or July 2, 1614).

Tun and Xopan Nahuatl, sun priests to the governor Hun Uitzil, the East priest of the Toltec Xiu at Uxmal under Mayapan, who was to rule 3 Ahau, have prepared him and spoken for him in Ni Tun Tz'ala and Pacat Ha. He has had me count 5 Ahau legitimately, adding one katun. This I have done at Bacalar. I have written it in glyphs which will be checked by the sage to see if I am right. In the district of Salamanca at the capital in the territory of Chetumal, division of

Y etel Na Puc Tun
   Y etel Ah *Xupan Nauat*
U y ah kin
   Noh hal ach uinic
Hun *Uitzil*
   Chac
Tutul Xiu
   Ti Uxmal
T u lumil *Mayapan*
   May cu
Ti u ch'abal u lac
   Ah ox Ahau
Bai bic
   Uchic
U alic
   U than
Uai Ni Tun Tz'ala*
   Uai Pacat Haa*
Ti chul te
   T in tzolah u ch'ich' katun
T u hahil sihanil
   Ychil u cuch katun
Likul ti
   Hun tz'it katun
Lai t in tzolah
   Uai Bak Halal e*
T in hoksah
   Ti uooh*
Ti ual bin u toh cin
   Ah miatz bin y ila
Ua ma toh
   U binel uchic
In tzolic
   Uai t u lumil
T u cabil
   Salamanca*
Ti tzuc peten
   Uai tan cah
Chac Temal*
   T u lumil tzucub te*

And Puc Tun
   And Xopan Nahuatl,
2935 The sun priests
   Of the great governor
Hun Uitzil,
   The rain priest
Of the Tutul Xiu
2940   At Uxmal
In the lands of Mayapan
   The cycle seat,
Which was taking the plate
   Of 3 Ahau
2945 To humble,
   Soften,
And speak
   His word
At the place called Ni Tun Tz'ala,
2950   The place called Pacat Ha,
Who may have occasioned
   That I count the bird *katun*
In the truly born
   Within the burden of the *katun*,
2955 Raising it
   By one *katun* piece.
That is what I counted
   Here at Bacalar.
I have manifested
2960   In glyphs
Which return will have been corrected,
   And the sage will see
If it is not correct,
   What may come to pass
2965 That I have counted
   In the lands,
In the country
   Of Salamanca,
In the groves of the country
2970   Here at the capital,
Chetumal
   In the lands of the sacred grove,

2949. Ni Tun Ts'ala 'squeezed noseplug', a town near Chetumal.
2950. Pacat Ha 'water view', a town near Chetumal.
2958. Bacalar, on the lake of the same name. Roys 1957: 159 translates Bak Halal as 'surrounded by reeds'.
2960. The continued insistence on glyphs is of interest. See also line 2976.
2968. Montejo founded several Salamancas in honor of his birthplace. This appears to be the one near Chetumal. See Tozzer 1941: 8.
2971. Chac Temal 'red steps': pyramids or ceremonial benches of the east. This is the modern Chetumal.
2972. The sacred grove of Bacalar.

Uaymil, I have finished the glyphs on 11 Chuen 18 Zac, February 15, 1544. (2980)

Tah*
  Uaymil*
Ti tz'oc in tz'aic
  Uooh*
Lae t u uaxac lahun te Sac
  Ti buluc huen
T u ho lhum pis kin *Febrero*
  1544 hab.*

Division of
  Uaymil.
2975 I have finished giving
  These glyphs
  On the eighteenth of Zac
  On 11 Chuen
  On the fifteenth day of February,
2980 The year 1544.

2973. *Tah* 'division' could be a place-name, as Roys would have it, but I don't think so.

2974. Uaymil *'guaya* tree', the modern Uaymil, also near Chetumal.

2976. In preceding passages (see line 2643) the author makes it clear that he is reading from a hieroglyphic manuscript, presumably a prophetic one covering the pseudo-*katun* from 1541 to 1561. It is not possible that this glyphic document was transcribed as early as 1544, as is implied below. Here, however, I think the assertion to be that he completed translating the glyphic prophecy on the date given but in 1596.

2980. 11 Chuen 18 Zac (February 21, 1544, or February 8, 1596). The date cited is incorrect because it suppresses the leap year correction, choosing to relate the correlation to a base year 1 Kan 1 Pop, July 16, 1581. The author is aware that there is a seven-day error (the difference between this base and the true base year of 1 Ix 1 Pop, July 16, 1555), but he doesn't bother to note it. The correct interpretation of the date for the composition of the manuscript is therefore 11 Chuen 18 Zac, February 8, 1596. He writes the year 1544 to emphasize that he is basing his prophecy on the fifty-two-year cycle—but he is also aware that this involves a thirteen-day leap year correlation, which he also doesn't bother to enter. See also note 2410.

I believe both dates, and the claimed authorship of this document, to be fictional. If there were a glyphic document for the pseudo-*katun* 1541 to 1561, it would presumably have been written around 1566. If the second document were the 'finished' word for the pseudo-*katun* 5 Ahau it purports to describe, it would probably date to around 1618 to 1623. Since it seems to reflect actual history in both *katuns*, I incline to the latter supposition. Kauil Ch'el, Xopan Nahuatl, and Puc Tun were already named in a prophecy for 13 Ahau (1539); see lines 562 ff., which, however, may have been put into present form as much as two *katuns* later: 9 Ahau (1559). Kauil Ch'el may well have been Spokesman of the Jaguar at the beginning of 9 Ahau (1559)—see note 1239—but I don't believe he prepared the present text in 1596, let alone in 1618. Whoever did simply used his name.

3 Ahau

23. Merida under the Gallows

3 Ahau was the fifth in the Itza katun series. Merida was its seat. The West priest Coc Ay the Crier was its lord, and Cib Yan and Muk Yan and Pat Yan tried hard to exorcise the devil. All three were hanged by God's command. (2998)

There were Locusts and Jaguars, Monsters, Ants and Bees,

(16v) Ox Ahau
  U ho tz'it
Katun
  C u xocol
Ich Can Si Ho
  U hetz' katun
Ek Coc Ay Mut u u ich*

  Tan y ahaulil
Cib Yan u u ich
  Muk Yan u u ich
Pat Yan u u ich
  Sitz'il tz'utal
Tz'ut u tza cisin i
  Ti y emel ox ualah
U le
  Silil i
U than Hunab Ku
  Canal
Sakal Habil*
  Balam Habil
Sac Pat Ay Chacil*

  Thul Can Chacil*

3 Ahau
  Was the fifth part
Of the *katun*
  To be counted.
2985 Heaven Born Merida
  Was the seat of the *katun.*
The West priest Coc Ay Mut was the person
  Who was in the lordship.
Cib Yan was his face;
2990 Muk Yan was his face;
Pat Yan was his face.
  Desire was sharpening.
Sharp was the exorcism of the devil.
  There descended three turns
2995 Of the noose
  Which was rolled up,
The word of the Sole God
  On high.
There were the Locust scouts,
3000 And Jaguar scouts,
The North priest Pat Ay of the Monsters,
  Thul Can of the Monsters,

2987. Ek Coc Ay Mut 'black turtle grease crier', a West priest who seated the *katun* in Merida. He was opposed by the Center priest Coc Ay of Zuyua (possibly a brother) and by Cib Yan 'wax direction', Muk Yan 'strength direction', and Pat Yan 'wait direction', the last three of whom were apparently caught and hanged.

2999. There follows a list of the military orders active around Merida at this time. While the orders were generally pro-Christian and propeasant, they probably opposed the taxes of both Merida and Zuyua. They include Sakal Habil 'locust scouts', Balam Habil 'jaguar scouts', Chacil 'monsters', Sinic 'ants', Balamil 'honeybees', Pan 'flags', and Ch'in Ch'in 'chiggers'. Of these, the Monsters and the Chiggers are not mentioned elsewhere.

3001. Pat Ay 'wait grease', a North priest and leader of the Monsters.

3002. Thul Can 'rabbit snake', another leader of the Monsters.

Flags and Chiggers! Three trials of peasants were staged in this katun. Three times in seven years there were hangings, and burnings began in the center of Merida, destroying the robe of the East priest Bol Ay before the three pyramids on the plaza. Copal fires and many, many hangings were held, and the burden of suffering and fear fell on the fly-by-night lords by the true will of the risen God, O peasants. The ceremonial insignia were taken from the cen-

Sinic
  Balamil
Pan
  Ch'in Ch'in
Ox ch'uilah xotem
  Ox cuch-hom y al max

Ulom ix u esil
  Ti bal cah i
Ti tal i
  U cuch katun uch i
Uuc ppel hab
  U chibal
Ox ualah u le
  Silil i
Hopom
  Kak
T u Xulub Yuc*
  Ich Can Si Ho
Haulahom u keulel
  Chac Bol Ay*
Tan kiuic
  Ox mul tun tzekil
Ix pom
  Kakil
Ban ban hich' cal
  U cuch katun
Ti tal i
  U cuch
Num ya
  Cotz'bal u u ich
Ah ca kin pop
  Ah ca kin tz'am
T u tz'oc u than katun
  Ma tus i
U than ku
  Likul canal
Cex
  U itz'in ex e
Okom bul cum
  Okom yax cach
T u can xai be
  Ti tali ob
Tan y ol che
  Ti ual

Ants,
  Bees,
3005 Flags,
  And Chiggers.
Three sentences of hanging—
  Thrice burdened was the monkey
  child
Which came about and was manifested
3010   On earth.
He came:
  The *katun* was carried.
Seven years
  Was his term.
3015 Three turns of the noose
  Were rolled up.
There flamed
  The fire
At the Goat Horns
3020   In Heaven Born Merida.
Carved up is the hide
  Of the East priest Bol Ay
In the middle of the plaza
  Of the three stone pyramids,
3025 And copal
  Fires,
Piles and piles of hangings
  Were the burden of the *katun*.
There came
3030   The burden
Of suffering,
  Rolling of eyes
Of the two-day mat people,
  The two-day throne people.
3035 The word of the *katun* was done.
  It does not lie—
The word of God
  Who ascended into heaven,
O ye
3040   Younger brothers.
Gone are the beans and squash,
  Gone are the green flies
From the four crossroads.
  They have come
3045 Among the trees
  And returned

3019. Xulub Yuc 'goat horns' is unidentified but sounds like a *cantina* that may have been the site of a memorable fire. My guess is that it was known as Los Cabrones.

3022. Chac Bol Ay and Yax Bol Ay were both active in the politics of 5 Ahau and 3 Ahau (1598–1638). Both had namesakes in 8 Ahau (1461).

ter to the wilderness, and Ol
Zip accepted the nomination.
(3048)

T u kamic u matan   To accept the request
  Ah Uuc y Ol Sip ual e.*   Of the 7 priest Ol Zip again.

3048. Ol Zip, lord of Emal, was priest of the *katun* off and on in 5 Ahau
(1602–1618) and again at the beginning of 1 Ahau (1638–?).

---

24. Days of the Year

*This text, the final one in the
manuscript, is a calendar of the
Christian year 1626 with corresponding dates in the tzol kin
and divinations. The day-by-
day auguries are either "good"
(utz) or "bad" (lob) or else they
are not given. Some 199 days
are "bad"; 118 are "good." The
first 105 days are repeated at
the end of the year, 15 of them
with different auguries. A sec-
ond-order translation is not
necessary, as the language is
not ritual and the texts make
peasant sense as they stand.*

   *The calendar is accompanied
by three contemporary texts,
dating it to the first half of
3 Ahau (1618) and mentioning
Sotuta. A reference to Corpus
Christi makes it probable that
the Julian calendar was still in
use. The note for 10 Kan (1629)
records a plague of locusts; that
for 3 Muluc (1622) describes a
famine; and that for 8 Ix (1627)
describes another plague of
locusts.*

(22r) *Enero* (31)			**January (31)**	
1. lahun Oc	utz*		1. 10 Oc	good
2. buluc Chuen	utz	3050	2. 11 Chuen	good
3. lahca Eb	utz		3. 12 Eb	good
4. oxlahun Ben	utz		4. 13 Ben	good
5. hun Hix	lob*		5. 1 Ix	bad
6. ca Men	lob		6. 2 Men	bad
7. ox Cib	utz	3055	7. 3 Cib	good
8. can Caban	utz		8. 4 Caban	good
9. ho Etz'nab	utz		9. 5 Etz'nab	good
10. uacil Cauac	utz*		10. 6 Cauac	good
11. uuc Ahau	utz		11. 7 Ahau	good
12. uaxac Ymix	lob*	3060	12. 8 Imix	bad
13. bolon Ik	lob*		13. 9 Ik	bad
14. lahun Akbal	lob		14. 10 Akbal	bad
15. bulucil Kan	utz*		15. 11 Kan	good
16. lahca Chicchan	lob		16. 12 Chicchan	bad

3049. The first marginal note, for January 1, reads: *U hopol kak* 'the flaming of
the fire'. This marks the second phase of the Oc fire ceremonies, begun on January 1, centered on January 21, and ended on February 10.

3053. *Licil cimil uinicob* 'as the death of people'.

3058. The use of the *-il* suffix with numerals appears to be euphonic rather
than syntactic or semantic. It is generally found with short rather than long day
names. Reading the present list of days aloud rapidly will make the point that it is
the rhythm of the count that is at issue.

3060. *Licil u cutal Yaax* 'as the seating of Yax'. If Yax is seated on 8 Imix, the
yearbearer for this year would be 10 Imix, implying yet another calendar with
Type I yearbearers (Imix, Cimi, Chuen, Cib). Most (but not all) of the subsequent
seatings of the *uinals* in the notes to this chapter confirm this intention.

3061. *U kukum tok ch'apahal y an i* 'the quetzal feather knife has been
seized'. Perhaps a reference to sacrifice: if so, it is a very late one!

3063. *U xul u kaxal ha i* 'the end of the dropping of water'. The observation
has no perceptible relation to the Yucatecan rainy season, which begins in May. It
could be a reference to baptism.

The extensive marginal notes, added substantially later, give Catholic saints' days in Gregorian dates and correlate the tzol kin with the Mayan year in a new calendar with new year-bearers, and there are additional calendrical notations which are simply aberrant or erroneous. Other marginal notes relate to the cult of the Burners (see chapter 40), and there are also notes on ceremonies, taxes, weather, agriculture, and other matters—some of them quite obscure. These notes are reproduced in the following footnotes. I believe them to belong to katun 9 Ahau, which began in 1848.

17. oxlahun Cimi	utz*	3065	17. 13 Cimi	good
18. hun Manik	utz*		18. 1 Manik	good
19. ca Lamat	lob		19. 2 Lamat	bad
20. ox Muluc	lob		20. 3 Muluc	bad
21. canil Oc	*		21. 4 Oc	
22. ho Chuen	lob	3070	22. 5 Chuen	bad
23. uac Eb	utz*		23. 6 Eb	good
24. uuc Been	lob		24. 7 Ben	bad
25. uaxacil Hix	lob		25. 8 Ix	bad
26. bolon Men	lob		26. 9 Men	bad
27. lahun Cib	lob	3075	27. 10 Cib	bad
28. bulucil Caban	utz		28. 11 Caban	good
29. lahca Etz'nab			29. 12 Etz'nab	
30. oxlahun Cauac	utz		30. 13 Cauac	good
31. hun Ahau	lob*		31. 1 Ahau	bad

(22v) Febrero (28)   February (28)

1. ca Ymix	lob*	3080	1. 2 Imix	bad
2. oxil Ik	lob		2. 3 Ik	bad
3. can Akbal	lob		3. 4 Akbal	bad
4. hoil Kan	lob		4. 5 Kan	bad
5. uac Chicchan	lob		5. 6 Chicchan	bad
6. uuc Cimi	utz*	3085	6. 7 Cimi	good
7. uaxac Manik	utz		7. 8 Manik	good
8. bolon Lamat	lob		8. 9 Lamat	bad
9. lahun Muluc	lob		9. 10 Muluc	bad
10. bulucil Oc	utz*		10. 11 Oc	good
11. lahca Chuen	*	·3090	11. 12 Chuen	
12. oxlahun Eb	lob		12. 13 Eb	bad
13. hun Ben	lob*		13. 1 Ben	bad
14. ca Hix	lob		14. 2 Ix	bad
15. ox Men	*		15. 3 Men	

3065. *U sian chaac* 'born is the rain'.

3066. *U kalal u koch mehen palal* 'the collection of the tax on boy children'.

3069. *Y al kaba ah toc* 'the dawn of the Burner'. This is the third phase of the quarter–tzol kin fire ceremonies of Oc.

3071. *Sut ti kax u ti al ah ceehob* 'return to the forest for the deer people'. Perhaps a survival of the old hunting ritual.

3079. *U hokol chac mitan chac; che tun cimi* 'the appearance of red plague rot; stick and stone death'. Compare line 2774. With Roys, I read *chac mitan ch'oc*.

3080. *Licil u cutal Sac* 'as the seating of Zac'.

3085. *U tup (kak ah toc); hai xan* 'the Burner quenches his fire; there is a flood too'. The phrase in parentheses is crossed out in the manuscript, and the assertion is reentered below on the correct date, February 10 (11 Oc).

3089. *U tup kak ah toc* 'the Burner quenches his fire'. This ends the first (Oc) of the four quarter–tzol kin fire ceremonies. It is described by Landa 1929: 2: 78 in some detail and by Villa 1945: 79, 116 in the twentieth century.

3090. *U koch ah kin; ppix ich* 'the sun priest's tax; vigil'.

3092. *Ch'apahal chocuil* 'getting hot'.

3094. *U ch'a kak ah toc* 'the Burner takes the fire'. The beginning of the Men fire ceremonies.

16. can Cib	lob*	3095	16. 4 Cib	bad
17. ho Caban	*		17. 5 Caban	
18. uac Etz'nab	lob		18. 6 Etz'nab	bad
19. uuc Cauac	lob		19. 7 Cauac	bad
20. uaxac Ahau	lob*		20. 8 Ahau	bad
21. bolon Imix	lob*	3100	21. 9 Imix	bad
22. lahun Ik	lob		22. 10 Ik	bad
23. buluc Akbal	*		23. 11 Akbal	
24. lahca Kan	*		24. 12 Kan	
25. oxlahun Chicchan	lob		25. 13 Chicchan	bad
26. hun Cimi	lob	3105	26. 1 Cimi	bad
27. ca Manik	lob		27. 2 Manik	bad
28. ox Lamat	lob*		28. 3 Lamat	bad

10 Kan (1629)

En 6 de Juño
   1629 años ti ban i
Sak y okol nalob
   Muk tun y an nal
C uch i
   T u hach man
Kinal
   *Corpus**
Sat i
   Col
T u hanal ob
   T u y ukul
Cahtal
   Ti chikin
Tal Cupul*
   Tal Ppol e*
Man i
   U hanal sak nak pucil*

10 Kan (1629)

On the sixth of June
3110   Of the year 1629 there fell
      Locusts on the corn-ears
         And the ears rotted,
      Which happened
         On the very passing
3115 Of the time
         Of Corpus,
      And destroyed
         The fields.
      They ate
3120   And drank,
      Starting to come
         From the west,
      Coming to Cupul,
         Coming to P'ol,
3125 And passed
         The devouring locusts near the
      Hills.

3095. *Ti ppix ich i* 'which is a vigil'.

3096. *U lubul u koch ah manob* 'the posting of the tax of the buyers'.

3099. *U nup tun cisin* 'the opposing *tun* of the devil'. Obscure. The date is 8 Ahau, which may have something to do with it.

3100. *U cutal Ceeh* 'the seating of Ceh'.

3102. *U koch ah kulelob* 'the tax of the officials'.

3103. *U koch ah uil uinicob* 'the tax of the poor people'. The manuscript adds: *x S. Mateo Ap.* 'St. Matthew the Apostle'. The date is Gregorian.

3107. A dummy line has been counted at line 3108 so as not to disrupt the numbering of the following couplet.

3116. 4 Chuen 7 Pop, June 6, 1629, Corpus Christi. The date is Julian.

3123. *Cu Pul* 'seat of *guayaba*', probably Cupul. The province of Cupul was centered around Valladolid (Roys 1957: map).

3124. *P'ol* 'head(land)', a town on the east coast near Cozumel.

3126. *Pucil* 'the hills': the only hills in Yucatan, the Puuc. The sense is that the locusts spread clear across the peninsula from west to east.

Hex te	And it was there
Sututa e*	At Sotuta
U tabah u cal*	That there hung herself
U ch'upil D. Fran^co Cocom* 3130	Don Francisco Cocom's girl
T u men satc i	Because of the destruction
U col	Of the fields
Y ah canan hunob*	Of the guardian of books
T u hanal sak	By the devouring locusts.
Hach otzil cahob 3135	Very miserable were the towns.
T u men uih ob	Because of hunger.
Pecnah i	Oppressed
Cah t u lacal t u men num ya	Were all the towns by suffering,
Hex y al sakob	And there were the locusts' offspring,
Chan u ne sak 3140	Small-tailed locusts,
U ca . . . lal nal	Which . . . occupied the corn-ears
T u hanal ob	And ate them.
Cahlah i	The residents
Ma u tocic u nal ob	Couldn't pick the ears:
T u hanal sak ma chaanh i 3145	The locusts ate them before they were ripe
Tocsah i.	For picking.

(23r) *Marso* **(31)**			**March (31)**	
1. can Muluc	utz*		1. 4 Muluc	good
2. hoil Oc	lob		2. 5 Oc	bad
3. uac Chuen	lob*		3. 6 Chuen	bad
4. uuc Eb	lob	3150	4. 7 Eb	bad
5. uaxac Ben	lob		5. 8 Ben	bad
6. bolon Hix	lob		6. 9 Ix	bad
7. lahun Men	*		7. 10 Men	
8. buluc Cib	lob		8. 11 Cib	bad
9. lahca Caban	lob*	3155	9. 12 Caban	bad
10. oxlahun Etz'nab	*		10. 13 Etz'nab	
11. hun Cauac	lob		11. 1 Cauac	bad
12. cabil Ahau	lob		12. 2 Ahau	bad

3128. Sotuta, a town near Izamal. Roys 1935: 8 translates the name as 'water in a circle'.

3129. This is the only reference to suicide in the Tizimin. Suicide and hanging are associated with the goddess Ix Tab (Tozzer 1941: 132).

3130. Francisco Cocom, an unidentified man from Sotuta. This is the only Indian with a Christian first name mentioned in the Tizimin, with the possible exception of Antonio Martínez.

3133. The guardian of books may have been the local keeper of the *Book of Chilam Balam*, often elsewhere the choirmaster or the *sacristán* of the church.

3147. *U kin u pec chac i* 'the day of the hard rain'.

3149. *U kalal hub* 'the taking of conch'.

3153. *U hopol u kak ah toc; u pec chac i* 'the flaming of the fire of the Burner; hard rain'.

3155. *Chikin chac y an i* 'in the west there is rain'.

3156. *Y oc uiil payan be c u kaxal ha i* 'germinate plants before it rains'.

13. ox Ymix	lob*	
14. canil Ik	lob	3160
15. ho Akbal	lob	
16. uacil Kan	utz*	
17. uac Chicchan	utz	
18. uaxacil Cimi	utz	
19. bolon Manik	lob	3165
20. lahun Lamat	lob	
21. buluc Muluc	utz	
22. lahcabil Oc	lob	
23. oxlahun Chuen	lob	
24. hun Eb	lob	3170
25. ca Been	lob	
26. ox Hix	lob	
27. can Men	utz*	
28. ho Cib	utz	
29. uacil Caban	utz	3175
30. uuc Etz'nab	utz*	
31. uaxacil Cauac	utz*	

13. 3 Imix	bad	
14. 4 Ik	bad	
15. 5 Akbal	bad	
16. 6 Kan	good	
17. 7 Chicchan	good	
18. 8 Cimi	good	
19. 9 Manik	bad	
20. 10 Lamat	bad	
21. 11 Muluc	good	
22. 12 Oc	bad	
23. 13 Chuen	bad	
24. 1 Eb	bad	
25. 2 Ben	bad	
26. 3 Ix	bad	
27. 4 Men	good	
28. 5 Cib	good	
29. 6 Caban	good	
30. 7 Etz'nab	good	
31. 8 Cauac	good	

3 Muluc (1622)

1622 años
  Li hab uchc i
Chac mitan uiih
  T u hach
Yukul peten
  T u lacal e
Otzilh on
  La ix hokc i
U pectzil chibc i
  Ca lakob
T u man ixim ob
  Te
Ti kax e
  Nak Uitzil e
T u men ah col cabob
  Ma ix bin uiih u cah ob
C uch i e
  He ix t on e
Cahan tah u pak huhub*
  Kum che*

3 Muluc (1622)

The year 1622
3180   Was the year there occurred
Red hunger plague.
  It emptied
The whole country
  Entirely.
3185 We were miserable
  And there appeared
Rumors of devouring
  Our neighbors.
They bought corn
3190   There
In the wild
  Near the mountains
Because the farmers of that land
  Had no famine in their villages
3195 That had occurred,
  And here we were
Living on pine tree fruit
  And squash trees.

3159. *Uai c u cutal Mac* 'here is the seating of Mac'.
3162. *T u hopol ha i* 'which is the beginning of water'. I read *hop'ol.*
3173. *Y al kaba ah toc* 'the dawn of the Burner'.
3176. *Y oc uiil te la* 'generate sprouts thereon'.
3177. A dummy line has been counted at line 3178 so as not to disrupt the numbering of the following couplet.
3197. *Huhub* 'plums'.
3198. *Kum che* 'squash tree'. Genus *Jacaratia.*

U pachahal yab palal cim ob			Afterward many children died	
Y etel nucuch uincob		3200	Together with grown people	
T u men uih			Because of hunger.	
Ma tz'etz' num ya			No small thing was the suffering	
Y anh i			That had come	
T oon.			Upon us.	

(23v) *Abril* (30)   ## April (30)

1. bolon Ahau	utz*	3205	1. 9 Ahau	good
2. lahun Ymix	lob*		2. 10 Imix	bad
3. buluc Ik	*		3. 11 Ik	
4. lahcabil Akbal	utz		4. 12 Akbal	good
5. oxlahun Kan	*		5. 13 Kan	
6. hun Chicchan	utz	3210	6. 1 Chicchan	good
7. ca Cimi	utz		7. 2 Cimi	good
8. ox Manik	utz		8. 3 Manik	good
9. can Lamat	utz		9. 4 Lamat	good
10. ho Muluc	lob		10. 5 Muluc	bad
11. uacil Oc	lob	3215	11. 6 Oc	bad
12. uuc Chuen	lob		12. 7 Chuen	bad
13. uaxacil Eb	utz		13. 8 Eb	good
14. bolon Ben	utz		14. 9 Ben	good
15. lahun Hix	utz		15. 10 Ix	good
16. buluc Men	utz*	3220	16. 11 Men	good
17. lahca Cib	utz		17. 12 Cib	good
18. oxlahun Caban	utz		18. 13 Caban	good
19. hun Etz'nab	lob		19. 1 Etz'nab	bad
20. cabil Cauac	lob		20. 2 Cauac	bad
21. ox Ahau	*	3225	21. 3 Ahau	
22. can Ymix	lob*		22. 4 Imix	bad
23. hoil Ik	lob		23. 5 Ik	bad
24. uac Akbal	lob		24. 6 Akbal	bad
25. uucil Kan	lob*		25. 7 Kan	bad
26. uac Chicchan	lob	3230	26. 8 Chicchan	bad
27. bolon Cimi	utz		27. 9 Cimi	good
28. lahun Manik	lob		28. 10 Manik	bad

3205. *U ch'aal ba ku* 'the god prepares himself'. The day being 9 Ahau, the name day of the *katun* is one *uinal* later.

3206. *U cutal Kan Kin* 'the seating of Kankin'.

3207. *U hokol y ik hub; u kin haa* 'the appearance of the conch wind; the time of water'.

3209. *U coi kinal kuu* 'the abstention period of the god'.

3220. *U tup kak ah toc* 'the Burner quenches the fire'.

3225. *U ch'a kak ah toc* 'the Burner takes the fire'. This is the beginning of the Ahau fire ceremonies.

3226. *U cutal Moan; y oc uiil* 'the seating of Muan; germinate plants'.

3229. *U hun te Pop* 'the first of Pop'. See June 14, September 27. The three dates form a series of new year dates (5 Ix, 6 Cauac, 7 Kan) in the Mayapan calendar, but the Gregorian equivalents make no sense, implying years like 1373, 1723, 1883, or 1987. A more likely 7 Kan 1 Pop would be 1666.

29. buluc Lamat	lob		29. 11 Lamat	bad
30. lahca Muluc	*		30. 12 Muluc	

8 Ix (1627)

En I de Mayo
  De 1627 años
Ca ul i
  Sak sat i
Nal t u hanal ob
  Y etel buul
Y etel kumob
  Ibob
Yuklah
  Hi u ximbal sak la e

Hex ba tabob e
  U hach kubah ob sak
T u tan *juesob*
  U bin ob
U tohl ob sak
  Y etel hemob
Chirin chulob*
  Tzitzac i
Ha u kamsib
  Sak la e.

8 Ix (1627)

3235 On the first of May
  Of the year 1627
Then came
  The destroying locusts.
They ate the corn-ears
3240 And beans
And squashes
  And lima beans
Everywhere.
  That was the coming of the locusts
  then.
3245 And the chiefs
  Set the locusts directly
Before the judges
  Who went
To judge the locusts
3250 And the grubs,
(?) to douse
  And sprinkle them.
Water will be the death
  Of these locusts.

(24r) *Mayo* (31)

I. oxlahun Oc	utz*	3255	1. 13 Oc	good
2. hun Chuen	lob		2. 1 Chuen	bad
3. ca Eb	lob*		3. 2 Eb	bad
4. ox Ben	lob*		4. 3 Ben	bad
5. can Hix	*		5. 4 Ix	
6. ho Men	lob	3260	6. 5 Men	bad
7. uac Cib	lob*		7. 6 Cib	bad
8. uuc Caban	lob*		8. 7 Caban	bad
9. uaxacil Etz'nab	lob*		9. 8 Etz'nab	bad

May (31)

3234. *U ua be hun ch'ab tan; ox ppel kab pix ich i* 'the raising of the road of 1 Ch'ab Tan; three nights' vigil'. I read *akab p'ix*.

3251. There is no *r* in colonial Yucatec, and I have not been able to come up with a sensible reading of *chirin*. My sense of the couplet rests on *chul* 'drip' and *tzitz* 'sprinkle'.

3255. *U kin haa* 'a day of water'.

3257. *Santa Cruz; y oc uiil i* 'Holy Cross; germinate plants'. The date is Gregorian.

3258. *Sut ob ti kax* 'they return to the wild'.

3259. *U takal u keban ahauob i* 'the engendering of the sins of the lords'.

3261. *Xinximbal ti kax* 'wandering in the wild'.

3262. *Pasar ceh utz i* 'passing deer is good'.

3263. *Ti kuyan uinicob* 'who are bent people'.

10. bolon Cauac	utz*		10. 9 Cauac	good	
11. lahun Ahau	*	3265	11. 10 Ahau		
12. buluc Hix	lob*		12. 11 Imix	bad	
13. lahca Ik	lob*		13. 12 Ik	bad	
14. oxlahun Akbal	lob*		14. 13 Akbal	bad	
15. hun Kan	lob*		15. 1 Kan	bad	
16. ca Chicchan	lob	3270	16. 2 Chicchan	bad	
17. ox Cimi	lob		17. 3 Cimi	bad	
18. can Manik	utz		18. 4 Manik	good	
19. ho Lamat	utz		19. 5 Lamat	good	
20. uac Muluc	utz*		20. 6 Muluc	good	
21. uucil Oc	lob	3275	21. 7 Oc	bad	
22. uaxac Chuen	lob		22. 8 Chuen	bad	
23. bolon Eb	lob		23. 9 Eb	bad	
24. lahun Ben			24. 10 Ben		
25. buluc Hix	lob		25. 11 Ix	bad	
26. lahca Men	lob	3280	26. 12 Men	bad	
27. oxlahun Cib	utz		27. 13 Cib	good	
28. hun Caban	utz		28. 1 Caban	good	
29. ca Etz'nab	utz*		29. 2 Etz'nab	good	
30. oxil Cauac	utz		30. 3 Cauac	good	
31. can Ahau	lob*	3285	31. 4 Ahau	bad	

(24v) *Juño* (30)   June (30)

1. ho Ymix	lob*		1. 5 Imix	bad	
2. uacil Ik	lob		2. 6 Ik	bad	
3. uuc Akbal	lob		3. 7 Akbal	bad	
4. uaxacil Kan	lob		4. 8 Kan	bad	
5. bolon Chicchan	utz	3290	5. 9 Chicchan	good	
6. lahun Cimi	utz		6. 10 Cimi	good	
7. buluc Manik	lob		7. 11 Manik	bad	
8. lahca Lamat	lob		8. 12 Lamat	bad	
9. oxlahun Muluc	utz		9. 13 Muluc	good	
10. hunil Oc	utz*	3295	10. 1 Oc	good	
11. can Men	lob*		11. 2 Men	bad	
12. ox Eb	lob		12. 3 Eb	bad	
13. can Been	lob		13. 4 Ben	bad	

3264. *Ti y ahaulil cabob* 'who are lords of the land'.
3265. *U hopol u kak ah toc; u k(in) ha i* 'the flaming of the Burner's fire; day of water'.
3266. *Ti ba tabob; u cutal Paax* 'who are chiefs; the seating of Pax'.
3267. *Ik tan y ol uinc i* 'clever-hearted people'.
3268. *Licil pix ich* 'as a vigil'.
3269. *Cup ikal* 'calm winds'.
3274. *U xocol y oc kin* 'the counting of movement of the sun'.
3283. *Utz cahtal te la* 'good to live here or there'.
3285. *Y al kaba ah toc* 'the dawn of the Burner'.
3286. *Licil u cutal Kayab* 'as the seating of Kayab'.
3295. *U kin noh chac* 'the day of the great rainstorm'.
3296. The manuscript has Men for Chuen.

14. hoil Ix	lob*		14. 5 Ix	bad
15. uac Men	lob	3300	15. 6 Men	bad
16. uuc Cib	lob		16. 7 Cib	bad
17. uaxac Caban	lob		17. 8 Caban	bad
18. bolon Etz'nab	utz		18. 9 Etz'nab	good
19. lahun Cauac	utz		19. 10 Cauac	good
20. buluc Ahau	*	3305	20. 11 Ahau	
21. lahca Imix	utz*		21. 12 Imix	good
22. oxlahun Ik	lob		22. 13 Ik	bad
23. hun Akbal	lob		23. 1 Akbal	bad
24. cail Kan	lob*		24. 2 Kan	bad
25. oxil Chicchan	*	3310	25. 3 Chicchan	
26. can Cimi	utz*		26. 4 Cimi	good
27. ho Manik	utz		27. 5 Manik	good
28. uac Lamat	lob		28. 6 Lamat	bad
29. uuc Muluc	lob*		29. 7 Muluc	bad
30. uaxacil Oc	utz	3315	30. 8 Oc	good

(25r) *Julio* (31)   **July (31)**

1. bolon Chuen	lob		1. 9 Chuen	bad
2. lahun Eb	lob		2. 10 Eb	bad
3. buluc Ben	lob		3. 11 Ben	bad
4. lahca Ix	*		4. 12 Ix	
5. oxlahun Men	utz*	3320	5. 13 Men	good
6. hun Cib	lob		6. 1 Cib	bad
7. ca Caban	lob		7. 2 Caban	bad
8. ox Etz'nab	utz		8. 3 Etz'nab	good
9. can Cauac	lob*		9. 4 Cauac	bad
10. ho Ahau	lob	3325	10. 5 Ahau	bad
11. uac Ymix	utz*		11. 6 Imix	good
12. uucil Ik	lob		12. 7 Ik	bad
13. uaxac Akbal	lob		13. 8 Akbal	bad
14. bolon Kan	utz*		14. 9 Kan	good
15. lahun Chicchan	utz*	3330	15. 10 Chicchan	good

3299. *U hun te Pop* 'the first of Pop'. See also note 3229.

3305. *U tup kak ah toc* 'the Burner quenches his fire'.

3306. *Ti al u cutal Cumku* 'for the seating of Cumku'.

3309. *San Juan* 'Saint John's day'. The date is Gregorian.

3310. *U ch'a kak ah toc* 'the Burner takes the fire'.

3311. *U sian ku* 'God is born'.

3314. *S. Pedro Ap.* 'St. Peter the Apostle'. The date is Gregorian.

3319. *U kin balam habil* 'the day of the jaguar year period'. This corresponds to 12 Ix and Ix is the day of the jaguar.

3320. *U nahal ppolom; ppix ich* 'fulfillment of trade; vigil'.

3324. *Payab te la; accunabal siil* 'divided here and there; settlement of gifts'.

3326. 6 Imix 1 Uayeb, but the manuscript does not note it.

3329. *Ti u tz'abal sil te la; y oc chicam* 'which is given gifts here and there; germinate gourdroot'.

3330. *Ti u hopol kak ah toc* 'which flames the Burner's fire'.

16. buluc Cimi	utz*		16. 11 Cimi	good		
17. lahca Manik	utz*		17. 12 Manik	good		
18. oxlahun Lamat	lob		18. 13 Lamat	bad		
19. hun Muluc	utz*		19. 1 Muluc	good		
20. cail Oc	utz	3335	20. 2 Oc	good		
21. ox Chuen	utz		21. 3 Chuen	good		
22. can Eb	utz*		22. 4 Eb	good		
23. ho Ben	*		23. 5 Ben			
24. uacil Hix	lob		24. 6 Ix	bad		
25. uuc Men	utz	3340	25. 7 Men	good		
26. uaxacil Cib	utz		26. 8 Cib	good		
27. bolon Caban	utz		27. 9 Caban	good		
28. lahun Etz'nab	utz		28. 10 Etz'nab	good		
29. bulucil Cauac	lob		29. 11 Cauac	bad		
30. lahca Ahau	utz*	3345	30. 12 Ahau	good		
31. oxlahun Imix	utz		31. 13 Imix	good		

(25v) *Agosto* (31)   ## August (31)

1. hunil Ik	utz*		1. 1 Ik	good	
2. ca Akbal	lob		2. 2 Akbal	bad	
3. oxil Kan	lob		3. 3 Kan	bad	
4. can Chicchan	lob*	3350	4. 4 Chicchan	bad	
5. ho Cimi	lob*		5. 5 Cimi	bad	
6. uac Manik	lob*		6. 6 Manik	bad	
7. uuc Lamat	lob		7. 7 Lamat	bad	
8. uaxac Muluc	*		8. 8 Muluc		
9. bolon Oc	lob	3355	9. 9 Oc	bad	
10. lahun Chuen	*		10. 10 Chuen		
11. buluc Eb	lob		11. 11 Eb	bad	
12. lahca Ben	lob		12. 12 Ben	bad	
13. oxlahun Hix	lob		13. 13 Ix	bad	

3331. *Uai c u cutal Pop* 'here is the seating of Pop'. See also note 3060. The year 10 Imix is followed here by 11 Cimi (1 Pop). This is consistent with the seatings of the other *uinals* in this calendar but not with the notes for April 25, June 14, and September 27, which are in the Mayapan calendar. See also note 3229.

3332. *U ti al pakal* 'for planting'. A reasonable date for planting, well north on the Yucatan Peninsula.

3334. *Cup canil u ti al pakal* 'cut sprouts for planting'.

3337. *U ti al ah ceehob* 'for the deer people'. See also note 3071.

3338. *Kal ikal; u chibal tok* 'seizing the winds; bite of the knife'.

3345. *Licil u sihil ah miatzob* 'as the birth of sages'.

3347. *U ti al al mehenob* 'for the nobles'.

3350. *Y al kaba ah toc* 'the dawn of the Burner'.

3351. *Licil u cutal Uoo* 'as the seating of Uo'.

3352. *Trasfigurasion* 'Transfiguration'. The date is Gregorian.

3354. *Ka lob; ppix ich* 'just bad; vigil'. Oddly, there is no general prognostication for this day.

3356. *U sian che tun cimil; S. Lorenso; chac ikal y an i* 'the origin of stick and stone death; St. Lawrence; there was a hurricane'. The date for San Lorenzo is Gregorian.

14. hun Men	*	3360	14. 1 Men	
15. caa Cib	lob*		15. 2 Cib	bad
16. ox Caban	lob		16. 3 Caban	bad
17. can Etz'nab	lob		17. 4 Etz'nab	bad
18. hoil Cauac	lob*		18. 5 Cauac	bad
19. uac Ahau	*	3365	19. 6 Ahau	
20. uuc Ymix	lob		20. 7 Imix	bad
21. uaxacil Ik	lob		21. 8 Ik	bad
22. bolon Akbal	lob		22. 9 Akbal	bad
23. (lahun Kan)			23. (10 Kan)	
24. buluc Chicchan	*	3370	24. 11 Chicchan	
25. lahca Cimi	lob*		25. 12 Cimi	bad
26. oxlahun Manik	lob		26. 13 Manik	bad
27. hun Lamat	*		27. 1 Lamat	
28. ca Muluc	lob		28. 2 Muluc	bad
29. oxil Oc	lob*	3375	29. 3 Oc	bad
30. can Chuen	lob		30. 4 Chuen	bad
31. hoo Eb	lob		31. 5 Eb	bad

(26r) *Septiembre* (30)   September (30)

1. uac Ben	lob		1. 6 Ben	bad
2. uuc Hix	lob		2. 7 Ix	bad
3. uaxac Men	lob	3380	3. 8 Men	bad
4. bolon Cib	utz		4. 9 Cib	good
5. lahun Caban	*		5. 10 Caban	
6. buluc Etz'nab	utz		6. 11 Etz'nab	good
7. lahcabil Cauac	utz		7. 12 Cauac	good
8. oxlahun Ahau	utz*	3385	8. 13 Ahau	good
9. hun Imix	utz		9. 1 Imix	good
10. cabil Ik	utz		10. 2 Ik	good
11. ox Akbal	utz*		11. 3 Akbal	good
12. canil Kan	utz*		12. 4 Kan	good
13. ho Chicchan	utz	3390	13. 5 Chicchan	good

3360. *Ti ulah che tun cimil i* 'which brought stick and stone death'.

3361. *Asumpsion* 'Assumption'. The date is Gregorian.

3364. *Chac ikal* 'hurricane'.

3365. *U hokol chac mitan ch'oc* 'the appearance of red plague rot'. See also note 3079.

3370. *U tup kak ah toc; S. Bartolome* 'the quenching of the fire of the Burner; St. Bartholomew'. The date is Gregorian.

3371. *Licil u cutal Sip* 'as the seating of Zip'.

3373. *U takal u kak balam* 'the engendering of the jaguar's fire'. Roys' transcription suggests reading *u kab balam*.

3375. *U cha kak ah toc; ik y an i* 'the Burner takes the fire; there is wind'. Like Roys, I read *ch'a*.

3382. *U sian ahauob* 'the birth of the lords'.

3385. *Natiuidad; ik y an i* 'Christmas; there is wind'. I have no explanation for Christmas in September.

3388. *Hahaal te la e* 'scattered thunderstorms'.

3389. *Hahaal te la e* 'scattered thunderstorms'.

14. uac Cimi	utz*		14. 6 Cimi	good
15. uuc Manik	lob		15. 7 Manik	bad
16. uaxac Lamat	*		16. 8 Lamat	
17. bolon Muluc	lob		17. 9 Muluc	bad
18. lahun Oc	*	3395	18. 10 Oc	
19. buluc Chuen	utz		19. 11 Chuen	good
20. lahca Eb	utz		20. 12 Eb	good
21. oxlahun Ben	utz		21. 13 Ben	good
22. hun Hix	lob*		22. 1 Ix	bad
23. cail Men	lob	3400	23. 2 Men	bad
24. oxil Cib	utz*		24. 3 Cib	good
25. can Caban	utz		25. 4 Caban	good
26. ho Etz'nab	utz		26. 5 Etz'nab	good
27. uacil Cauac	utz*		27. 6 Cauac	good
28. uuc Ahau	utz	3405	28. 7 Ahau	good
29. uaxac Imix	lob*		29. 8 Imix	bad
30. bolon Ik	*		30. 9 Ik	

(26v) *Octubre* (31)   ## October (31)

1. lahun Akbal	lob		1. 10 Akbal	bad
2. bulucil Kan	utz*		2. 11 Kan	good
3. lahca Chicchan	lob	3410	3. 12 Chicchan	bad
4. oxlahun Cimi	*		4. 13 Cimi	
5. hun Manik	*		5. 1 Manik	
6. ca Lamat	lob		6. 2 Lamat	bad
7. ox Muluc	lob		7. 3 Muluc	bad
8. canil Oc	lob*	3415	8. 4 Oc	bad
9. ho Chuen	lob		9. 5 Chuen	bad
10. uac Eb	utz*		10. 6 Eb	good
11. uuc Ben	lob		11. 7 Ben	bad
12. uaxacil Hix	lob		12. 8 Ix	bad
13. bolon Men	lob	3420	13. 9 Men	bad
14. lahun Cib	utz		14. 10 Cib	good
15. buluc Caban	utz		15. 11 Caban	good

3391. *U sian ku; u cutal* 'the birth of god; the seating of Zotz''. The manuscript omits Zotz'.

3393. *U nich' co; hun Ahau Can* 'the teething of a tooth; one Lord Snake'.

3395. *U hopol kak ah toc* 'the Burner flames his fire'.

3399. *Licil u sihil ahauob* 'as the birth of the lords'.

3401. *U pakal cab i* 'planting the land'.

3404. *U hun te Pop* 'the first of Pop'. See also note 3229.

3406. *San Miguel* 'Saint Michael'. The date is Gregorian.

3407. *U kukum tok ch'apahal y an i* 'the quetzal feather knife has been seized'. See also note 3061.

3409. *U kaxal ha i* 'the dropping of water'. See also note 3063.

3411. *U sian chac; u cutal Seec* 'the birth of rain; the seating of Tzec'.

3412. *U lubul u koch palal; ch'apahal y an i* 'the posting of the tax on children; there are seizures'. Compare note 3407.

3415. *Y al kaba ah toc* 'the dawn of the Burner'.

3417. *Sut ti kax ximbal* 'return to the wild, walking'.

16. lahca Etz'nab	*		16. 12 Etz'nab		
17. oxlahun Cauac	utz		17. 13 Cauac	good	
18. hun Ahau	lob*	3425	18. 1 Ahau	bad	
19. ca Imix	lob		19. 2 Imix	bad	
20. oxil Ik	lob		20. 3 Ik	bad	
21. can Akbal	utz		21. 4 Akbal	good	
22. hoil Kan	lob		22. 5 Kan	bad	
23. uac Chicchan	lob	3430	23. 6 Chicchan	bad	
24. uuc Cimi	utz*		24. 7 Cimi	good	
25. uaxac Manik	*		25. 8 Manik		
26. bolon Lamat	lob		26. 9 Lamat	bad	
27. lahun Muluc	lob		27. 10 Muluc	bad	
28. bulucil Oc	*	3435	28. 11 Oc		
29. lahca Chuen	*		29. 12 Chuen		
30. oxlahun Eb	lob*		30. 13 Eb	bad	
31. hun Ben	lob*		31. 1 Ben	bad	

(27r) *Noviembre* (30)   ## November (30)

1. cail Hix	lob*		1. 2 Ix	bad	
2. ox Men	*	3440	2. 3 Men		
3. can Cib	*		3. 4 Cib		
4. ho Caban	lob		4. 5 Caban	bad	
5. uac Etz'nab	lob		5. 6 Etz'nab	bad	
6. uucil Cauac	lob		6. 7 Cauac	bad	
7. uaxac Ahau	lob	3445	7. 8 Ahau	bad	
8. bolon Imix	lob		8. 9 Imix	bad	
9. lahun Ik	lob		9. 10 Ik	bad	
10. buluc Akbal	*		10. 11 Akbal		
11. lahca Kan	*		11. 12 Kan		
12. oxlahun Chicchan	lob*	3450	12. 13 Chicchan	bad	
13. hun Cimi	lob*		13. 1 Cimi	bad	

3423. *Hac lob; cimil y an i* 'very bad; there is death'. Like Roys, I read *hach lob*.

3425. *U hokol chac mitan ch'oc* 'the appearance of red plague rot'.

3431. *U sian chac; u cutal Xul* 'the birth of rain; the seating of Xul'.

3432. *U kin ha i; utz* 'the day of water; good'. There is no general augury.

3435. *U tup kak ah toc* 'the Burner quenches the fire'.

3436. *U lubul u kob ah kinob; u kin ppix ich* 'the posting of the sun priests' tax; vigil day'. Like Roys, I read *koch* for *kob*.

3437. *U kin ppix ich* 'vigil day'.

3438. *Ch'apahal y an i* 'there are seizures'.

3439. *Mnium. S. M.* 'All Saints''. Like Roys, I reconstruct Omnium Sanctorum. The date is Gregorian.

3440. *U cha kak ah toc; finados* 'the Burner takes the fire; the ends (?)'.

3441. *U lubul u koch ah menob; ppix ich* 'the posting of the curers' tax; vigil'.

3448. *U lubul u koch a kulel; cimil* 'the posting of the tax of the officials; death'.

3449. *U cimil ahauob, ti cimil ix . . .* 'the death of the lords, which is also the death . . .'.

3450. *S. Diego* 'St. James'. The date is Gregorian.

3451. *U cutal tz'e Yax Kin* 'the seating of the birth of Yaxkin'.

14. can Manik	lob		14. 2 Manik	bad
15. ox Lamat	lob		15. 3 Lamat	bad
16. can Muluc	utz*		16. 4 Muluc	good
17. hoil Oc	lob	3455	17. 5 Oc	bad
18. uac Chuen	*		18. 6 Chuen	
19. uuc Eb	lob		19. 7 Eb	bad
20. uaxac Ben	lob		20. 8 Ben	bad
21. bolon Hix	lob		21. 9 Ix	bad
22. lahun Men	*	3460	22. 10 Men	
23. buluc Cib	lob		23. 11 Cib	bad
24. lahca Caban	lob		24. 12 Caban	bad
25. oxlahun Etz'nab	*		25. 13 Etz'nab	
26. hunil Cauac	lob*		26. 1 Cauac	bad
27. can Ahau	lob*	3465	27. 2 Ahau	bad
28. ox Ymix	lob		28. 3 Imix	bad
29. canil Ik	lob		29. 4 Ik	bad
30. ho Akbal	lob*		30. 5 Akbal	bad

(27v) *Diciembre* (31)   December (31)

1. uacil Kan	utz*		1. 6 Kan	good
2. uuc Chicchan	utz	3470	2. 7 Chicchan	good
3. uaxac Cimi	*		3. 8 Cimi	
4. bolon Manik	lob		4. 9 Manik	bad
5. lahun Lamat	lob		5. 10 Lamat	bad
6. buluc Muluc	utz		6. 11 Muluc	good
7. lahca Oc	lob	3475	7. 12 Oc	bad
8. oxlahun Chuen	lob*		8. 13 Chuen	bad
9. hun Eb	lob		9. 1 Eb	bad
10. ca Been	lob		10. 2 Ben	bad
11. ox Hix	lob		11. 3 Ix	bad
12. can Men	lob*	3480	12. 4 Men	bad
(13. ho) Cib	utz		(13. 5) Cib	good
(14. uac) Caban	utz		(14. 6) Caban	good
15. uuc Etz'nab	utz		15. 7 Etz'nab	good
16. uaxac Cauac	utz		16. 8 Cauac	good
17. bolon Ahau	*	3485	17. 9 Ahau	
18. lahun Imix	lob		18. 10 Imix	bad

3454. *U pec chac y an i* 'there was a hard rainstorm'.
3456. *Uchic u kalal hub* 'occurred the taking of conch'.
3460. *U hopol u kak ah toc* 'the Burner flames his fire'.
3463. *Y oc noh uah pai be ocsah* 'germinate the big food before sowing'.
3464. *Ceel y an i* 'there is fog'.
3465. *Ceel y an i* 'there is fog'.
3468. *S. Andres* 'St. Andrew'. The date is Gregorian.
3469. *U hoppol ha i* 'the beginning of water'.
3471. *U cutal Mol* 'the seating of Mol'.
3476. *Consepsion* 'Conception'. The date is Gregorian.
3480. *Y al kaba ah toc* 'the dawn of the Burner'.
3485. *U ch'aal ba ku* 'the god prepares himself'. The date is again 9 Ahau: see note 3205.

19. bulucil Ik	*		19. 11 Ik	
20. lahca Akbal	utz		20. 12 Akbal	good
21. oxlahun Kan	*		21. 13 Kan	
22. hun Chicchan	utz	3490	22. 1 Chicchan	good
23. ca Cimi	utz*		23. 2 Cimi	good
24. ox Manik	utz		24. 3 Manik	good
25. can Lamat	utz*		25. 4 Lamat	good
26. ho Muluc	lob		26. 5 Muluc	bad
27. uacil Oc	lob	3495	27. 6 Oc	bad
28. uuc Chuen	lob		28. 7 Chuen	bad
29. uaxac Eb	lob		29. 8 Eb	bad
30. bolon Ben	utz		30. 9 Ben	good
31. lahun Ix	utz*		31. 10 Ix	good
		3500		

3487. *U kin chac i* 'a day of rain'.
3489. *U coi kinal ku* 'the abstention time of god'.
3491. *U cutal Ch'een* 'the seating of Ch'en'.
3493. *Natibidad* 'Christmas'. The date is Gregorian. The omission of Lent, Holy Week, and Easter from the Tizimin is striking.

3499. A dummy line has been counted at line 3500 so as not to disrupt the numbering of the following couplet.

25. The Seven-Day Week

Like the preceding chapter, this text does not require an interpretative translation. It begins with a table for predicting the abundance of corn according to which day of the week initiates the Christian year— thus reinterpreting the seven days of the week as seven year-bearers. Each day is associated with its corresponding planet or with the sun and moon, and the auguries are laconic, implying feast, famine, or average conditions. The years are listed by fours, implying an awareness of leap years.

(21r) U ti al u pat-hal yxim*
  Ba ix maxan.

				For the usage of corn		
				And likewise cornmeal:		
Domingo	*Sol*	tz'oc lukan		Sunday	Sun	gulped
Lunes	*Luna*	tan coch		Monday	Moon	halfway
Martes	*Marte*	uiih	3505	Tuesday	Mars	hungry
Miercoles	*Mercurio*	tan coch		Wednesday	Mercury	halfway
Viernes	*Venus*	tz'oc lukan		Friday	Venus	gulped
Sabado	*Saturno*	uiih		Saturday	Saturn	hungry
Domingo	*Sol*	tz'oc lukan		Sunday	Sun	gulped
Lunes	*Luna*	tan coch	3510	Monday	Moon	halfway

3501. It is of some interest to note that 1620 in the Julian calendar and 1752 in the Gregorian one (!) were years in which the Christian count began on New Year's Day on Sunday. The pattern of the count here presented repeats each twenty-eight years (see lines 3531 ff.). The pattern of the following auguries is the first such in the Tizimin which (tacitly) acknowledges leap years, omitting each fifth weekday "yearbearer."

Note 1 speculates about a twenty-eight-year cycle—presumably because the whole text is playing with sevens and fours. Note 2 reports a hurricane in 1628. Note 3 repeats the report of the 1629 plague of locusts, emphasizing the damage near Merida (see the preceding chapter). And note 4 specifies that these were red-spotted locusts and that they came in April.

The remainder of the text details the yearbearer-divinatory significance of the days of the Christian week, emphasizing agricultural implications and specifying the expected corn harvest. The order of the days is peculiar (Thursday, Friday, Saturday, Tuesday, Wednesday, Sunday, Monday), and I have no explanation for it.

Miercoles	Mercurio	tan coch		Wednesday	Mercury	halfway
Juebes	Jupiter	tz'oc lukan		Thursday	Jupiter	gulped
Biernes	Benus	tz'oc lukan		Friday	Venus	gulped
Sabado	Saturnoo	uiih		Saturday	Saturn	hungry
Lunes	Luna	tan coch	3515	Monday	Moon	halfway
Martes	Marte	uiih		Tuesday	Mars	hungry
Miercoles	Mercurio	tan coch		Wednesday	Mercury	halfway
Juebes	Jupiter	tz'oc lukan		Thursday	Jupiter	gulped
Sabado	Saturno	uiih		Saturday	Saturn	hungry
Domingo	Sol	tz'oc lukan	3520	Sunday	Sun	gulped
Lunes	Luna	tan coch		Monday	Moon	halfway
Martes	Marte	uiih		Tuesday	Mars	hungry
Juebes	Jupiter	tz'oc lukan		Thursday	Jupiter	gulped
Viernes	Venus	tz'oc lukan		Friday	Venus	gulped
Sabado	Saturno	uiih	3525	Saturday	Saturn	hungry
Domingo	Sol	tz'oc lukan		Sunday	Sun	gulped
Martes	Marte	uiih		Tuesday	Mars	hungry
Miercoles	Mercurio	tan coch		Wednesday	Mercury	halfway
Juebes	Jupiter	tz'oc lukan		Thursday	Jupiter	gulped
Viernes	Benus	tz'oc lukan	3530	Friday	Venus	gulped

(Note 1)

Hun kal
    Ca tac uaxac pel hab
Y an ichil
    Lei hun canal la e
He ix ca bin tz'aloc u xoc

    Tac cabal e
Ca nacac u xoc t u ca ten
    U ti al u nup hab
La t u lah
    U tz'ocol u xoc e
Ca ix chumpahac canal
    T u ca ten*
Lei t ob hay tun canal o
    Lai li c u sat cab
Ba hun hab
    Lei tux y an *Domingo* lo
La t u ppis u
    Hayal cab.

(Note 2)

1628 años
    Lei hab

Note 1

One twenty
    And then eight years
Are in
    This one sky
3535 And that is when the count will have to be given
    Of hidden land.
Then is to approach the count again
    For the opposite year
That completes
3540   The ending of the count
And when the pile is to be set up
    Again.
This they (?) the fire stone of the sky
    In the same way come the lands
3545 Of that many years
    That is where Sunday is:
That it measures
    The amount of land.

Note 2

1628.
3550   That was the year

3542. Text obscured.

Y an ca uch i
  Noh chac ikal
Ichil akab ca hop i
  Ik lub lah i
Cheob
  Naob
He bal canal tac ob e
  Lubi t u men ik.

There occurred
  The hurricane
During the night, when there began
  A wind that devastated
3555 Trees
  And houses.
Everything that was close to the sky
  Was felled by the wind.

(Note 3)

1629 años
  Lei hab uchc i
U hach satal nal
  T u men saak
Lic u tupul u u ich
  Kan tub ai sak
Ma chanh i
  Cimsah i
Tac T Ho sin
  Lic sak c uch i
La t u lah ti Cupul
  Manan y oc.

Note 3

1629.
3560   This was the year there occurred
The great destruction of corn-ears
  By locusts
Like the quenching of the face
  That was there where the locusts
3565 Did not appear
  They died.
Near Merida it was flattened
  As the locusts occurred
When they returned to cut it
3570   There wasn't a sprout.

(Note 4)

He le *en 19 de Abril*
  De 1629 años ul i
U y anal sak
  Chac nicen u pach ob
Sati kax
  T u hanal ob
T u hach hitz' yax kin
  Chac sak*
Ti ul i
  Bai chachacil ti.

Note 4

Then on April 19,
  1629, there arrived
The locusts
  With red-spotted backs
3575 To destroy it.
  They ate up the forest
And totally finished off the springtime
  The red locusts
That came
3580   And thus trampled it down.

(2Iv) *Jueves*

He t u lubul *Enero*
  Ti *Juebes* e
Matan
  Y antal
U lol cheob i
  U ti al cabob i
Bin y anac yax kin i
  Bin y anac u kaxal ha i
Bin ix chuplahac
  Yoc haob i

Thursday

This is on the posting of January
  On Thursday.
It is expected
  That there will be
3585 Flowers on the trees
  So that the lands
Will have spring.
  They will have the falling of rain
And will be stuffed
3590   With sprouting water.

3578. Text obscured.

Bin il   There will be
  Ti bilac   Someone
Ch'apahal ob i   To help them gather it.
  T u lacal cah   All the towns
Bin y an heb   3595   Will have a turn.
  Bin patai yxim i.   There will be the expected corn.

Viernes   ### Friday

He t u lubul *Enero*   This is on the posting of January
  Ti *Biernes* e   On Friday.
Utz   It is good
  T lobal   3600   That befalls.
Bin y anac chauac yax kin i   There will be a long spring
  Bin ix y anac ch'apahal i   And there will be a harvest.
Bin y anac ya ich i   It will have pain in it.
  Pec otzil u talel   Grinding poverty is coming.
Ma okolal ob i   3605   They do not believe
  T katunob i   In the *katuns*
T u men num ya   Because suffering
  Bin talac ob   Will trouble them.
Bin pata Yxim i   There will be the expected corn
  Tz'etz'il i   3610   But little
Nahal   That is useful
  Y an i.   Will there be.

Sabado   ### Saturday

He t u lubul *ero**   This is the posting of January
  Ti *Sabado* e   On Saturday.
Bin y anac kin tun y abil i   3615   It will have a calendar round
  Bin ix cohac yxim xan i   And will pound corn too,
Ma ix mac bin hach conic   But there will not be very much to sell,
  Tz'etz'il i   Just a little.
Bin pat heb ixim i   The corn will be expected to turn.
  Bin y anac chocuil i   3620   There will be a heat wave
La ob i   And it
  Box i   Will be black.
Ti u cimlahal no xi cabob i*   That will be the dying off of the adult men of the lands
  Bin lublahac kak i   Who will be felled by fever,
Bin ix hokoc nucuch kak y okol   3625   And it will appear as a great fire over
uinicob i   the people.
  Bin ix y anac ch'uhuc ob i   And they will be sweet:
U u ich   The fruits
  Cheob i   Of the trees.

3613. I read *enero*.
3623. I read *noh xib*.

T u lacal ocsah ob e i
   T u lacal ocsah ob e
Bin hauac
   Bin cimlahac y ikil cabob i.

They will sow everything . . .
3630   Everything they sow
   Will be finished:
      Will be killed by the winds of the
      lands.

Martes

He t u lubul *Enero*
   Ti *Martes* e
Bin y anac y nohil thanal
   Than i
He x ti y ahal cab
   Ychil hab la e
Bin y an y anac yeeb
   Bin y anac kin tun y abil xan
Bin cohac (u tohol) yxim i*
   Y okol conol ob i
He ix ppolomob ti chem e
   Ma t u yabhal u na balob i
T u men num ya
   Bin ma ya cimil
U nucil al mehenob i
   Ma t an u pattal ixin
Tz'etz'il i
   Bin y anac i.

Tuesday

This is on the posting of January
   On Tuesday.
3635 They will have the right words
   To say.
And this is at the dawn
   Of the year.
It is going to be having fog;
3640   It will have a calendar round also.
It will pound the straight corn
   They go to sell.
And those who are traders in boats
   Will not have their houses sicken,
3645 Because the suffering
   Will be painless death,
The complaint of the nobility.
   Not half the expected corn
And little
3650   Will it be.

Miercoles

He t u lubul *Enero*
   Ti *Miercoles* e
U y utz hab
   Utz ix yax kin xan i
Bin utzac u bel
   Ah tanlahob i
Bin y anac ch'uhucob i
   Bin y anac pah subtal i

Utz u cambaltabal cux olal i
   T u men ah ma cux ol e
Bin choc uac
   Lum i
He ix ah ximbalte
   Y etel ah numul beob e
Y an bin cimic ob i
   Cimlahac
Tatan
   Celemob i

Wednesday

This is on the posting of January
   On Wednesday.
Good is the year
   And good is the spring too.
3655 It will be a good road
   For half of the people.
They will have sweets.
   It will have to be able to shame
   them.
Good is its instruction in happiness
3660   Because those who are not happy
Will have to oversee
   The land.
And there are the travelers
   And those who suffer the roads.
3665 They will die
   And must die:
Old men
   And youths,

3641. *U tohol* crossed out in the manuscript.

Ix tam pamob i   Beautiful girls
  Y etel palalob i   3670   And children.
Bin ix y anac uih   And there will be hunger
  Tz'etz'ec i   And very little
Hanilte   To be eaten
  Uinicob e   By the people,
Bin cimic ob i   3675   Who will die
  T u men ti   Because of it.
C u lubul   They are posting
  U koch ob i   Their arrival
Tan coch   Half will be expected
  Bin pat heb yxim i.   3680   Of the measure of corn.

Domingo   ## Sunday

He t u lubul *Enero*   This is on the posting of January
  Ti *Domingo* e   On Sunday.
Lic u y antal kin tun y abil i   As it has a calendar round,
  Ca hatz u cah *Dios* i   Then it divides the town of God,
Ix ma can tan coch i   3685   And it is not the sky half—
  Kin tan coch i   The sun half.
He x canaltac ob e   And this is to elevate them:
  Bin cabalac t u lacal   It will descend to bear everything.
He *uacaxob* e   These are the cattle
  Y etel u chayan bal cheob e   3690   And the other animals
Bin y okoc ob   Who will leave
  T u men ukah   Because of thirst,
Bin paxlahac cabob i   And will destroy the lands,
  Bin y anac y ah pau lob   And it will have ghost giants.
Bin y anac ch'uhuc ob i   3695   It will have them burned,
  Y etel lauacbal pakalbil ob e   And that is the return of their
      expectations.
Bin y anac katun ti uinicob   There will be war for men
  T u men ix ma okolalob i   Also because of the infidels
Bin ix uluc u nohol anumal i   Who must also arrive at the right
  speedily,
  Bin xococ   3700   And must come
Ti noh thanil   Into the right word.
  Bin y anac tuk olal i   It will have a groaning spirit.
Bin patai yxim i   There will be the expected corn
  T u y uklalil.   For drinking.

(22r) Lunes   ## Monday

He t u lubul *Enero*   3705   This is on the posting of January
  Ti *Lunes* e   On Monday.
Bin y anac u tz'ayal   It will have the giving
  Tzil *Dios* i   Of the remainder of God
Bin ix lubuc   And it will have to post
  U hach nohil chacil ha i   3710   The rightest rainwater.

Bin hach sisac lum i | It will be very numbing to the earth.
Bin y anac u nohol | It will have the south
Chapahal i | Taken.
Oox e | Three then
U cuch | 3715 Are its burdens,
Bin ix hokoc | And there must arrive
Ah chalamat | The possibly evil people,
Lai u tus ci uchc i | That is who have lied—
U ch'a haal | The taking of water
Kaknab | 3720 From the sea.
Ma t u ci ci pat-hal yxim i | Not the best expectation of corn,
Tan cochil i. | Just half.

26. Zuyua

Zuyua was the seat of katun *3 Ahau. As fated, Zuyua got the lordship. Ahau Can as Jaguar ruled in Merida. With the return of the constellation Nok, the Center priest Coc Ay the Crier was lord. (3738)*

(14r) Ox lahun *Suiua*
U hetz'
Katun
Ti ox Ahau
Lic u than
U bel
Suiua
U hetz' y ahaulil.
Hau lic u keulel Ahau Can

Bai lic u keulel Balam*
Ich Can Si Ho
Ti ox kin
U sut ekel
Nok canal.*
Yax Coc Ai Mut u u ich*

Y ahaulil.

13 Zuyua
Was the seat
3725 Of the *katun*
In 3 Ahau.
Like its word,
Its road,
Zuyua
3730 Was the seat of the lordship.
Divided like the skin of the
Rattlesnake,
Just like the skin of the Jaguar
In Heaven Born Merida.
In three days
3735 Was the return of the stars
Of Nok on high.
The Center priest Coc Ay Mut was the person
In the lordship.

3732. Ahau Can 'lord snake, rattlesnake', like Jaguar, is a title of the lord of the *katun*, who wore both jaguar and rattlesnake skin robes. Landa 1929: 1: 72 gives the full title as *ahau can may* 'rattlesnake of the cycle' and equates it with *ah kin may* 'sun priest of the cycle'. Ahau Can was also the personal name of notables at Chichen Itza in 8 Ahau (1461) and at Merida in 5 Ahau (1598).

3736. *Nok* 'clothes' may be an unidentified constellation, presumably one visible in Yucatan at the approach of the half *katun*: 2 Ahau 2 Zac, December 27, 1628. On the offhand guess that the reference was to Halley's Comet, I've checked it out. The only occurrence of that comet within a recent 3 Ahau was in 1378.

3737. See note 2987. Landa 1929: 2: 28 considers Yax Coc Ay Mut a god name.

*It was clear weather but
windy as the sky was searched
for the approach of the mid katun. (3746)*

*The lord was overthrown in
office. Cut was the throat of the
ruler by the peasants and the
East priest Bol Ay of the northeast lineages, causing mourning
for the poor lords because of the
northeast demons, scouts, and
peasants. (3768)*

*And God in heaven knew
that Merida and all the world
were puffed up with pride. The
land was flattened and broken*

Sac
  Patai habil
Chen ik
  Bin ma nanac i
Pacatnom
  T u canil
T u tzicil
  T u tepal Buluc Ch'ab Tan

Paaxlahom
  Y ahaulil cab
T u pop
  T u tz'am
Xotom
  U cal
Ah tem pop
  Ah tem tz'am
U balmil cab*
  Chac Bol Ai
Chac bob
  Sac bob
Num y ol ualac
  Y acan
T u pach y ahaulil cab
  Otzilhom ob
Chac uen co
  Sac uen co
Ah chin coot*
  Ah chin pacat*
Ah mab yum
  Ah mab na
Uchom u tz'oc sitz'il
  Uchom mac tzil
Ti caan
  Hunab Ku y ohel uchom
Ich Can Si Ho
  Yuklah bal cah
Bin uchbal
  Ppuluxhal
Uesahom cab
  Uecsahom peten
Chochpahom u u ich
  Chochpahom u kab
Chochpahom y oc
  Ua Pa Cabal

Bright
3740 Clear years;
Only the wind
  Will be unusual.
They searched
  In the sky
3745 For the glory
  For the rule of the 11 priest Ch'ab
  Tan.
Destroyed
  Was the lordship of the land.
On the mat
3750 On the throne.
Cut
  Was the throat
Of the step mat lord,
  The step throne lord
3755 By the Honeybees
  And the East priest Bol Ay
The red stalks
  And white stalks.
Sadness will arise
3760 And be covered up
After the lords of the land
  Are impoverished.
Red nightmare,
  White nightmare
3765 Eagle porters
  And lookout porters
The fatherless
  And motherless.
Ended is envy;
3770 Come are the brave.
In heaven
  The Sole God knew.
Merida
  And the whole world
3775 Underwent
  Puffing up.
Spread over the land,
  Spread over the jungle
Flattened was the face,
3780 Flattened was the hand,
Flattened was the foot
  Whether of the Fort of the Lands,

3755. See note 2999.

3765. *Ah chin coot* 'bearer eagles': the porters of the Eagles, a military order.

3766. *Ah chin pacat* 'bearer lookout', a military scout, presumably also a
porter of the Eagles; these were peasants or "orphans," as the following lines state.

*even in Mayapan by sacrifices
in 3 Ahau. The ruler was ill and
hemorrhaging during his brief
and illegitimate rule, abandon-
ing his office, capital, and
throne to the peasants. And
lesser nobles took over. (3804)*

Ua ma ya cimlal
   Ua hai cabil
Y an ichil y ahaulil
   Ox Ahau katun
He x ah tem pop
   Ah tem tz'am e
Bin u xee u lukah e
   Ti u hoyabal u cal i
Ah ox kin tepal i
   Ah ox kin tz'am
Ah ma mahan
   Nail
Okom yax cach
   Okom bul cum
T u ho can be
   Bin y okte
U tz'am
   U pop
Ah mab yum
   Ah mab na
Uch cutal tz'itz'iil al
   Tz'itz'iil mehen i.

Or of the sacrifices,
   Or of the devastated lands
3785 That were under the lordship
   Of *katun* 3 Ahau.
And he was the lord of the step mat
   Of the step throne,
Who will vomit and spew forth
3790   With the discharge of his throat.
The three-day rulers,
   The three-day thrones
Of these unknown
   By matriline.
3795 Departed are the green flies;
   Departed are the bean gourds
From the four crossroads.
   They will be made to leave
The throne,
3800   The mat
Of the fatherless,
   The motherless.
There have been seated the mean born,
   The mean engendered.

I Ahau

27. The Last Jaguar of Merida

Emal was the seat of katun *1 Ahau, bringing warfare to the time of Puc Ol Ha and Ual Icim. There were three terms of office, three terms of rule. It will be seen who supports the lords. Then Amayte Kauil was lord and beat down both the*

(14r) Emal*
  U hetz'
Katun
  Ti hun Ahau.
Ti y emel tab i
  Ti y emel sum i
T u kin y an
  Ca em
Ix Puc y Ol Ha*
  Ix Ual Icim*
Ox kas u ta*
  Ox kas u toon
Ox kas ti y ahaulil
  Ox kas u tucul
Bin y ilab max cuxan
  Kosan ahauob i
He ahau la e
  Amaite Kuil u u ich*
(14v) Bin pecnac peten i
  Pecnom bal cah i

3805 Emal
  Was the seat
  Of the *katun*
  In 1 Ahau,
  Which was to lower the rope,
3810   Which was to lower the cord.
  At this time it was
  That there came down
  Also Puc Ol Ha
  And Ual Icim;
3815 Three divisions of his word;
  Three divisions of his secret;
  Three divisions of the lordship;
  Three divisions of his thought.
  It will be seen who has experienced
3820   And served the lords.
  This was the lord:
  Amayte Kauil was.
  The country will be made aware,
  The world informed,

3805. Emal, which had served as the seat of the *katun* in 11 Ahau and 5 Ahau, had already been designated as the seat of 1 Ahau with Ol Zip as lord (see also note 3048). The claim was contested by Amayte Kauil of Merida, though no Merida text on the point has survived. This was the last time that Merida claimed to seat the *katun*, having become sufficiently Christianized to lose interest in the traditionalist competition. It may be about this time that Merida ceased to style itself Born of Heaven and became simply *ti Ho* again.

3813. Puc y Ol Ha 'hill heart water', perhaps a relative of Puc Tun (see also line 3883). Barrera 1948: 110 translates this as 'she who destroys the heart of the water'.

3814. Ual Icim 'fan owl', an otherwise unidentified lord. See also line 3884, which gives Ual Ecuy. Barrera 1948: 110 has 'owl with her wings spread'. Icim is the horned owl (*Bubo*) according to Tozzer 1941: 202.

3815. See line 3885, which gives *than* for *ta*.

3822. I read Amayte Kauil. See also line 3890, where he is identified as a sage and lord. A namesake was prominent in 7 Ahau.

country and the city, even Merida to the north. (3828)

The usurper of the throne and lordship was dealing in land. Son of a sun priest and a street mother, he abandoned his duty. The world was mad. The destroyer then calmed down again in his brief term in office. Then spoke the northeast lineages to end it, restoring the ceremonies and ending 1 Ahau.

Pecnom chumuc cab
  T u pol peten*
Ich Can Si Ho
  Ti y an y okol
Ah cotz matan i
  Ah mahan koh
Ah mahan tz'am
  Ah mahan pop
Ti y ahaulil
  Cuch lum tam ba*
Bin tz'ocebal
  Ah sitz'bic ahaulil*
U mehen ah kin
  Y al ti ti be
Okom yax cach
  Okom bul cum*
Coopahom bal cah i
  Bin u co co u Ba Cab i
Ah taxtal
  Ah actal
Ca bin tz'em
  Actum e
Y ua ua than katun
  U hun kin tepal
Ah tem pop
  Ah ten tz'am
Ti u pul
  Than
Chac uen co
  Sac uen co
Bi ba o
  Bi uil
Much*
  Coc-hom e
Ox y al
  Ah toc*
U tz'oc sitz'il
  Ti hun Ahau ual e

3825 The center of the land informed
      At the head of the country
    In Heaven Born Merida,
      That he is over
    The office seekers
3830   As the announced mask lord,
    The announced throne lord,
      The announced mat lord
    In the lordship.
      Bearing the land for each other.
3835 That will be the termination
      Of the coveter of the lordship,
    Son of a sun priest
      And born of a whore.
    Departed are the green flies;
3840   Departed are the bean gourds.
    The world has been driven mad;
      The land will go mad.
    The flattener
      The diminisher
3845 Will be calm
      And small anew
    Is the agonizing word of the *katun*
      Of one-day rule,
    Lord of the step mat,
3850   Lord of the step throne.
    That will be the casting
      Of the word
    Of red nightmare,
      White nightmare.
3855 Thus it follows;
      Thus is its moon.
    It was twisted
      And cleared.
    Three loads
3860   Of the Burners
    Ended the covetousness
      In 1 Ahau again.

3826. *T u pol peten* 'at the head of the country' describes the geographical position of Merida. I read *p'ol*.

3834. *Cuch lum tam ba* 'bearing the land for each other'; bearing land is claiming title to it.

3836. Barrera 1948: 111 translates this as 'maestras', but on page 116 he agrees with me.

3840. A repeated couplet alluding to the disappearance of spirits and insignia at the end of a *katun*.

3857. Barrera 1948: 111 has 'who look like frogs, those of big testicles, those of flint'.

3860. *Ah toc* 'burner': the god and priest who presided over the fire ceremonies on certain Chicchan, Oc, Men, and Ahau days. Each Burner ruled a sixty-five-day cycle, or a quarter *tzol kin*. See lines 3049 ff., 5000 ff. The Burners are more or less equated with the Ba Cabs (Tozzer 1941: 136).

The peasants returned and made peace with the minor nobles of the west. It was a sad time in 1 Ahau. (3874)

Sutpahom ah cuc lum
   Itz'in ob i
Yuklah cab u than
   Ti tal u habil
Tz'itz'iil al
   Tz'itz'iil mehen i
Mucui al
   Mucui mehen i*
Okom y ol y ahaulil
   Ti ulom u y anal than i

T u cuch
   Hun Ahau katun ual e.

Returned were the bearers of the land,
   The younger brothers.
3865 Across the land was the word
   That came of the year
Of the mean born,
   The mean engendered,
Dove born,
3870   Dove engendered.
The lordship sorrowing
   At the arrival of the essence of the word
In the burden
   Of *katun* 1 Ahau again.

3870. Mucuy 'dove', a town not far from Acanceh.

---

28. The Surrender of Merida

Katun 1 Ahau was the sixth in the Itza katun series. Emal was its seat, and there were both Puc Ol Ha and Ual Ecuy. There were three factions and three terms of office. (3888)

And it was the sage Amayte Kauil who was lord and brought

(16v) Hun Ahau
   Katun
Uac tz'it
   Ti katun
Ich cah Emal
   U hetz' katun
Ti tal i
   U y emel
Ix Puc y Ol Ha i
   Ix Ual E Cuy i*
Ox kax u than
   Ox kax u toon
Ox kasap u tucul
   Ox kasap y ol*
Ti y ah miatzil i
   Amaite Kauil u u ich*

3875 1 Ahau
   Was the *katun*,
The sixth part
   In the *katun* cycle
In the town of Emal,
3880   The seat of the *katun*.
There came
   The descent
Also of Puc Ol Ha
   And Ual Ecuy.
3885 Three divisions are their word;
   Three divisions are their secret;
Three divisions are their thought;
   Three divisions are their span.
It was the sage
3890   Amayte Kauil

3884. Ual Ecuy 'enemy hard', another rival for the lordship of the *katun*. Compare Ual Icim, line 3814.

3888. There were three factions, led by Ol Zip (traditionalist), Amayte Kauil (pro-Christian), and Hun Pic and Can Ul (representing the military orders). What may be the ideology of the third faction is spelled out in the following text, which also identifies it with the Chan lineage of Emal. Cozumel and Izamal may also have been involved, and there was a Xiu-Itza dimension to the scrap as well.

3890. Amayte Kauil 'paper-tree god' (see also line 3822) was apparently successful in gaining the lordship in 1 Ahau. He is not to be confused with his

(note continued on following page)

the true prophecy to the world from edge to center, with justice, the word of God, and taxes. (3902)

And Hun Pic and Can Ul came to power, the latter for seven years and the former for seven years. Then came the land tax and the Chan rising, the Chan war. This was the martyrdom of the Spaniards by 240 darts, they say. It was the rulers of the port who lost. It was not the lords, who were judged and accepted if legiti-

T an y ahaulil
  Ti y ulel
U y anal than i
  U y anal (17r) can i
Bin okomac
  Y ol bal cah i
Pecnom u xik cab

   Pecnom chumuc luum i

Ti y emel *justisia*
  Likul ti can i
U than hahal ku
  U koch bal cah
Ti y ulel Hun Pic ti Ax*

   Ti y emel Can Ul ti chibal i

Uuc ppel hab u chibal Can Ul

   Uuc ppel hab u chibal Hum Pic
ti Ax i
Ti tal i
  Y emel
U koch Chakan i
  Ti u likil Chan*
Ti bateel i
  U Chanal katun
Ti y emel u tzicil
  Ah ben tenal tz'ul i
Ox much' hom
  Yala
Ah canan sus
  Ah canan kaknab ti y emel

Ma xul ahau i
  Xotom ahau

Who was in the lordship,
  The bringer
Of the existing word,
  The existing teaching
3895 To be brought
  Into the hearts of the world,
To the awareness of the wings of the earth,
  To the awareness of the middle of the land.
That is the descent of justice
3900   Rising up to heaven
The word of the True God,
  The taxation of the world.
That will be the coming of Hun Pic from Ax;
  That will be the descent of Can Ul by succession.
3905 Seven years will be the succession of Can Ul;
  Seven years will be the succession of Hun Pic from Ax.
Then came
  The descent
Of the tax on fields
3910   Which was the rising of the Chans
In arms,
  The war of the Chans.
That was the descent of their worships,
  The foreign people who go to die:
3915 Three piles of darts
  It says here.
It was the guardians of the sands,
  The guardians of the sea who descended.
It was not the end of the lords.
3920   The lords were judged

(note continued from preceding page)

namesakes who held office in 7 Ahau and 8 Ahau or with Amayte Ku, who was prominent in Emal in 5 Ahau. The present Amayte Kauil was a leader of the Christian faction in Emal.

3903. Hun Pic 'strong bedbug' ti Ax 'from blister', an unidentified village, was a pro-Christian who was lord in the *katun* from 1651 to 1658 and again in the following *katun* from about 1664 to 1670. He followed Can Ul in his first term and Yax Chuen (1658–1664) in his second and was succeeded by Pat Ay (1670–1671). He was supported by the merchants, peasants, and military companies against the priests and curers. Accused of illegitimacy because his mother was a commoner, he was executed by the traditionalists in 1670.

3910. Chan 'molar', a lineage prominent in Emal and Chab Le in the sixteenth and seventeenth centuries (see note 4289). Hun Chan was lord of *katun* 10 Ahau in Chab Le.

*mate, declaring peace and sup-
pressing the military orders.
Then came the imposition of
tribute, Christianity, and hangings, and there were sacrifices
and plague and famine in 1
Ahau. There was a ceremonial
removal of the insignia from
the center, and they were hidden, to end the ambitions of the
poor at katun time. (3950)*

Ix mektan
  Ca sih i
Hoyic u u ich
  U maxil katun*
Xotic y ich'ac Ch'uyum Thul*

  Ah Cab Coh
Ti y emel u cuch patan i
  Ti tali *xptianoil* i
Ti y emel sum
  Tal canal i
Ti tali chac sitz'il
  Ma ya cimlal
Xe kik
  Chac mitan uiih
U cuch
  Hun Ahau katun
Ocnal
  Kuchil
Okom yax cah
  Okom bul cum
T u ho can be
  T u ho can heleb
T ix u mucul nicte i
  C u xul muc u cuch katun

Ti u tz'oc sitz'il
  U tz'oc cotz
Ti ah tz'utul
  Tz'utob
T u kin
  T u katunil ual e.

And were embraced
  When they were born.
Sprinkling the face
  Of the shields of war,
3925 Cutting the nails of the Hanging
  Rabbits,
  The Earth Lions.
Then came the burden of tribute;
  Then came Christianity.
Then descended the rope
3930   Coming from the sky.
Then came red desire,
  Painless death,
Blood vomit,
  Great hunger plague,
3935 The burdens
  Of *katun* 1 Ahau.
The progression
  And arrival
Of the departed green flies,
3940   Of the departed gourd bowl
At the four crossroads
  At the four rest stops
Where the flowers are to be hidden
  And the burden of the *katun* is
  hidden
3945 Which is the end of the desire,
  The end of the plucking
Of those who
  Are the most needy:
At that time
3950   In this *katun* period.

3924. Apparently a ritual of peace. See also line 4134.
3925. Ch'uyum Thul 'hanging rabbits', a military order.

29. A Word from Mani

*The song of the Spokesman of
the Jaguar of Mani for 13 Ahau*

(10r) U *profesia* Chilam Balam*

  T ix kayom

The prophecy of the Spokesman of the
Jaguar
  Which is also sung

3951. Although it is identified with Mani, this text appears to express the
position of Izamal as well in the continuing religious debate of *katun* 1 Ahau.

(note continued on following page)

was the end of the capital. God
was set up on the cross, forgiv-
ing the whole world. (3968)

The Xiu are jealous when we
come bearing God as priests. At
once He may rouse the world in
the northwest and the god
Itzam Na at the place of the
Itza and the sculpture. (3984)

Welcome then the Spaniards,
the bearers of God. The word of

Cabal Chen
    Mani*
Ox lahun Ahau u hetz' i
    Uil katun
Ualac uil Ytza
    Ualac uil tan cah e*
Yum
    U chicul hunab ku canal
Ulom uaom che
    Etsahom ti cah e*
Uchebal
    U sas-hal
Y okol cab e
    Yum
Tz'uni moc tam ba
    Tz'uni sauinal*
Ca tal on
    Ti pul chicul ku uchmal
Ah kin uinic e
    Yum
Hun auat
    Hun lub i
Uil u tal
    Ahom uil cab
Hun xaman
    Hun chikin
Ahom
    Itzam Na Kauil*
Talel u cah
    A yum Ytza
Talel u cah
    (U) sascun tan tun e
Kam
    A u ula
Ah mexob
    Likin cabob
Ah pulob
    Ti chicul ku yum

In the lands of the well
    At Mani.
3955 13 Ahau was the seating
    Of the moon of the *katun*,
To return the moon of the Itza,
    To return the moon of the capital.
The father,
3960   The sign of the Sole God on high
Who came on the standing tree
    Was placed in the town,
Occasioning
    His forgiveness
3965 Of the whole world
    As father.
The Xiu tie each other in knots;
    The Xiu are jealous
When we come
3970   Who bear the blessed god:
The sun priest men,
    The fathers.
One shout,
    One stop
3975 And he may come
    And may awaken the earth.
One north
    One west.
Awakened
3980   Is Itzam Na Kauil,
Coming to the place
    Of your Itza fathers,
Coming to the place
    Of the clarified front stone.
3985 Receive them
    Welcome them—
The bearded ones,
    The eastern landers,
The bearers of him
3990   Who is the blessed father god.

(note continued from preceding page)
Like the preceding texts, it refers back to the authority of the Spokesman of the Jaguar in a plea for Christian orthodoxy.

3954. Mani 'buying', a major town of central Yucatan, notable as the first permanent seat of the Franciscan missionary effort and the origin of one of the *Books of Chilam Balam*.

3958. Tan Cah 'front town', hence capital. Mani was the capital of the province of Tutul Xiu.

3962. Roys n.d. suggests *ti bal cah e* 'in the world'.

3968. Tz'uni 'needles', apparently a lineage. If we read Tz'unun 'hummingbird' the reference would be to the Xiu.

3980. Itzam Na Kauil: Itzam Na the God.

God is good. He is the light of our lives. O God the Creator whose word is good, Father and guardian, be established and manifest in the cross, to the sorrow of the yearbearer priests beyond the ceiba. This is the Sole God of the Itza. Worship Him on high with true faith as the True God. Enter into the word of your Redeemer, O Itza, now. Love one another, I say, for that is God's word. I shall unite it in 1647. (4038)

Utz kau than ku
   C u talel k icnal e
Talel u cah u thanl
   U kin ca cuxtal e
Ma a sahtic y okol cab e yum
   T ech hunab ku ch'abtic oon
Utz tum ba
   U than ku e
Yum
   (Y ah canul ca pixan)
Ca u acunte u chicul canal
   Ca a u acunto
Ca pacte hele e
   Ca u acunto u uaom che
Numtetah u kex
   Ah okol hele e
U hel t u pach u yax cheel cab
   Etsahom helel ti bal cah e
La u chicul hunab ku canal
   (10v) Talom e
La a kult ex
   Ah Itza ex
Ca a kulte hel e
   U chichil ku
Likul canal e
   Ca c kulte to
T u hahil kolah
   Ca c kulte to
Ca hahal ku e
   Oces t a ba
U than hunab ku
   Tal i
Canal au ah thanul e
   Cuxcint a u ol
Ah Ytza
   Ahom uil cab ti ob
Ocsic ti y ol
   Ychil u y anal katun ual e
Yab t u ba
   In than
C en
   Chilam Balam
Ca in tzolah
   U than hahal ku
In bin hunac
   Tzuc ti cab
T u bolon pis y abil
   Ah hun Ahau ual e.*

Good is the word of God
   Which is coming before us,
Coming to begin the words,
   The sun of our lives here.
3995 Do not frighten the world, Father,
   Thou, Sole God, created us.
Good is the news—
   The word of God,
The Father,
4000 (Guardian of our souls).
Establish his grace on high;
   Establish it
And manifest its change.
   Establish his standing tree
4005 To pain his replacement,
   The believer in change:
The change behind the ceiba land
   Placed as a change in the field
That is the blessed Sole God on high
4010 Who is come.
That is your God,
   O ye Itza.
Worship the replacement
   Of the powerful God
4015 Rising to heaven.
   Let us worship him
With true devotion;
   Let us worship him
Our True God.
4020   Enter yourselves
Into the word of the Sole God
   Who is come
To raise your spokesman
   And resurrect your hearts,
4025 O Itza,
   That the earth may be awakened
By those who are brought to his heart
   In the period of this *katun*'s return.
Love one another
4030   Is my word,
Mine
   As Spokesman of the Jaguar.
For I am recounting
   The word of the True God.
4035 I shall unite
   And assemble it on earth
In the ninth year's time
   Of him who is again 1 Ahau.

4038. That is, 1647, possibly the date of the composition of this text.

12 Ahau

---

30. Valladolid Fights On

Valladolid was the seat of ka-tun 12 Ahau. Yax Chuen was the lord. He united the sha-mans and magicians and was seated as a sun priest on the throne with insignia for six years. The lords and people were righteous everywhere, and

(14v) Sacl Ac Tun*
  U hetz'
Katun
  Ti lah ca Ahau.
Yaxal Chuen u u ich*
  U y ahaulil
Ti uchom
  Hunac ah menil*
Hunac ah itz'atil
  Hunac ah esil
Hokom
  Y an ti can
Ah kin
  Cumlahom
T u tz'am
  T u pop
Ti balam
  Kokob*
Uac tz'ac
  U tepal uchom*
Ci ci ba tabil i
  Ci ci ahaulil i

Valladolid
4040 Was the seat
Of the *katun*
  In 12 Ahau.
Yax Chuen was the person
  In the lordship
4045 Who achieved
  Unifying the curers,
Unifying the seers,
  Unifying the sorcerers.
Seated
4050 He is on high,
A sun priest
  Seated
On the throne,
  On the mat
4055 In the jaguar robe
  And rattles.
Six steps
  His rule lasted.
Righteous were the chiefs;
4060 Righteous were the lords;

4039. Valladolid was the undisputed seat of the *katun* when 12 Ahau began, but the lordship nonetheless changed hands twice. At the outset it was claimed by Yax Chuen of the anti-Christian party; he was succeeded by Hun Pic (pro-Christian), and he in turn was succeeded by Pat Ay, who was anti-Christian again. Both this and the following text are Itza and anti-Christian.

4043. Yaxal Chuen 'green monkey', lord of Valladolid and a sun priest and priest of *katun* 12 Ahau. The Yax were a Xiu lineage prominent in Merida in the sixteenth century, and another Yax Chuen was an early victim of the Spanish there in the 1540s.

4046. *Ah menil* 'curers', *ah itz'atil* 'seers', *ah esil* 'sorcerers'. These practitioners are not otherwise mentioned in the Tizimin. Yax Chuen achieved peace and stability by incorporating the lower orders into the power system. He was opposed by the military orders and the merchant class, who were pro-Christian.

4056. 'In the jaguar robe and rattles': signs of lordship.

4058. Yax Chuen was overthrown in 1664.

*the priest designate awaited his
legitimate rule. And Yax Chuen
cleared the area of the woods
for the poor villagers, eliminating the soldiers and assaulters and sacrificers. Such was
12 Ahau. It produced order even
though hungry. (4088)*

*It ended with sacrifices at
Mayapan, and finished was the
term of the monkey katun with
the Death God. There were six
good and six bad years and
then the final ceremonies. The*

Ci ci uniicil i
    Ci ci al mehenil
Yuklahom
    Ti cab
Cuch
    Pach-hom
Ah holil
    Och i
Bin u ppat u mahan pop

    U mahan tz'am*
Ca xic nak
    Tan cab nak
Poc
    Che
Ci otzilhom uinicil
    Utzhom cah i
Manan Cab Coh i
    Manan Ch'amacob
Manan Hom Sabin i
    Manan Ah Coc ahaulil i
Manan Ah Coc tepal i
    Manan hom al letz' ahaulil*
Ma uchom ah mahan koh i
    Lai u cuch lah ca Ahau katun
Y an u tepal
    Y an y ahaulil
Y anahom u tzic
    He uac manahom u uah
Pa Cabal u tz'oc
    Ua ma ya cimlal*
T u tz'oc
    U y anhal
U max kin
    U max katun
Ah Puch'*
    Tun
Uac te ti hab utz i
    Uac te ti hab lob i
Ca utzac t u ca ten
    Yambil tam*

Righteous were the people;
    Righteous were the nobles
Everywhere
    In the land.
4065 Burden
    On his back,
The ender
    Of the count
Will await the announcement of his
mat,
4070   The announcement of his throne,
Then go nearby
    Before the nearby land,
The thickets
    And trees,
4075 Telling the impoverished people
    That the town has been improved.
There are no Earth Lions,
    There are no Foxes,
There are no Dart Weasels,
4080   There are no Turtle Lords,
There are no Turtle Rulers;
    There are no darts of the lord lickers.
The mask announcer has not come.
    That is the burden of *katun* 12 Ahau.
4085 He had his rule;
    He had his lordship;
He had his honor,
    Whether in fact he finished his food
And ended at Mayapan
4090   Or in painless death.
That completed
    The existence
Of the monkey time,
    The monkey *katun*:
4095 The Death God
    Idol.
Six of the years were good;
    Six of the years were bad.
Then it was possible again
4100   That it be changed,

4070. Yax Chuen was punctilious about the traditional ritual. He started on his
ceremonial circuit only four days after assuming office (see line 4126), bearing to
the villages the official count of the *katun*, confirming titles, and holding the
drinking ceremonies.

4082. Yax Chuen cleared the woods of the military companies. This must have
been between 1638 and 1645.

4090. And he was installed at Mayapan, holding sacrifices.

4095. Ah Puch' 'crusher', the god of death. See Tozzer 1941: 132.

4100. This text omits direct reference to the six-year rule of Hun Pic

(note continued on following page)

katun *ended in the selection of*
the new lord, eliminating the
soldiers, assaulters, and sacri-
ficers and reviving the land in
12 Ahau. (4116)

Pel eb
  Xot eb katun
Bin tohcintic
  Bin chaanac
U than hun kul ahau i
  Bin utzac cah i
Manan hom u Ch'amacil
  Manan Coh i
Manan Sabin i
  Manan hom Ah Chibal i
Hotz'om
  Ych'ac Coh i
Cuxlahom cab
  Cuxlahom peten
Ti y ox lahun uutz'
  Ah lah ca Ahau ual e.

The danger step,
  Cut step *katun.*
There will be sought;
  There will be found
4105 The word of one divine lord
  To improve the town.
There will be no darts of Foxes;
  There will be no Lions;
There will be no Weasels;
4110 There will be no darts of the nobility.
Pulled
  Are the claws of the Lions
Who lived on the land,
  Who lived in the country.
4115 This was the thirteenth fold
  Of the divider 12 Ahau again.

(note continued from preceding page)
(1664–1670), which is described in the following chapter, skipping to the re-establishment of Mayan orthodoxy in 1671.

31. Class War

12 Ahau was the seventh of
the Itza katun *series. Valladolid*
was its seat. Yax Chuen was its
lord, and on the fourth day he
left, bearing the result of the
count in the Mayan tradition

(17r) Lah cabil Ahau
  U uuc tz'it
Katun
  C u xocol
Sacl Ac Tun
  U hetz' katun
Yaxal Chuen u u ich*
  U y ahaulil
Okom y an t u canil kin

  Y an t u canil akab
Cuch
  Pach-hom
Holil
  Och
Ti y emel chac tun
  Ah u sil

The twelfth Ahau
  Was the seventh part
Of the *katuns*
4120 To be counted.
Valladolid
  Was the seat of the *katun.*
Yax Chuen was the face
  Of the lordship,
4125 And departed to be there on the fourth day
  On the fourth night,
Bearing
  Loaded on his back
The ending
4130 Of the count.
That was the descent of the red stone,
  The witches.

4123. Compare lines 4043 ff., a briefer account of this *katun* which is nonetheless in general agreement. Yax Chuen was the traditionalist lord from 1658 to 1664.

and declaring peace. Bitter and defeated were the merchants over the confusion of katuns, their lordship, their processions, and their ceremonies. This was the katun *of families, children, and young men. (4152)*

The merchants and headmen rebelled at once at the lordship of the beginning of the katun, *bringing on the pain of division and war. It was half-bad, half-good: six years bad, six good, making twelve years. And what they wanted, the merchants, was the seventh year in the cen-*

Hoyic u u ich
  U maxil katun
Cicilnac
  Papalnac
Hom u pucsikal
  Y ah belnalil cab i
T u men u saual katun
  Katun tepal
Katun ahaulil
  Katun than
Katun hanal
  Katun ukul
Katun ximbal
  Katun belnalil
Ti tali u katun no xib
  U katun ix nuc
U katun palal
  (. . . . .)*
U katun hol can
  U katun tan celem
Ti tali sisitz' belnalil
  Sisitz' ba tabil
Hun kin
  Hun uay
U tz'am
  U pop
Al kab
  Katun
Oc yail
  Tepal
Ti u likil che
  Y etel tunich ti bateel i
Tan koch utz i
  Tan koch lob i
Uac ppel hab lob i
  Uac ppel hab utz i*
La t u lah
  Lah ca tz'acab katun
Ti u katal
  Okolal
Ti y ah belnalilob cab i
  Tu u katal
Uuc tz'acab
  Y ibnel cab i*

He sprinkles the faces
  Of the shields of war.
4135 Throbbing
  And shattered
Are the darts in the hearts
  Of those who travel about the earth
Because of envy of the *katun*:
4140 The *katun* of rule;
The *katun* of lordship;
  The *katun* of the word;
The *katun* of eating;
  The *katun* of drinking;
4145 The *katun* of walking;
  The *katun* of traveling;
The *katun* of husbands;
  The *katun* of wives;
The *katun* of children;
4150 (. . . . .)
The *katun* of warriors;
  The *katun* of youths.
Then came the passion of travelers,
  The passion of chiefs.
4155 One day,
  One sleep away
Was the throne
  The mat
Of the dawn
4160 Of the *katun*,
The coming of pain
  And division
Which was the raising of sticks
  And stones in battle.
4165 Halfway good,
  Halfway bad:
Six years bad;
  Six years good.
That completes twelve
4170 Steps of the *katun*.
That was the desire
  And belief
Of those who roam the earth
  Where they wish.
4175 The seventh step
  Is the navel of the earth,

4150. Line missing.

4168. War broke out again in 1684 to 1685.

4176. Seven may again symbolize Christianity, though the implication of six plus seven produces a cycle of thirteen. Presumably an Itza-Christian syncretism is implied, possibly the one represented by weekday divination.

ter as the local books said. For the merchants, God is coming: accept and welcome Him. He is coming immediately. (4184)

And Hun Pic took power as one of the three lords of the katun, to demand a parent for the snarled katun, a new one. God was installed in the lordship of the rich katun 12 Ahau. This ended the fighting around the country, and the warriors fled to the forest and the lordship was established. The merchants were beaten. (4208)

New lords were nominated for the end of the katun, to do away with the irresponsible nobles. The sun priest was executed, the son of a street mother. Tribute was imposed

Ti u katal
  U *libroil* cah i*
Ti y ah belnalil cabob i
  U than ku lic u talel
Kam
  A u ula ex
Hun lub
  Hun auat u tal
Hum Pic ti Ax*
  U cuch katun
Ox kasap y ol
  Ox kasap u than
Bin u tza u yum
  Y etel u na t u saual katun
Kekex yum
  Kekex na
Hunab ku
  C u tza i
Okol kan che u cah
  T u pop
(17v) Lah cabil Ahau
  Ayikal katun
Bay hol i
  Xan *punob* cal
Punob peten
  Punob tan chumuc cab*
Sutnom halal
  Tan chumuc peten
Ti tali u y anhal
  Y ahauil bal cah i
Ti y uchul ban meyah i
  Ti u baxtabal y ah belnalil cahob i
Ti culh i
  Al cab katun
Hul katun
  Tz'on katun
Bin y anac
  U tz'on
Co co al
  Co co mehen
T u tza katun
  Satnom y al
Ix ti ti be*
  Ti tali patanhal i

Which is the desire
  Of the books of the place.
That is the travelers of the earth;
4180 The word of God as it is coming.
Receive
  And welcome it.
In one rest,
  One shout it is coming.
4185 Hun Pic from Ax
  Was the bearer of the *katun.*
Thrice blocked its heart;
  Thrice blocked its word.
He will demand a father
4190 And a mother for the envy *katun:*
A substitute father,
  A substitute mother.
The Sole God
  Is installed
4195 On the throne of his place,
  On the mat
Of 12 Ahau,
  The rich *katun.*
Thus it is finished,
4200 As well as ending the Flags:
The Flags of the country,
  The Flags in the middle of the land.
Returned are the arrows
  In the middle of the country.
4205 Then came the realization
  Of the lordship of the world.
Then were occurring piles of work.
  Then was the beating down of the travelers of the towns.
Then was seated
4210 The dawn of the *katun,*
The pierced *katun,*
  The shot *katun.*
It is going
  To be the end
4215 Of the insane born
  And insane engendered children.
The *katun* was removed.
  Destroyed were the born children
Of the street mother.
4220 Then came the tribute system.

4178. *Libroil* 'books': the locally written prophecies.
4185. *Hum*: I read *hun.* Hun Pic ruled from about 1664 to 1670. See also note 3903.
4202. *Panob* 'flags' from Nahuatl *pantli*: a military company.
4219. See line 3838. I surmise that it was Hun Pic whose parentage was ques-

(note continued on following page)

and the duumvirate ended. Pat Ay became lord and imposed new officials and taxes. He united the curers and made his circuit of the wilderness, judging the lords and warriors of the military orders, burning villages, and destroying the orders. Great and rich was the katun. *And the headmen rejoiced everywhere. The count was accepted by country and city for the* katun *and the calendar round. But disease struck as the lord feasted, and it was neither good nor bad in that* katun *again. (4262)*

Ti y emal ahau ca ppel u pol i

　Baxtic y ah belnalil cabob i
Ek Pat Ai u u ich*
　T u men u saual katun
T ix u hatzal u cuch bal cah i
　Ti u katabal u takin ahau i

Hunac ah menil
　Hunac ah tz'acil*
Ti tal i
　U hokol
Ich lumil che
　Ich lumil tunich i
Xotom ahau i
　Xotic y ich'ac
Ah Chuyum Thul i
　Ti u lachlam pach
Cab Coh i
　Y etel Ch'amac i
Elom
　Y ac tunil
Manan tun Ch'amac
　Manan tun Cab Coh
Noh uah
　U uah
Katun
　Ayikal katun
Ci ci ba tabil
　Ci ci olal bin y anac
Ti bal cah
　T u chi kaknab
U ch'aic y och tan y ol che
　U hetz'
U katunil ual e
　Kin tun y abil
Xe kik
　U tz'oc ci ci olal
Ti u katabal natal nat
　Ti hanal i
Manan tun num ya
　Ci ci olal
T u kin
　T u katunil ual e.

There will descend the lord with two heads
　And beat the travelers of the lands.
The West priest Pat Ay was the face
　For the envy *katun,*
4225 And he divided the burden of the world
　And demanded the money of the lords:
To unite the shamans,
　To unite the curers.
There came
4230 His appearance
In the lands of trees,
　In the lands of stones.
Cut are the lords;
　He cuts the claws
4235 Of the Hanging Rabbit people,
　Which is the scratched back
Of the Earth Lion
　And the Fox.
Burned
4240 Are the springs.
There are then no Foxes;
　There are then no Earth Lions.
Great food
　Is the food
4245 Of the *katun;*
　Rich is the *katun.*
Happy are the chiefs.
　Rejoicing is to be
On earth
4250 And at the edge of the sea.
They get the count among the trees,
　The seat
Of the *katun* period again,
　Of the calendar round.
4255 Blood vomit
　Ended the rejoicing
Of him who was asked to comprehend,
　Who was eating.
There was neither then suffering
4260 Nor rejoicing
On that day,
　On that *katun* period again.

(note continued from preceding page)
tioned (note the atypical name) and who was executed by the traditionalists in 1670.
　4223. Pat Ay 'wait grease', lord of the *katun* from about 1670 to 1671. A traditionalist, he attacked the military orders and merchants.
　4228. See note 4046.

10 Ahau

---

32. Christian Victory

---

10 Ahau was the eighth in the Itza katun cycle. Valladolid was its seat. The Chab Le founded Uat Hom in the wilderness, claiming title in poverty and burning and destroying the north coast. Christianity was regretted throughout. (4284)

(17v) Lahun Ahau
  U uaxac tz'it
Katun
  C u xocol
Sacl Ac Tun
  U hetz' katun.*
Lahun Chab Le y ulelob
  T u cahal ob Can Uat Hom*
U kax eb
  Cheob
Y okol y ahaulil
  Cabob
Oxil uah
  U uah ob
Elom u Ku Ch'ich'*
  Ua Kom Chal Tun
Elom Tz'itz'
  Elom Mucuy t u chi kaknab

U than ku canal
  Bin tz'oc lucuc
Tac pach
  Tac tan ual e.

10 Ahau
  Was the eighth part
4265 Of the *katun*
  To be counted.
Valladolid
  Was the seat of the *katun*.
The 10 Chab Le people were to arrive
4270   And settle Can Uat Hom,
Its forests
  And trees
Over the lordship
  Of their lands.
4275 Breadnut food
  Is their food.
Burned is Ku Ch'ich'
  And Kom Chal Tun;
Burned is Tz'itz';
4280   Burned is Mucuy at the edge of the sea.
The word of God on high
  Will end in lamentation
Both behind
  And before it again.

4268. Valladolid again claims to seat the *katun* and accuses the people of Chab Le of burning and looting in the name of Christianity.

4270. Can Uat Hom 'four length sink', an unidentified place, probably near Emal.

4277. These appear to be place-names: U Ku Ch'ich' 'god of birds' and Kom Chal Tun 'pit flat stone'. Tz'itz' may be Tz'itz'om Tun. For Mucuy, see note 3870.

33. Christian Defeat

Chab Le was the seat of ka-tun 10 Ahau. Hun Chan was the ruler. Whether blessed or waning, the woods and gods wait in the sky. It was a misera-ble time of hunger and thirst, and the lords were tied and de-stroyed in the penitential cere-

(14v) Lahun Chab Le
  U hetz'
Katun
  Ti lahun Ahau.
Hun Chaan u u ich*
  Cit bolon ua u u ich t u canil*

Cit bolon
  Ua u u kin*
U kax eb
  Cheob
Can lot*
  Pat-hom be
Te
  Ti caan e
Satai habil y an i
  Manan hom uah
Ox
  Y etel cup*
U uah
  Y etel y aal
(15r) Kaxan u u ich
  Kaxan y ahaulil
Satan hal ach uinicob i
  Y etel u cucteelob*
Uiih u cuch
  Y oklal u keban bal cah i

4285 10 Chab Le
  Was the seat
Of the *katun*
  In 10 Ahau.
Hun Chan was the person.
4290   Either the Remote Nine were the face in heaven,
Or the Remote Nine
  Were the moon of the sun
Of the forests
  And trees.
4295 The four twins
  Awaited their road
There
  In heaven.
Needy years they were;
4300   Gone was the bright food.
Breadnut
  And gourdroot
Were its food
  And drink.
4305 Tied was its face;
  Tied the lordship.
Destroyed were the governors
  And officials.
Hunger was the burden.
4310   Weeping for the sins of the world,

4289. Hun Chan 'book molar' of Chab Le 'sapote leaf' contested the seating of the *katun* with Valladolid (line 4269). I believe Chab Le to be on or near the site of Chan Santa Cruz or the modern Felipe Carrillo Puerto. See also note 777. The end of this *katun* marked the conquest of the Peten Itza; but the Tizimin does not mention it.

4290. *Cit bolon* 'remote nine' is a pregnant religious pun. It refers to the approach (in the next *katun*) of the end of the Xiu nine cycle on 8 Ahau. The nine lords of the night, like the thirteen lords of the day, were "holy and remote." They symbolically represent the (black) west and the Xiu, as the day gods represent the (red) east and the Itza. *Bolon*, furthermore, connotes 'great'. The Itza were under-standably perturbed as the end of the Xiu cycle approached, particularly so since they also had to cope with the mysterious seven cycle of the Christians.

4292. *Ua u u kin* 'or the moon was its sun': see note 1558. Either Valladolid was justified in its grandiose pretensions, or it had it upside down. That was indeed the question. Were the Ba Cab priesthoods doubled? Old and new perhaps?

4302. *Cup*, also called *chicam* in Maya, is identified variously as jicama or camote (*Pachyrrhizos* or *Calopogonium*). See Tozzer 1941: 196. It was considered an undesirable food.

4308. *Cuchteel ob* 'those who were arranging for them to be borne', hence landowners. Bearing land was owning it.

monies of the four Fathers of
the Land behind the ceiba. And
the stars brought the word of
the end of the katun *and re-*
demption. 10 Ahau was a sad
period. (4326)

Pecnahom pax
   Pecnom sot
Pecnahom
   Can tul Ba Cab i
Ti u ch'abal
   U pach u yax cheel cab i
T ix u colabal
   Y ekil cal
C u cup u hahal than
   U catz' pop*
Kaspahan ti ualac
   U xihul bal cah e*
T u cuch lahun Ahau ual e
   Okom olal y an i
Ti y ahaulil
   T u cuch hab ual e.

Sounded was the drum,
   Sounded the rattle—
Sounded
   The four Fathers of the Land,
4315 Who are doing it
   Behind the ceiba grove.
And that is the cultivation
   Of the starry voice,
Releasing the true word
4320   Of the fold of the mat,
Preventing the arising
   Of the stain of the world.
He bore 10 Ahau again
   And there was sorrow
4325 In the lordship
   Bearing the year's return.

4320. *Catz'* may be an error for *uatz'*. I so read it.
4322. *Xihul* 'stain' refers to the "sins of the world"; see also line 4310.

THE EIGHTEENTH CENTURY

8 Ahau

34. The Final Battle for Mayapan

Katun 8 *Ahau was seated at Mayapan, and in the south Chab Le was the seat of* katun 8 Ahau. *Amayte Kauil was the lord and leader and proceeded on Xiu doctrine to sacrifice and war. No one could provide his village with food and drink. Fields and hills were poor and*

(15r) Uaxac Ahau
  Katun
Culh i
  Ca uch i
Pa Cabal
  Mayapan
Ti nohol
  Y an i
Lahun Chab Le
  U hetz'
Katun
  Ti uaxac Ahau*
Amaite Kauil u u ich
  Y ahaulil
Ti u uah
  Ti y aal
Oclis t u ba
  Ti xul i
Cit bolon ua*
  U u ich
Tokil uah
  Tokil haa
Hol can
  U can
Ma mac u tzic
  Ti besah u cah
T u uah
  T u y aal
Otzilhom chakan
  Otzilhom uitz

8 Ahau
  Was the *katun*
That was seated
4330 When it occurred
At the Fort of the Lands,
  Mayapan.
In the south
  It was.
4335 10 Chab Le
  Was the seat
Of the *katun*
  In 8 Ahau.
Amayte Kauil was the person
4340 Of the lordship.
He was its food;
  He was its drink,
Collecting himself
  At the end.
4345 Or the Remote Nine
  Were the face:
Flint food,
  Flint water.
The captains
4350 Were its guardian.
No one succeeded
  In teaching the towns
Their food,
  Their drink.
4355 Idled the plains,
  Idled the hills.

4338. The leading lineages of Emal apparently emigrated to Chab Le, which again claimed to seat the cycle under Amayte Kauil. The southern part of Quintana Roo was becoming a refuge for traditionalist Mayas, as it has been since, though the lordship continued in the northeast "from Chichen Itza to the sea" under Kak Mo, heir to the tradition of the pro-Christian Itza. The primacy of Mayapan continued to be respected by both parties, at least ritually.

4345. See note 4290. This *katun* ends the Xiu cycle.

cursed by all; fields and hills were without water for the land everywhere. (4362)

The Fathers of the Land were in the flats and brought Kak Mo to power, and he ruled the country directly for the scouts and peasants from Chichen Itza to the sea. The north went Ba Cab (anti-Christian), and taxes were suspended as the rule broadened. And war broke out over the many, many lords and rulers, heirs of the Itza and street women, who were dispossessed and taxed by the Death God, by power seekers.

Bin tzaclabac
  T u men t u lacal
Manan u y aal chakan i
  Manahom ix y alil uitz i
Yuklah ti cab
  Yuklah peten
T u sinil
  Y an Ba Cab i
Ti emom
  Kin Ich
Kak Mo
  T u tepal i
Ti emom ix
  U y anal cab
Ti y uchul cha
  Toh
T u men ah chin cot
  Ah chin pacat
T u men ah mab na
  Ah mab yum
U koch y ahaulil t u Chi Ch'en
  Y etel y ahaulil u chi kaknab

Ah xaman cab
  Y an Ba Cab
Ca bin tac u koch i
  Uil t u lacalob
Lic y ahaulil
  Cochom e
Emom halal
  Emom *chimal*
Y okol paxebalob
  Ah yan yan tepalob*
Ah ten tz'am*
  Ah ten popob
U mehenob
  U hoyob Ah Iza
Y alob ix
  Ix hihitz' be
Koch
  U than katun a
Puch'*
  Tun y an i
Pa Cabal u tz'oc*
  T u men ah sisitz' ahaulilob

They will be cursed
  By all:
No juice of the plains
4360 And no juice of the hills.
All over the world,
  All over the country.
In the plains
  There were the Fathers of the Land,
4365 Who brought down
  The Sun Eye,
Kak Mo,
  To his rule,
And who brought down
4370 The existing earth
And made it adequate
  And correct
For the Eagle bearers
  And Scout bearers,
4375 For the motherless
  And fatherless.
The tax of the lordship at Chichen
  And the lordship at the edge of the sea.
The north country
4380 Has the Fathers of the Land.
Then they will stop the tax,
  Perhaps altogether,
As the lordship
  Is broadened.
4385 Arrows descending,
  Shields descending
Over the destructions
  Of the owners of the rules,
The step throne lords,
4390 The step mat lords,
The engendered sons
  And little ones of the Itza.
And those born
  Of streetwalkers
4395 Are the tax
  And word of this *katun.*
The Death God
  Idol is there.
The Fort of the Lands is finished
4400 By the coveters of the lordship.

4388. *Yan yan:* I read *yaan* from *ya* 'exact'. It has the sense of the Spanish *mero mero:* the veriest rulers.
4389. *Ten:* I read *tem.*
4397. See line 4096.
4399. I read Pa Cabal to be Mayapan.

Such was the evil power of Kak Mo in katun *8 Ahau. (4406)*

Seizing Mayapan, Kak Mo came and divided the priesthoods and raised the peasants. The priesthoods were divided and village governors were exalted. The real lords were captured or in hiding and dispossessed by the ruler. The peasants were raised, and the indigent seized property. So they abandoned the insignia and the capital. Thus was 8 Ahau. (4434)

Alas, the prophecy was fulfilled at Mayapan. Its ancient doom returned. The sun priest has spoken and written the character of the katun *in 8 Ahau. (4448)*

Bai chacanil
  Bin u lobal
Ah kin ich
  Kak Mo
Ichil uaxac Ahau
  Katun ual e
Pa Cabal
  Bin ocbal
Ah kin ich
  Kak Mo e
Ti tal i
  Haulahom caan
Noclahom luum
  Ti uchom
Haulahom can e
  Sipc i
Bin chacanac ob
  U hal ach uinicilob cah e
Bin ix thilac
  U calob y ahaulil cab i
Muc
  Chehan ob
T u men ah ten tz'am
  Ah ten popob e
Hex oc
  Ti nocpahom luum e
Ah chincunah bailob
  Ah ma balob
T u tz'oc okom yax cach
  Okom bul cum
Tu ho cam be
  U y okol ob
Lai u than
  Uaxac Ahau ual e
Heklai
  Uchc i
Pa Cabal
  Mayapan
Kas u than katun
  Bai li bin labal u than
Ca bin sutnac
  T u ca ten
T u than ah kin
  Chilam*
Ca t u tz'ibtah
  U u ich
Katun
  Ichil uaxac Ahau e.

Thus was the trampling,
  Thus the evil
Of the glorious
  Kak Mo
4405 In 8 Ahau,
  The returned *katun.*
The Fort of the Lands
  Will be stolen.
It is the glorious
4410 Kak Mo
Who came
  And divided the sky.
Raised was the land
  When he did it,
4415 And he divided the sky
  To permit it.
They will appear,
  The governors of the towns,
And will stop
4420 The throats of the lords of the land.
Hiding
  And beaten
Are the step throne lords,
  The step mat lords,
4425 And so they come
  To the raised land
The bearers of such evil,
  The destitute.
The green fly is mourned;
4430 The bean gourd is mourned
At the four crossroads.
  They weep.
That is the word
  Of 8 Ahau again,
4435 The events
  Occurring
At the Fort of the Lands,
  Mayapan.
Stopped is its word,
4440 So its word will just be old
When it shall return
  For the second time.
The sun priest has spoken,
  The Spokesman.
4445 Then he has written
  The character
Of the *katun*
  In 8 Ahau.

4444. Like the prophet of line 3951, this one claims the mantle of the Spokesman of the Jaguar to justify a vision of the Xiu apocalypse for the Itza.

6 Ahau

---

35. Chic Kalac Rebels

Teabo was the seat of katun *6 Ahau. Kak Mo of Uxmal was the lord. (4456)*

And Chic Kalac rebelled, promoting himself as legitimate lord, raising himself to the sky as legitimate, but it was a lie. Secret punishment appeared and the people suffered and died in the middle of 6 Ahau, starving and dying as he sat in

(15v) Uuc y Ab Nal*
  U hetz'
Katun
  Ti uac Ahau.
Kin ich
  Kak Mo
Uxmal
  U u ich ti*
Ti y ahaulil
  Chic Kalac u u ich
Co u than
  Ti uchom
Oclis t u ba i
  Ti u u acuntic u ba
Ah ten pop
  Ah ten tz'am
Oclis t u ba t u canil
  T u y ekil
T u sihnalil
  Bin u tusub
Homol tza
  Hoc
Mucuc tza
  U uinicil yah
T an lahul
  Ah uac Ahau
Uiilnom che
  Uiilnom tunich

7 Ab Nal
4450 Was the seat
Of the *katun*
  In 6 Ahau.
The glorious
  Kak Mo
4455 Of Uxmal
  Was the face of it.
In the lordship
  Chic Kalac was the face.
Mad was the word
4460 That occurred.
He summoned himself
  And elevated himself.
The step mat lord,
  The step throne lord
4465 Summoned himself to the sky,
  To the stars
By having been born to it—
  But it will be lies.
Dart removal,
4470 Uprooting,
And burial removal
  Of the people of pain:
That was the completion
  Of 6 Ahau:
4475 Starved trees,
  Starved stones;

4449. Like the preceding prophecy, this shows a degree of confusion between this *katun* and the preceding one of the same name, seated at Uxmal. Kak Mo continued to claim the lordship from the previous *katun*, presumably still in the northeast. He was opposed around 1728 by Chic Kalac 'coati resting' of Teabo, who was anti-Christian and represented the southwest. Toward the end of the *katun* (around 1732) a third claimant arose, Cup Uah 'cup food', who ambushed and killed the other two. Itza history is increasingly concentrated in the east.

4456. Compare lines 367 ff., which agree that Uxmal was the seat of the *katun*.

*state killing village headmen
and abusing the neighborhood.
Because the agents just divided
the land, they began to say, per-
manently, and he wanted to do
this even in the wild. (4492)*

*The third time this happened,
war broke out and famine. At
Mayapan there were three rules
and rulers, and in 1719 they
were ambushed, the rulers, and
finished off. And the lands were
confirmed again because it
wasn't time to replace the
lords, not time for the installation. That is the* katun *fate
and what happened in* katun
6 Ahau. (4526)

Chac mitan uih
　U cuch cimom
Culan ti pop
　Culan ti tz'am
Xotom u cal
　Hal ach uinicilob cah i
Bin culac ob nak
　Cot nak tan cab
T u men ah macil
　Tah be lo bi
T u men ppis u cah la
　U cah t u than manan u xul

T u tz'i y ol
　Ti u hokol
Ich lumil che
　Ich lumil tunich i
Ti ox ten uchom
　Cahom i
U chacil
　Cupil
Uah
　Chac mitan uiih
Pa Cabal
　Uchom i
Ox kas tepal i
　Ox tul
Ah ten tz'am
　Ah tem pop
Bin y anac i
　T u can pis tun
U pactic
　U pach
Ti an tepal i
　Ti an ahaulil i
T u tz'oc e
　Ma on t kin
Bin haulac luum e
　Ca noclac t u ca ten
Mamanom kin
　T u thical
Ah ten pop
　Ah ten tz'amob i e
Ma ix bal put-hom
　Ti y ahaulil
Lai u than katun
　C u talel e
He lai u u ich
　U uohil
Ah uac Ahau
　Katun ual e.

The red plague of hunger,
　The burden of the dead,
Seated on the mat,
4480　Seated on the throne.
Cut were the throats
　Of the governors of the towns.
They are to be seated nearby,
　Cleared nearby before the land
4485 By the people
　Dividing it that way.
Because they surveyed the town there
　And began to say that it was
　　permanent,
Which they wanted
4490　And asked for
In the lands of trees,
　In the lands of stones.
The third time it happened
　It was set:
4495 The chopping
　And cutting
Of food:
　Red hunger plague.
At the Fort of the Lands.
4500　There occurred
Three divisions of rule:
　Three people,
Step throne lords,
　Step mat lords
4505 Who will be there
　In the fourth *tun.*
Looking
　Back
There were rulers:
4510　There were lords.
That's finished—
　Not now
When the land is divided:
　When it is raised again.
4515 Time has passed
　And unraveled
The step mat lords
　The step throne lords,
And nothing is carted
4520　To the lords.
That is the word of the *katun*
　That is coming.
Indeed, that is the character
　Of the glyphs
4525 Of 6 Ahau,
　The returning *katun.*

36. Early History

In 8 Ahau was destroyed the city of Mayapan by the hill tribes, 280 years ago. (4534)

In 6 Ahau and 4 Ahau sacrifices were held in the Fort. (4538)

In 2 Ahau was the great fire. (4540)

In 13 Ahau the water priest died. Six years before the end of the katun, an east year (2 Muluc) when 4 Kan fell on 16 Pop and 5 Kan on 15 Zip. Add three, and on 9 Imix 3 Ceh

(19r) Uaxac Ahau*
  Paxc i
Cah
  Mayapan
T u men uitzil
  Tz'ul*
Lahun kal hab
  Ca tac can kal hab i*
Uac Ahau
  Can Ahau uchc i
Ma ya cimlal ocnal
  Kuchil Ych Paa*
Cabil Ahau uchc i
  Noh kakil*
Ox lahun Ahau uchc
  U cimil Ah Pul Ha*
Uac ppel hab u binel
  Ca tz'ococ u xoc ox lahun
  Ahau c uchi e
Ti y an u xocol hab
  Ti lakin c uchi e
Canil Kan cumlahc i
  Pop
Hool Kan
  T u ho lhun Sip
Ca tac
  Ox ppel i

8 Ahau (1461)
  There was destroyed
The city
4530 Of Mayapan
By the Hummingbird
  Foreigners.
Two hundred years
  And then eighty years:
4535 6 Ahau (1480),
  4 Ahau (1500) passed.
Painless death was brought,
  Appearing inside the walls.
Second Ahau (1520) passed
4540 The great fire.
13 Ahau (1539) occurred
  The death of Water Thrower.
Six years were to come:
  Then came the end of the count of
  13 Ahau.
4545 It lay in the counting of the year
  That occurred in the east:
  4 Kan was included
  In Pop.
  5 Kan
4550 Was on the fifteenth of Zip.
So then
  There were three.

4527. This unusual text is incomplete and different in character from the remainder. On its own testimony it was written at Mani in 1732. It constitutes a highly summary account of the major events from the destruction of Mayapan in 1451 to the first census in 1611, where it breaks off. It manifests far more attention to Spanish affairs than does the rest of the Tizimin.

4532. Uitzil Tz'ul 'mountain or hummingbird foreigners': the Mexicanized western lineages.

4534. That is, Mayapan was destroyed 280 years before the composition of the present text, which therefore dates to 1732.

4538. Sacrifices continued at Mayapan into the seventeenth century. It continued to be considered the seat of the cycle by some Itzas into the nineteenth century.

4540. Other sources agree laconically that there was a "great fire" in 2 Ahau. Nobody knows where. Barrera 1948 remarks in another context which I cannot relocate that forest fires are rare in Yucatan, and I surmise that this fire was in Mayapan.

4542. Pul Ha 'throws water', a water priest (see Tozzer 1941: 54) and probably lord of the *katun* at Merida in 13 Ahau, since no other is mentioned. Barrera 1948: 65 gives his name as Pot Xiu 'blouse grass'. The emphasis on dating his death may be related to the arrival of the Spanish.

the water priest died, in 1536.
_(4556)_

In 11 Ahau there arrived the
Spanish missionaries from the
east here in this land. (4564)

In 9 Ahau there began Chris-
tianity and there arrived the
first bishop, Toral, in 1544.
_(4574)_

In 7 Ahau Bishop Landa died,
and in 5 Ahau our town priest
died at Mani. In 1550 he came
over to settle and in 1552 they

Bolon Imix*
  U kinil cimc i
Ah Pul Ha
  Lei tun hab _1536_ c uch i*
Buluc Ahau
  Ulc i
Tz'ulob
  Kul uincob*
Ti lakin u tal ob
  Ca ul ob
Uai
  Tac lumil e
Bolon Ahau
  Hoppc i
Xp̃tianoil uchc i
  Ca put si
Lai li ichil u katunil
  Ulc i
Yax _obispo_
  Toral*
He ix hab c u ximbal c uchi e
  _1544_
Uuc Ahau cimc i
  Obispo Landa ychil u katunil*
Hoo Ahau ca yum cah i
  Padre Mani*
Lai hab c u ximbal c uch i
  La _1550_
Lai hab c u ximbal
  Ca cahi ob
Y ok ha*
  _1552_ c uch i

9 Imix
  Was the time of death
4555 Of Water Thrower.
  That was then the year 1536.
11 Ahau
  Was the arrival
Of the foreigners,
4560   The people of the gods.
From the east they came
  When they arrived
Right here
  In this land.
4565 9 Ahau
  It began:
Christianity occurred,
  Second birth.
It was just in this _katun_ period
4570   That there arrived
The first bishop,
  Toral.
And this was the year he came:
  1544.
4575 7 Ahau there died
  Bishop Landa on the _katun_ date.
5 Ahau the Father of our town,
  The priest of Mani.
This was the year he came:
4580   It was 1550.
This was the year they came
  And settled our town
Above the water:
  It happened in 1552.

4553. Brinton 1882: 149 has this as 9 Imix 18 Zip.

4556. A very confusing bit of chronology here: the scribe appears to be calculating out loud. He first mentions 1533, six years before the end of _katun_ 13
Ahau. He then takes us to 1530, which began on 2 Muluc 1 Pop, remarking
correctly that it was an East year and that 4 Kan fell on (16) Pop and 5 Kan on 15
Zip. How this digression helps his calculation is obscure to me. He then goes
back to 1533 (which began on 5 Kan 1 Pop) and adds three years, bringing him to
1536 (which began on 8 Cauac 1 Pop), then adds the two days to get to Imix. That
lands him on 10 Imix 3 Pop, and he can then figure (though he does not say so)
that Pul Ha died on 9 Imix 3 Ceh. The mention of an East year may relate to the
coming of the Spaniards from that direction. The thirteen years from 1529 to 1542
were East years.

4560. The Spanish reached Merida in 1541, the second year of 11 Ahau.

4572. Francisco de Toral arrived in 1562 (Barrera 1948: 65). The first missionaries reached Merida in 1549.

4576. Diego de Landa died in Merida on April 19, 1579 (Julian), in the first year
of 7 Ahau (Barrera 1948: 66; Ancona 1878: 2: 115). It was 4 Imix 13 Muan, the 101st
day of the _katun_ and the 201st day of the Mayan year.

4578. The word _padre_ does not otherwise occur in the Tizimin. Who was the
priest of Mani in 5 Ahau?

4583. _Y ok ha_ 'above the water': probably the well of Mani.

settled at Mani. In 1559 the Auditor came. In 1560 the Doctor came: Quijada, the first governor here. In 1562 there were hangings. In 1563 the Marshal arrived. In 1569 was the fire. (4598)

In 1610 they hung the prisoners. In 1611 was the judge's sentence . . . (4602)

1559 hab ca ul i
   Oydor ca pak ispital*
1560 u habil ca ul i
   Doctor
Quixada
   Yax hal ach uinic*
Uai
   Ti lum e
1562 hab ca uch i
   Ch'ui tab*
1563 hab ca ul i
   Mariscal*
1569 hab ca uch i
   Kakil*
1610 u habil ca hich i
   U cal Ah Kaxob*
1611 hab ca tz'ibtab i

   T u mene jues . . .*

4585 1559 was the year when there arrived
   The Auditor (? of our hospital).
   1560 was the year when there arrived
   The Doctor,
   Quijada,
4590   The first governor
   Here
   In this land.
   1562 was the year when there occurred
   The hanging of the rope.
4595 1563 was the year when there arrived
   The Marshal.
   1569 was the year when there occurred
   The fire.
   1610 was the year when they knotted
4600   The necks of the Tied Ones.
   1611 was the year when there was written
   The settlement by the judge . . .

4586. Tomás López, oidor, founded the hospital in Merida in 1562 (Barrera 1948: 66).

4590. Diego Quijada was named alcalde mayor in 1560; he arrived at Merida in 1562 (Ancona 1878: 2: 81) and remained until 1565 (Barrera 1948: 66).

4594. Hangings were instituted by Landa as punishment for heresy in 1562 (Barrera 1948: 65).

4596. Mariscal: Barrera 1948: 66 identifies the marshal as Governor Luna de Arellano (1604–1612).

4598. Another fire? Brinton 1882: 149 and Barrera 1948: 66 say 'smallpox'.

4600. There is general agreement that this refers to the punishment of the rebellion of Tekax (Ancona 1878: 3: 201).

4602. Barrera 1948: 67 refers to a census conducted by Judge Diego Pareja in 1611.

4 Ahau

37. The War Is Over

Teabo was the seat of katun 4 Ahau. There were seven uprisings at Chichen. Mac Chahom was the ruler in the south. Both parties fought each other and the military companies were cleared out. But Mac Chahom died of starvation and thirst, and it was the old nobility that got the mandate by fate. (4622)

It was both mad and just, a period without honor, disreputable but straight. Only in

(15v) Uucil y Ab Nal*
  U hetz'
Katun
  Ti can Ahau.
Uuc ten u yail
  T u Chi Ch'en
Mac Chahom u u ich
  Ti nohol
Y ah es u ne
  Sas tam ba
Ah bal cab
  Cochom
Macan u u ich
  Cimen u u ich
Y ok u uah
  Y okol y aal
Lic u tzicil ob u than
  U kat tzicil
Ma y olah tzic
  Bai u bel y ahaulil cabob

Co
  Cach
T u uah
  Ti y aal
Bin tz'oc oc ti
  T u tzicilil
Hum pai y ol
  Ma t an u tzic halic i

Teabo
  Was the seat
4605 Of the *katun*
  In 4 Ahau.
Seven times was it rising
  At Chichen.
Mac Chahom was its face
4610   In the south.
The tailed sorcerers
  Cleared each other up.
The animal people
  Were cleared up.
4615 His face was not tired:
  His face was dead.
Tears were his food,
  And weeping his drink.
As they honored his word,
4620   He sought honors,
Not being honorable:
  That was the road of the lordship of
  the lands.
Mad,
  Broken
4625 In his food,
  In his drink.
He will finally get to it—
  To glory.
One part of his heart
4630   Wants honor to be true.

4603. Teabo continued to claim the lordship under Mac Chahom 'cover embittered'. Christianity made continuing inroads on the Itza, culminating in the Valladolid calendar reform of 1752. The reform repeated *katun* 4 Ahau on a new twenty-four-year basis (1752–1776) while retaining the Mayapan calendar yearbearers (see below). But Sunday was also the Christian yearbearer in 1752 (note 3501)!

the west was its rule, with sacrifice and destruction of lords:
bloody and Christian. There
was little food with the western
lineages, the branches of the
wild, the barbarian lineages.
They suppressed the tribute to
Chichen. (4654)

The katun was half-good,
half-bad, and came to be ruled
by Chicum Ek, Yax Lam, Yax
Ah, and Coc Ay the Crier, who
kept bad vigils because they
were sleepyheads, each and

T u cal tzicil
   T u hunal e
Chikin
   T an hom
U pop
   U tz'am
Ma ya cimil u cuch
   Ti tal i
Satai ba tabil i
   Much'lahom u hal ach uinicilob
cah i
Xe kik u cuch katun

   T u kin y anhom
A u ex
   Sac a nok i
Ix chamben uah
   U uah
Ulom kuk
   Ulom yaxum
T u kab
   Kax te
Ulom ah kayom mut
   Ulom ah tzimi tepoi*
Ulom ah tzimin
   Mucuc patan t u Chi Ch'en
Tan coch katun utz i
   Tan coch ix ma utz i
Lai bin tepalnac
   Ah Chicum Ek t u canil*
Yax lam*
   Yax Ah
Coc Ai Mut e*
   Ah Ahsa*
Ma ix mac ahom
   T u men mut e
Ch'en ch'en
   U xicin
Ti babal
   T u lacal
Te
   T u u ich

It has sought honor
   By itself.
The west
   Is half-gone:
4635 Its mat,
   Its throne.
Painless death is the burden
   That is coming,
Destroying the chieftainship,
4640   Choking off the governors of the
towns.
Blood vomit is the burden of the
katun
   Of the time there was.
(White) your pants,
   White your clothes.
4645 And reduced food
   The food.
Come is the quetzal,
   Come the blue bird
In the branches
4650   Of the wild tree.
Come is the news crier,
   Come is the official horseman,
Come is the rider
   To suppress the tribute at Chichen.
4655 Half the katun is good;
   And half is not good.
It will be ruled
   By the Seven Stars in heaven,
The Turtle,
4660   The Green Cane,
The firefly Announcer,
   The Wakener.
And there is no one awake
   For the vigil:
4665 Totally at rest
   Were the ears
Of each
   And every one.
There
4670   In the face

4652. I read tzimin tepal.

4658. There follows a series of references to stars, beginning with the Pleiades:
Chicum Ek (Nahuatl chicome 'seven').

4659. Yax lam: Barrera 1948: 106 reads yax ac lam 'new turtle sinking' and
identifies it with Ac Ek 'the turtle stars', a three-star constellation in Gemini.

4661. Yaxal coc ay mut 'announcer of the green turtle': another constellation.
Cocah Mut has been identified as Itzam Na (Tozzer 1941: 145–146).

4662. Ah Ahsa Cab 'waker of the land': Venus.

every one of them. Such were
the lords of 4 Ahau. (4672)

Sacrifices began to be possible, and 4 Ahau was started
over at the new year (in 1752).
As the sun priest Spokesman
said of 4 Ahau, it was the time
of Chichen Itza and its katun
cycle. This is its real history,
which is known in writing and
appears in the books of Ni Tun
Tz'ala, Chetumal, the division
of Uaymil, and Hol Tun of the
Itza, and it is also seen correctly in a report book which is
completely accurate. It gives
the time for ending each part of
the katun cycle, with a standing memorial to recount the
suffering that comes day by

Can Ahau katun ual e
  Uchc i
Ma ya cimlal ocnal
  Kuchil
Bai bin uch
  Pahbal
T u uutz'
  T u ca ten*
Ti cutal
  T u cuch habil
Bay y alc i
  Ah kin Chilam*
T u cuch katun
  Can Ahau ual e.
(16r) Can Ahau
  U kinil t u Chi Chen Ytza
Can Ahau
  U katunil xan
U kahlai
  U miatz
Natil
  Ychil u anahteil
Uai c u hoksabal
  Ti y unil
Ni Tun Tz'ala
  Chac Temal
Tah
  Uaimil
Hol Tun
  Ytza
Ti ci ci ilab i xan
  T u tohil than
T u y un i
  Reportorio*
Manan sipan i
  Ca utzac y oheltabel
Ca bin kuchuc
  T u kinil u cumtal
Hun hun tz'it katun
  U cuch katunob
Licil u natabal
  Uabal

Of the returned 4 Ahau
  There occurred
Painless death, coming
  And arriving.
4675 Thus will occur
  The possibility
That it fold
  A second time
At the seating
4680   In the burden of the year.
Thus it is said
  By the sun priest Spokesman
In the burden of the katun
  Of the return of 4 Ahau.
4685 4 Ahau
  Was the time at Chichen Itza.
4 Ahau
  Was also the katun period:
The account
4690   Of the wisdom
And knowledge
  In the manuscripts.
This is the explanation
  In the books
4695 Of Ni Tun Tz'ala,
  Chetumal,
The division of
  Uaymil,
Hol Tun,
4700   And Itza,
Which are also perfectly visible
  In true language.
One book,
  The Reportorio,
4705 Has no errors.
  Then knowledge can be perfected.
Then one can arrive
  At the time of seating
Every single part of the katun,
4710   The burdens of the katuns,
As well as the memorials
  Erected.

4678. I read this to mean that 4 Ahau was to be repeated, which is substantially what happened.
4682. And the authority of the Spokesman of the Jaguar is invoked along with
the stars and written sources to legitimize the calendar change.
4704. Reportorio is an unusual Hispanicism in these texts. It may be a direct
reference to the 5 Ahau Emal prophecy (chapter 22) that initiates the Tizimin
manuscript, a speculation encouraged by the similarity of the preceding place-
names (see lines 2949 ff.).

day, whenever they come, the
monkey and turtle katuns *and*
their departure. (4722)

U cuch num ya
   Tzolantac
Ti u talel ti kin
   Licil u binil tz'acab kin
C u talel e
   Ha li be oclis t u ba ob

U maxil katun
   Coc ix u katunilob
Oklem ix
   U u ichob.

The burdens of suffering
   Will be recounted
4715 That are coming at the time,
   As well as the future steps of days
That are coming.
   However they will be brought
   together:
The monkey *katuns,*
4720   The turtle *katuns,*
And the departure
   Of their faces.

38. End of the Long Count

And this was the lord of the
south, 3 Cauac 1 Pop in 1752 in
katun *4 Ahau. There was a*
twenty-year cycle and then four
more and Cauac returns. Then
Kan speaks, making five days,

(18r) He x Ahau culh i*
   T u cuch hab ti nohol
Oxil Cauac
   U hun te Pop
T u habil
   Hi *1552* culh i
Can Ahau katun
   T u hach kinil
Hun hun kal hab u cuch ob
   Hun hun tul ti ob
Tun cam ppel i e
   Ix ma kaba
Licil u baxal ho ppel hab i
   Y etel Cauac bac ix
Ti lic u cutal katun i e
   Kaan

And that was the lord who was seated
   And bore the year in the south.
4725 On the third Cauac
   On the first of Pop
In the year
   1552 it may have been seated.
4 Ahau was the *katun*
4730   At that very time.
Each twenty years were their burdens,
   Each and every one of them.
Then there were four of them
   And they were without names,
4735 As they played five years
   And Cauac was once again
The one who was seating the *katun,*
   Kan

4723. This is the earlier of the two texts in the Tizimin dealing with the Valladolid calendar. Written in 1752, it is a concise summary of the state of the Mayan calendar at that time. It acknowledges the supremacy of the Spanish *año* (albeit still without recognizing leap year), lists the *tzol kin* second, then the *hab,* and finally the *katun* of *tuns*—for sacrifice and divination. It leaves unstated the premise of the change, which was that in a year beginning 3 Cauac 1 Pop the name day of the *katun* fell on May 27, 1752, the second day of the year: 4 Ahau 2 Pop. Calculating correctly that extending the *katun* from twenty *tuns* to twenty-four *habs* would make this circumstance permanent, the priests decided to do so, even though it meant giving 4 Ahau a span of thirty-nine years. They continued to peg the Mayan new year to an arbitrary July 16 in the Christian calendar and to carry the leap year correction "in their heads."

and the year and the katun *come out even. The fifth year completes the* katun. *(4748)*

These are the counts of the katuns: *there are four of them.*

1. The year (año) *of birth of Jesus Christ, the best count.*

2. The ancient Mayan count (tzol kin) *is the second.*

3. The yearbearers (hab) *make the third.*

4. And the katun *of tuns for sacrifice and divination. (4772)*

The new system that is for future use is in twenty-day uinals, *twelve in all, for the moon and*

Licil y alic u kaba
  Y etel u than t u lacal
Lei ho ppel kin
  Ix ma kaba
Amal hab e
  Ba ix amal
T u hitz'il
  Katun ual e
Ho ppel hab u baxal
  U mol box katun*
He x tun u tzolan
  U u ich katunob la e
Can tzolob
  He u yax chun u tzolol e
Lai
  Y abil u sian
C ah loh i
  Ti *Jesu Xp̄to* e*
U hach tohil xoc
  Y okol t u lacal xocob
La ix lic u tzulabal u pach
  T u men u uchben Maya xok i
La cab ob
  He u ca tzol e
Lei ah cuch habob e
  T u can tukil
Can ob e
  He y ox tzol e
Lei katunob
  Licil u natabal
U lamay tun
  U yail haab
Licil y uchul ma ya ciml ob
  Pec otzil t u than ob
He uac ma ocsah ben ti ol
  Hel e
Lae
  Ba ba hunil i
Uchac u ch'abal i e
  Heklai sansamal kin xoc
Y an ichil uinal
  Hun kal kin e
Bi lah ca cancun e*
  U nah y ilabalob i e

As its name says
4740 And its whole word.
These five days
  Without names
Square the year,
  And so squaring
4745 At the end
  Of the *katun* again.
Five years it plays
  And collects the cask of the *katun*,
And that then is counted
4750 As the faces of the *katuns*.
These are the four counts
  That are the new base for counting,
Namely:
  (1) The year of birth
4755 Of our Savior
  Who is Jesus Christ,
The quite correct count
  Over all counts.
(2) And this is like the ordering before
4760 By the ancient Maya count.
This is their land;
  That is the second count.
(3) These are the yearbearers
  In the four corners
4765 Of the sky;
  That is the third count.
(4) There are the *katuns*,
  As a reminder
Of the *tuns* to be removed,
4770 Of the pains of the years,
Like the painless deaths
  And grinding poverty they told.
However it may be introduced,
  This change,
4775 That is,
  Insofar as
It is to be accepted
  For breaking off future day counts,
It is in *uinals*
4780 Of twenty days.
So twelve are to be kept
  To complete their appearance,

4748. *Mol box* 'full cask': possibly a new coinage for the completion of the new *katun*.

4756. This is the only occurrence of the name Jesus in the Tizimin.

4781. A curious assertion, otherwise unconfirmed. Keeping twelve *uinals* of twenty days each would certainly not serve as an agricultural calendar. In point of

(note continued on following page)

planting beans, lima beans,
chile, and gourdroot, and farm-
ing. That counts time like the
cycles in the codices. Anyone
who knows how can read it
right, since the lords are listed
by fours. After the sixteenth
year it is the nameless part.
Then the katun *is folded be-*
cause the tun *ends, and it*

Oheltabal y oc uiil	To inform us of the coming of the moon phases,
U kin col	The time of planting,
Y oc buul	4785 The coming of beans,
Y oc ib	The coming of lima beans,
Y oc ic	The coming of chile,
Y oc *chicam*	The coming of gourdroot,
He cen c u pakal ti colob e	Who is planting in their fields
He tun u uac tzol e	4790 And where the count is supervised.
Lai uabal ti uinalil	That is the position that the *uinal* count is in;
Y an ichil lubantac ti kinbesabal	And so measuring in the passing of time
He tun u chayan kuyahma	Where is the adding of the bending
Y etel nahma	And the completion
Tz'ibtabal	4795 Of the writing
Y ub e	In color.
Ua mac y an y ol	If someone has the wit
Y ohelte	He will know
Ma hun ppel tub a	Without forgetting one
Uchac u tz'ibtabal t lob i e	4800 The occurrence of the writing that is evil,
Ti lic u tz'abal ti can ban tul	Which is like being given four at a time
Ti ahauob cuchic hun tz'it katunob*	Who are the lords of one section of the *katuns*—
Ti ci alabal can kal habil	Which is just said "four rolls of years."
Ca tac (18v) uac lahum pis	Then when it is the sixteenth measure
Y etel ix ma kaba katun amal u uatal	4805 And it is the nameless *katun* that is brought together,
Ua ix ma tub u chacanpahal e	And if one doesn't forget what is being manifested,
Y an u man u uutz' katun	It will be the passing of the fold of the *katun*.
Ti ma u caxantal	Which will not be found
T u men t u tz'oc tun e*	Because the *tun* has ended.
Mol cab	4810 It is collected.

(note continued from preceding page)
fact all nineteen of the *uinals* were retained, at least into the nineteenth century,
but there was an increasing awareness of the twelve European months and the
church calendar of saints' days. The former would approximately mark the moon
phases, and either or both would serve for agricultural purposes.

4802. The author notes that the yearbearers are retained, pointing out that they
rotate by fours. It is not clear what he means by saying that they are "squared,"
that is, come out even, after sixteen years, since the new *katun* "rolls" for twenty
years plus an additional "nameless" four.

4809. Due notice is taken of the fact that the true *tun* (of 360 days) is no more.
There had been an increasing tendency during the colonial period to equate it
with the *hab* (of 365 days), but as long as it timed the naming of the *katuns* (i.e.,

(note continued on following page)

starts over. At the time of the
tun, fourth, third . . . (4816)

Bin ual   It is going to return,
  Hebal   Turning
Ca bin y anac   When it may be
  U tunil   The time of the *tun,*
Ua can tz'it   4815 Either four counts,
  Ua ox tz'it.*   Or three counts . . .

(note continued from preceding page)

until 1752) it was implicitly present. This same date therefore marks the definitive end of the Mayan Long Count, four years before 12.7.0.0.0.

    4816. The text breaks off without clarifying what assertion is being made about the *tun.* The repetition of *katun* 4 Ahau leaves its second incarnation unaccounted for historically. None of the *Books of Chilam Balam* mentions the 1761 rebellion of Jacinto Canek at Cisteil (Villa 1945: 171). One wonders whether Canek was involved in the calendrical debates.

2 Ahau

---

39. The Valladolid Calendar

This text expands and confirms the report of the preceding chapter of the institution of the twenty-four-year katun *in 1752 at Zaciapan (Valladolid), making it plain that this calendrical reform was intended to make the initial day of the* katun *always fall on the second day of the 365-day year—as it did in 1752. The passage lists the yearbearers for two of the new* katuns, *1752 to 1775 and 1776 to 1799, counting the years (rather than the* tuns) *by twenties and transmuting the old concept of five Uayeb days to four "nameless" years to make up the count of twenty-four and "fill the cask" of the* katun.

(19r) He x Ahau		And these are the lords
Bin tac te la e		Who are going to be approaching then.
Cauac		Cauac
U hun te Pop*	4820	On the first of Pop
Y ahal cab		Is the dawn,
T u ca te		And the second
U kinil		Of the days
Hab		Of the year
Cutal	4825	Is the seating
Can Ahau		Of 4 Ahau.
Oxil Cauac culh i e		Third Cauac is seated;
Can Ahau katun.		4 Ahau is the *katun*.
1752 oxil Cauac		1752 3 Cauac
1753 canil Kan	4830	1753 4 Kan
1754 ho Muluc		1754 5 Muluc
1755 uacil Hix		1755 6 Ix
1756 uucil Cauac		1756 7 Cauac
1757 uaxacil Kan		1757 8 Kan
1758 bolon Muluc	4835	1758 9 Muluc
1759 lahun Hix		1759 10 Ix
1760 buluc Ahau*		1760 11 Cauac
1761 lah cabil Kan		1761 12 Kan
1762 ox lahun Muluc		1762 13 Muluc
1763 hunil Hix	4840	1763 1 Ix

4820. The new calendar of Valladolid was designed to make that city the seat of a new cycle—a cycle composed of twenty-four *katuns* instead of thirteen, which, nonetheless, began the epoch with the *katun* 11 Ahau of the conquest. This was a daring and desperate ideological innovation, since the end of the Itza cycle (13 Ahau) was near. In *katun* 2 Ahau Saciapan (Maya *zaci* 'whiteness', Nahuatl *-apan* 'water place'), the modern Valladolid, seated the cycle under Hun y Op Oc Ik 'one macaw foot wind' and claimed equal rank with Mayapan as being Born of Heaven. Adopting the Nahuatlized place-name may have been part of the plan. The object, quite obviously, was to avoid the doom of 13 Ahau and double the life-span of the Itza, which would have extended to 2088.

4837. The manuscript has Ahau for Cauac.

1764 cabil Cauac	1764 2 Cauac
1765 oxil Kan	1765 3 Kan
1766 canil Muluc	1766 4 Muluc
1767 hoil Hix	1767 5 Ix
1768 uacil Cauac	4845 1768 6 Cauac
1769 uucil Kan	1769 7 Kan
1770 uaxac Muluc	1770 8 Muluc
1771 bolon Hix	1771 9 Ix
U tz'oc u cuch	Ends the burden
Can Ahau katun	4850 Of *katun* 4 Ahau
Ca tun culac	And then are seated
Cam ppel hab	Four years
Ix ma kaba	Without names
U hitz'il katun	To complete the *katun*:
(19v) Ca culac	4855 Then is to be seated
Cabil Ahau	2 Ahau,
U mol box	The full cask
Katun	Of the *katun*:
1772 lahun Cauac	1772 10 Cauac
1773 buluc Kan	4860 1773 11 Kan
1774 lah cab Muluc	1774 12 Muluc
1775 ox lahun Hix	1775 13 Ix
He x cabil Ahau	And this is 2 Ahau
C u cutal	Who is seated.
Hun Cauac	4865 1 Cauac
Y ahal cab	Is the dawn;
T u ca ppel	It is the second
U kinil	Of the days.
Hun te Pop	The first of Pop.
Lai u than	4870 This is the word
Y an ychil u cuch	That is in its burden
Y etel u bel	And the road
Y an ychil u cuch hab i la e	That is the burden of the year.
Saciapan	Valladolid
U hetz'	4875 Is the seat
Katun	Of the *katun*
Ti cabil Ahau	Which is 2 Ahau.
Sacl Ac Tun	Valladolid
Amay cu*	Is the seat of the cycle,
Mayapan	4880 And City of the Cycle,
Oclis t u ba katun	Establishing the *katun* for itself.
T u kin y an emom sum	At the time there is the descent of the rope,
Emom saban	The descent of venom,
Emom ya	The descent of pain,
Ma ya cimlal	4885 Painless death,
Ox mul tun tzekil	The three pyramids.

4879. *Amay cu*: I read *may cu* and consider the following line to be a Nahuatl paraphrase.

Despite its late date, the text remains divinatory and traditional, predicting the final assimilation of the Itza (lines 4921–4928):

> *The time of arrival*
> *Of their older brothers*
> *Thus is coming*
> *To the poor Itza.*
> *You will intermarry with them;*
> *You will wear their clothes;*
> *And you will put on their hats,*
> *And you will speak their language.*

La u cuch
  La u chaan
Katun
  Ti Ah cabil Ahau
Kaxan u cuch
  Buluc Ch'ab Tan
Ca sih i
  Hun y Opol Ik
Oxil uah
  U uah
Cupil uah
  U uah
Tan coch u cuch habil
  Utz
Y anil u uah
  Y anil y aal
Y etel u tepal
  U y ahaulil
Tan coch ix chac tun
  Num ya i
Y anil u tz'am
  U pop
Y an u tzic t u pop
  Ti y ahaulil cabob i
Ti y an u chek oc
  U y anal cabob i
Lai oheltabc i*
  U kinob
Sac uinicob
  Ah mexob
Bai chacanpah
  C in
Ah kin
  Chilam
U kin y ulel
  U sucunob
Bai y ulc i ti ob
  Ah num Ytzaob
Bin a balint ex ob
  Bin ix a bucint ex u buc ob
A ppocint ex u ppoc ob
  Bin ix a thanint ex u than ob
He uac he u ppolmal e
  Bateil ppolmal
T u kinil u toppol nicte*
  Un crus nicte

That is the burden,
  That is the appearance
Of the *katun*
4890 That is 2 Ahau.
Tied is the burden
  Of the 11 priest Ch'ab Tan.
Then is born
  Hun y Opoc Ik.
4895 Breadnut food
  Is his food.
Gourdroot food
  Is his food.
Half of the burden of the year
4900 Is good.
There is food;
  There is drink,
And the glory
  Of the lordship;
4905 And half is red stone
  And suffering.
There is his throne,
  His mat.
There is his Honor on the mat,
4910 In the lordship of the lands,
Which is the pacing off
  Of the existing lands.
This is so they will be informed
  Of the days
4915 Of the white people,
  The bearded people
As has been manifested
  By me,
The sun priest
4920 Spokesman.
The time of arrival
  Of their older brothers
Thus is coming
  To the poor Itza.
4925 You will intermarry with them;
  You will wear their clothes;
And you will put on their hats,
  And you will speak their language.
Nevertheless there will be trade:
4930 War trading
At the time of the sprouting flowers,
  Of the flowers of the cross;

4913. That is, the purpose of this document is to bring the Mayan and Christian calendars closer together and to instruct the Maya in the new system.

4931. The following lines define yet another Mayan-Christian syncretism as the ideology of the new *katun*.

Ma ix macma lub on i
   T u kin ix tz'ib ol nicteil
Ca bin u luc ob
   (Tzol ox) Ahau ual e*
U tan ca mol boxtic
   U katunil buluc Ahau*
Lei culic Ah cabil Ahau
   C u cutal ti hunil Caua la e.*
1776 hunil Cauac
1777 cabil Kan
1778 oxil Muluc
1779 canil Hiix
1780 hoil Cauac
1781 uacil Kan
1782 uucil Muluc
1783 uaxac Hix
1784 bolon Cauac
1785 lahun Kan
1786 buluc Muluc
1787 lah cabil Muluc*
1788 ox lahun Cauac
1789 hun Kan
1790 cabil Muluc
1791 oxil Hiix
1792 canil Cauac
1793 hoil Kan
1794 uacil Muluc
1795 uucil Hix
U tz'oc
   Tz'oc u cuch Ah cabil Ahau
C u cutal
   U hitz'il katun
Cam ppel hab
   Ix ma kaba
Ca culac
   Ox lahun Ahau.
1796 uaxac Cauac
1797 bolon Kan
1798 lahun Muluc
1799 buluc Hix

But no one of us will rest,
   And on the day of painted flowers,
4935 Then will be their lamentation
   Of the count of 3 Ahau again.
We shall have half filled the cask
   Of the *katun* cycle of 11 Ahau.
There is seated 2 Ahau:
4940   He is seated on first Cauac.
1776 1 Cauac
1777 2 Kan
1778 3 Muluc
1779 4 Ix
4945 1780 5 Cauac
1781 6 Kan
1782 7 Muluc
1783 8 Ix
1784 9 Cauac
4950 1785 10 Kan
1786 11 Muluc
1787 12 Ix
1788 13 Cauac
1789 1 Kan
4955 1790 2 Muluc
1791 3 Ix
1792 4 Cauac
1793 5 Kan
1794 6 Muluc
4960 1795 7 Ix
It ends,
   And ends the burden of 2 Ahau,
Seating
   The ending of the *katun*.
4965 The four years
   Without names,
Then is to be seated
   13 Ahau.
1796 8 Cauac
4970 1797 9 Kan
1798 10 Muluc
1799 11 Ix

4936. Text blurred; Roys reads *Cabil* where I get *Tzol ox*.

4938. Meaning 2 Ahau is the twelfth *katun* counting from 11 Ahau, hence marking the halfway point in the new cycle of twenty-four *katuns*.

4940. Another syncretism is suggested here: that of holding the *katun* ceremonies on the first day of the year, since the next day is the day name of the *katun*. See also note 1554, emphasizing that the "dawn" of a ceremony goes back to the sixteenth century.

4952. The manuscript has Muluc for Ix.

THE NINETEENTH CENTURY

13 Ahau

40. The Burners

This text begins with a table correlating the Mayan and Christian years on the premise that the first day of Pop will always be July 16 and that the most convenient starting point is a year 1 Kan, the first year of the fifty-two-year cycle.

(20v) U kaba kin*
Amal y ahal cab ich uinal.

The names of the days
Squared with the dawn in the *uinal*.

hunil Kan	16 *Julio*	Pop*	4975	1 Kan	16 July	Pop
ca Chicchan	5 *Agosto*	Uo*		2 Chicchan	5 Aug.	Uo
ox Cimi	25 *Agosto*	Sotz'*		3 Cimi	25 Aug.	Zip
can Manik	11 *Septiᵉ*	Cip		4 Manik	11 Sept.	Zotz'
ho Lamat	04 *Octubre*	Zec*		5 Lamat	4 Oct.	Tzec
uac Muluc	24 *Octubre*	Xul	4980	6 Muluc	24 Oct.	Xul
uucil Oc	13 *Nobiᵉ*	Tz'e Yaxkin*		7 Oc	13 Nov.	Tz'e Yax Kin
uaxac Chuen	03 *Deciᵉ*	Mol		8 Chuen	3 Dec.	Mol
bolon Eb	23 *Deciᵉ*	Chen		9 Eb	23 Dec.	Ch'en
lahun Ben	12 *Enero*	Yax		10 Ben	12 Jan.	Yax
buluc Hix	01 *Febrero*	Sac	4985	11 Ix	1 Feb.	Zac
lah ca Men	21 *Febrero*	Mac*		12 Men	21 Feb.	Ceh
ox lahun Cib	13 *Marso*	Queh		13 Cib	13 Mar.	Mac
hun Caban	02 *Abril*	Kankin		1 Caban	2 Apr.	Kan Kin
ca Etz'nab	22 *Abril*	Muan		2 Etz'nab	22 Apr.	Muan
oxil Cauac	12 *Mayo*	Kayab*	4990	3 Cauac	12 May	Pax
can Ahau	01 *Juño*	Paax		4 Ahau	1 June	Kayab
ho Imix	21 *Juño*	Cumku		5 Imix	21 June	Cumku

4973. This text, beginning with a handy calculation table for computing dates, has a number of features of interest. It consists of three columns, listing (1) the thirteen sacred numbers (*xoc*) and the day names (*kin*), (2) the initial days of the Mayan months in Christian dates for a year beginning on July 16, and (3) the names of the Mayan months (*uinals*)—with three errors in their order.

4975. Marginal note: *hun hun kal* 'each one twenty'.

4976. Marginal note: *u cuch hum pel u* 'the burden of one month'.

4977. The manuscript inverts Zip and Zotz'.

4979. The handling of zero in this passage is of interest. See also lines 5130 ff.

4981. Tz'e Yaxkin: 'Yaxkin is born'. See also note 3451. It is not clear why Yaxkin is the only *uinal* that is habitually "born." At this date it began in the latter part of August.

4986. The manuscript inverts Ceh and Mac.

4990. The manuscript inverts Pax and Kayab.

The passage moves on to a description of the Burner (Ah Toc) fire ceremonies, of their periodicity and directional associations (see the footnotes to chapter 24). The four Burners appear to be a replication of the pattern of quadripartite gods represented also by the year-bearers, the Fathers of the Land (Ba Cabob), the sun giants (Pauahtunob), the rain giants (Chacob), and others.

uacil Ik	00 U tich kin	—5—*	6 Ik 00 enough days —5—
uucil Akbal			7 Akbal

Hun kal kin   4995   Twenty days
   Y an ichil u cuch   Are in the burden
Y uil   Of the moon period,
   Uinal   The *uinal*.
Lai u kaba ob la e*   These are their names.
   U kahlai   5000   This is the account
Ah Tocob   Of the Burners
   Y an ich uinal   That are in the *uinal*:
Can tul   Four of them,
   T u ba ob   By themselves.
He can Chicchan e   5005   There is 4 Chicchan,
   Lahun Chicchan u ch'a kak   And 10 Chicchan who gets the fire,
Buluc Chicchan u tup kak   And 11 Chicchan who quenches the fire,

   Ah cuch uinal ti lakin   The bearer of the *uinal* in the east.
He ah canil Oc e   There is 4 Oc,
   Lahunil Oc u ch'a kak   5010   And 10 Oc who gets the fire,
Bulucil Oc u tupic u kak   And 11 Oc who quenches the fire,
   Ah cuch uinal ti xaman   The bearer of the *uinal* in the north.
He can Men e   There is 4 Men,
   Lahun Men u ch'a kak   And 10 Men who gets the fire,
Buluc Men u tupic u kak   5015   And 11 Men who quenches the fire,
   Ah cuch uinal ti chikin   The bearer of the *uinal* in the west.
He Ah canil Ahau e   There is 4 Ahau,
   Lahun Ahau u ch'a kak   And 10 Ahau who gets the fire,
Buluc Ahau u tupic u kak   And 11 Ahau who quenches the fire,
   Ah cuch uinal ti nohol   5020   The bearer of the *uinal* in the south.
He lai Ah Tocob la e   These then are the Burners.
   Ti culan ob t u chun uinal e   It is they who are seated at the base of the *uinal*.

He t u hopol u xoc Kan e   Those that begin on the count Kan,
   Ti bin a caxante Chicchan t u   You will find Chicchan on the
ca ppel u xoc e   second of the count.
Ca a caxante hi tub y an lei can   5025   When you find wherever 4 Chicchan is,
Chicchan e
   Bai bin a caxantic u chucanil   Thus you will find all of the
   Ah Tocob ichil uinalob   Burners in the *uinals*,
Ua ichil Pop   Whether they are in Pop
   Ua ichil Uoo   Or in Uo.
Ca ix ua tub ci tan   And then wherever is exactly half
   A u ilic amal hab   5030   You will see the squaring of the

---

4993. The manuscript avoids mentioning the month of Uayeb by name.

4999. Here is a detailed account of the Burners (Ah Tocob), who governed fire ceremonies centered on a day with the numeral prefix 4 but involving the announcement of the cycle forty days beforehand, a ceremonial fire twenty days before, and the extinguishing of the fire twenty days after each of the significant dates.

The final lines imply divination from the sign of the European zodiac in which the moon lies, and the emphasis in the whole passage is agricultural— when to plant, expected harvest, etc. The continuing use of glyphic writing in the katun that began with the nineteenth century (line 5055) is noteworthy.

Ma t ech
  U (2lr) mahal
Cux olal hach kabeet
  U bilal ti ah colob*
Ca y oltah ob u ti al ca utzac
  U ci ci hokol u nal ob uchebal

U ci ci y antal u nalil
  Bin a u ila ti an ua tub u tich kin e
Ua tumbul hokol
  Ua ti an ti lakin ca bin ocsahnac ech e
Bin ban ban hatz'abac

  T u menel ch'ich'
Y etel i xan c au u ila
  Ua ti an u
T u *signo*
  Tauro
Cancro
  Virgo
Libra
  Capricornio
T u lacal lai *signos* la e
  Ma lob u ti al ocsah
Bin ci ci patac hi bal
  Bin a tz'ab ichil col e
Ti bin a u ila ichil u uohil
  Sansamal kin xoc
Y oc ti cin muc e
  Bai bin a u ilic
C ech
  Ah col e.

And never
  Will you stop.
Good judgment is very necessary
  To helping those who are planters.
5035 When they desire for it to be good,
  Politely requesting the filling in of the corn ears,
The ears will come out sweet.
  You will see they are whenever there are enough days.
Either the request is fulfilled
5040 Or it is to the east that you must sow.
It will be piles and piles to be bundled up
  Because of the birds.
And also you will see
  Whether there was a moon
5045 In the signs
  Taurus,
Cancer,
  Virgo,
Libra,
5050 Or Capricorn.
All of these signs
  Are not bad for sowing.
It will be pleasant to use something
  That you will plant in the field.
5055 That you will see in the glyph writing
  Of future day counts.
Go into what is hidden:
  Thus you will see,
You
5060 Planters.

5034. Here we change the subject to consider divination for agriculture, including the use of prayer, the moon, and the signs of the European zodiac. Most of the signs fall in the summer: Taurus (April 20 to May 20), Cancer (June 22 to July 22), Virgo (August 23 to September 22), Libra (September 23 to October 23), and Capricorn (December 22 to January 19).

41. The Word of Itzam Na

Katun *13 Ahau was seated the day before, on new year's day, 12 Cauac. Kin Chil of Coba seated* katun *13 Ahau. Maya-pan was the seat of the cycle. His prophecy was the word of Itzam Na: fighting and famine, five years of famine and locusts. And in the tenth year (?) he enumerated the solar years as follows. (5086)*

(19v) C u cutal ox lahun Ahau katun*
    Ti lah bil Cauac
Kin Chil
    Coba
U hetz' katun
    Ti ox lahun Ahau
May cu
    Mayapan*
Lai bin thanbal
    U than
Y an u chi
    Y alic u than Itzam Naa*
Chac sabin u u ich*
    Chac mitan uiih u cuch
Cupil uah u uah
    Oxil uah u uah
Ho ppel hab
    Em i*
Cup
    Ox te hab
Sakil y an u uah
    Sak y an ix y aal xan
Lahun tz'acab
    U (20r) . . .*
. . . xoc u buk
    Habob lai la*

Then is seated the *katun* 13 Ahau

    On 12 Cauac.
Kin Chil
    Of Coba
5065 Seated the *katun,*
    Which was 13 Ahau.
The cycle seat
    Was Mayapan.
There will be spoken
5070   His word.
There is the mouth
    To speak the word of Itzam Na.
Red weasel is his face;
    The red hunger plague is his burden.
5075 Gourdroot food is his food.
    Breadnut food is his food.
Five years
    There descend
Gourdroot
5080   And breadnut years.
Locusts will be his food,
    And locusts will be his water as well.
Ten steps
    His (?) . . .
5085 . . . enumerated the years,
    The solar years as follows.

5061. All sources agree that Kin Chil 'sun sailfish' of Coba 'chachalaca water' seated *katun* 13 Ahau. There is probably a relation with the previous *katun* of the same name, seated at Bach Can 'chachalaca snake'. The fact that this *katun* ends the old Itza cycle gives all the prophecies an apocalyptic tone. That of the Chumayel is Christian; that of the Mani is traditionalist. The Tizimin is somewhere in between.

5068. Documenting the fact that Mayapan was considered by some to be the seat of the cycle from 987 to 1824. See, however, line 4880, where Valladolid appears to be called Mayapan.

5072. Itzam Na 'alligator house' still lives!

5073. Chac Sabin 'red weasel': a personal name?

5078. Perhaps 1800 to 1805.

5084. Several words are missing.

5086. The following list gives the traditional yearbearers with their directional associations for fifty-two years from 1758 through 1809. The list is disjunctive with the dating of the yearbearers in the rest of the Tizimin, according to which the year 1 Kan would have been 1737, not 1758. This could have something to do with the new calendar, but I don't see it. In the nineteenth-century notes to the 3 Ahau calendar (lines 3049 ff.), a further change in yearbearers occurs. See also

(note continued on following page)

1758 hunil Kan ti likin		1758 1 Kan in the east
1759 ca Muluc		1759 2 Muluc
1760 oxil Hix		1760 3 Ix
1761 canil Cauac	5090	1761 4 Cauac
1762 hoil Kan		1762 5 Kan
1763 uac Muluc		1763 6 Muluc
1764 uucil Hix		1764 7 Ix
1765 uaxacil Cauac		1765 8 Cauac
1766 bolon Kan	5095	1766 9 Kan
1767 lahun Muluc		1767 10 Muluc
1768 buluc Hix		1768 11 Ix
1769 lah cabil Cauac		1769 12 Cauac
1770 ox lahun Kan		1770 13 Kan
1771 hun Muluc ti xaman	5100	1771 1 Muluc in the north
1772 cabil Hix		1772 2 Ix
1773 oxil Cauac		1773 3 Cauac
1774 canil Kan		1774 4 Kan
1775 ho Muluc		1775 5 Muluc
1776 uacil Hix	5105	1776 6 Ix
1777 uucil Cauac		1777 7 Cauac
1778 uaxacil Kan		1778 8 Kan
1779 bolon Muluc		1779 9 Muluc
1780 lahun Hix		1780 10 Ix
1781 bulucil Cauac	5110	1781 11 Cauac
1782 lah cabil Kan		1782 12 Kan
1783 ox lahun Muluc		1783 13 Muluc
1784 hunil Hix chikin		1784 1 Ix west
1785 cabil Cauac		1785 2 Cauac
1786 oxil Kan	5115	1786 3 Kan
1787 canil Muluc		1787 4 Muluc
1788 hoil Hix		1788 5 Ix
1789 uacil Cauac		1789 6 Cauac
1790 uucil Kan		1790 7 Kan
1791 uaxacil Muluc	5120	1791 8 Muluc
1792 bolon Hix		1792 9 Ix
1793 lahun Cauac		1793 10 Cauac
1794 bulucil Kan		1794 11 Kan
1795 lah cabil Muluc		1795 12 Muluc
1796 ox lahun Hix	5125	1796 13 Ix
1797 hunil Cauac ti nohol		1797 1 Cauac in the south
1798 cabil Kan		1798 2 Kan
1799 oxil Muluc		1799 3 Muluc
1800 canil Hix		1800 4 Ix
18001 hoil Cauac	5130	1801 5 Cauac

(note continued from preceding page)

note 3060. It is relevant to remark that the Mayan cycles are now synthesized, but there is still competition between Christian (weekday), *katun* (twenty-four-year), and *kin tun y abil* (fifty-two-year) divination.

These are the years in order.
After that the count ends on
13 Cauac and starts again
with 1 Kan as listed. One sec-
tion of the katuns *has been*
given with its four divisions. It
is a true count. (5154)

18002 uacil Kan
18003 uucil Muluc
18004 uaxacil Hix
18005 bolon Cauac
18006 lahun Kan
18007 bulucil Muluc
18008 lah cabil Hix
18009 ox lahun Cauac
Lai u xocan u bukubil
   Habob t in u alah e
Hun hun ppel hab u cuch
   Lai tzolantac ob la e
La t u pak
   U tz'ocol u xoc
Lai
   Ox lahun Cauac la e
Ca tun hoppoc u xocic
   Hunil Kan t u ca ten
Lai lic u sut e
   Bai tz'aanil canal lo
Hun tz'it katun u y alabal
   T u cam pelil
Lei
   Hah la e.

1802 6 Kan
1803 7 Muluc
1804 8 Ix
1805 9 Cauac
5135 1806 10 Kan
1807 11 Muluc
1808 12 Ix
1809 13 Cauac
This has enumerated the year periods.
5140   The solar years I have recited.
Each year is borne.
   This sets them in order.
When these are used up
   The count ends.
5145 That is
   13 Cauac then.
So then one must begin to count
   1 Kan a second time.
That is how it returns,
5150   As has been given above.
One part of the *katuns* is reported
   In their four divisions.
This then
   Is true.

11 Ahau

42. Antonio Martínez

This is the history of God by the priests and prophets Xopan Nahuatl, Puc Tun, Ahau Pech, and Kauil Ch'el—the true word and mystery. (5170)

The Spokesman of the Jaguar went into a trance before his house. He lay unseeing and

(7r) Lay u kahlai uchc i*
  Y emel
Hunab ku
  Ox lahun ti ku
Hum pic ti ku*
  T u than ob ah kinob
Profetaob
  Chilam Balam
Y etel Ah *Xupan*
  Na Puc Tun
Ah kin N Ahau Pech
  Ah Kauil Ch'el ca tzol i
U than almah xicin ti ob
  Tz'ab u ppisan than ti ob
He uac ma u natah ob i
  Lai than alab ti ob la e

He bin Chilam Balam e

  Chil cabal
Bin ichil u (7v) uay
  Ichil y otoch
Ma ix bin tan u likil
  Ma ix bin tan u y ilabal u u ich

5155 This is the account of the occurrence
  Of the descent
Of the Sole God,
  The 13 Gods,
The 400 Gods,
5160 In the words of the sun priests
And prophets,
  The Spokesmen of the Jaguar:
Xopan Nahuatl
  And Puc Tun,
5165 The sun priests Ahau Pech
  And Kauil Ch'el when they counted it,
The word entrusted to their ears,
  The measured word given to them
That perhaps they did not understand.
5170 These are the words entrusted to them then.
That will be the Spokesman of the Jaguar
  Stretched out on the ground
Going into his place,
  Into the house.
5175 And he will not be getting up
  And his eyes will not be seeing,

5155. Both the dating and the interpretation of this text present problems. It is one of the earlier texts in the Mani, Chumayel, and Tizimin manuscripts and hence must antedate 1837, when Juan Pío Pérez copied the Mani. The references to the French would appear to place it after the Napoleonic invasion of Spain, and the reference to the King of Havana as an enemy implies a date after the Revolution of Independence in 1821. The text itself claims to come at the end of fourteen *katuns* of Spanish rule, which would bring us to 1848. I believe therefore that it was written early in *katun* 11 Ahau (1824–1848) and that our extant copies of the Mani, Chumayel, and Tizimin were written slightly later but in any case fall between 1824 and 1837.

5159. I read *hun pic* 'four hundred'. In later colonial times it meant 'one thousand', but the intent is a very large number rather than a specific count.

someone spoke to him from
above, being lodged on top of
his house. And he spoke to the
assembled priests and preached
anonymously. The Fathers of
the Land spoke and people
arose to hear the Spokesman in
the first year of 11 Ahau at the
third moon (November–De-
cember 1824). And he attacked
the Itza and the Xiu with the
prophecy of their destruction
and of the obliteration of their
faces. (5216)

They may return in 1834
quoting him, but that is the

Ua ba hun u cah
  Max c u than
Y okol u nail
  Y otoch
T u men te
  Bin c u hecel
Y okol u nail
  Y otoch
Ca tun bin hoppoc
  U y alabal than la e
Ti tum bin hu mol ah kinob

  Y icnal Chilam
Ca hopp u y alabal than
  C u talel ti ob la e
Ma y oheltah ob
  Mac al ti ob i
Ca y alah ob e
  Noh can yum
Ci bin u thanob
  Ca bin noclah ob ti lum

U y ub ob
  Than la e
Profeta
  Chilam
Ohelte ti culh i
  T u hum pis katun
Ti culh i
  Nicte katun
Oc te uu culam
  Yum a
U netzil kuk
  Yaxum
Ti ual y anom u u ich

  Ti ual y anom bolon te uitz

U netzil uil kuk
  Yaxum
Ma mac bin natic ob
  Ch'ab t u kin
T u tan ob
  Ti y ahaulil c u talel e
Ma uil mac bin natic ob
  Ti ulac u talel ob e
T u lah ca pis katun
  Y alah u kaba
Lai
  Uil e

Inasmuch as there began
  Someone speaking
Over his dwelling,
5180 His house.
Because there
  He must have been supported
On his dwelling,
  His house.
5185 So then was to begin
  The speaking of this word.
There will then be a crowd of sun
priests
  Together with the Spokesman.
Then begins the saying of this word
5190 That had come to them there.
They were not informed
  Who was speaking to them.
Then spoke
  The four Great Fathers.
5195 They are just going to speak.
  Then they are going to rise from the
  land
And listen
  To the words
Of this prophet
5200 Spokesman.
Let it be made known that he is seated
  On the first measure of the *katun*,
He is seated on
  The Flower *katun*,
5205 The third moon having set.
  This father
Is the abasing of the quetzal
  And blue bird,
Which is the return of his previous
face,
5210 Which is the return of the previous
  ninth hill,
The abasing of the sight of the quetzal
  And blue bird.
No one will remember them
  Taken on the day
5215 Before their faces
  In the lordship that is coming.
No one will remember them
  That their coming is to return
On the tenth measure of the *katun*
5220 To speak his name.
That then
  Is the moon:

*end of the Jaguar priesthood.
Like mad dogs, they are sacrificing and celebrating. That is
not his message: it is false and
insane. He has not stolen the
peasants' land. The thieves will
be removed together with their
heirs. (5240)*

*So now all of you are to hold
the* katun *ceremonies, because
if it is not done properly you
will be exiled like wild animals. If you don't do it you will
suffer famine and pestilence
and eclipse at the shrine of the
cycle in the City of the Cycle,*

Balam u pol
  Uaan u co
Tzui tzui uinicil
  Ppec unicil*
Man ch'acat hulte t u uinicil

  T u pucsikal
Ci ix u y ukul
  Ci ix u hanal
Ma la t u than i
  Ma la bin y ub i
Bin ix u tus
  Coil than
Ma tub u tz'aic u ba
  Ix cuch lum itz'nil

Bi lukebal uai ti peten

  Bin baac ob ah cuch lum
ytz'inob
Ti y alancil
  Ix mehen lok
Bayen ob i ti samal cabeh e
  Ch'a ex a ba ex
C ex u itz'in
  Sucun ex e
Mans ex u cuch katun
  Lic u talel e
Ua ma tan a manes ex e
  Ti u bohhol
T a u oc ex e
  T ex ix bin u helinte ceeh e

Ua ma a mansic ex e
  T ex ix bin kuxic u motz che
U chun che
  Y etel u le xiu
Ua ma a mansic ex e
  Bai cim cehil uchebal u hokol

Uai ti cab
  Ca bin tac u kinil uchmal

Uai t u chumuc tzucub te
  May cu
Mayapan
  Siyah Caan u kaba

A jaguar head.
  Raised is the madness
5225 Of the canine people,
  The dog people,
Coming across that they might pierce people
  And hearts,
And just drinking
5230   And just eating.
That is not what he said;
  That is not what will be heard,
But there will be their lies
  And insane talk.
5235 Nowhere did he give himself up
  Or bear the land of the younger brothers.
They are to be removed here from the country
  The bearers of the land of the younger brothers will be absorbed,
Their offspring
5240   And adolescent sons
So be it: on the day after tomorrow
  You will take yourselves,
O younger
  And older brothers,
5245 And pass the burden of the *katun*
  As it should have come,
For if you do not pass it
  By the listing,
You shall leave,
5250   And shall also be transformed into deer then.
If you should not pass it,
  You will also gnaw the roots of trees,
The trunks of trees,
  And the leaves of grass.
5255 If you should not pass it,
  The occurrence of deer death will arrive
Here on earth.
  The hiding of the sun will then be brought about
Here amid the bunched trees
5260   Of the seat of the cycle,
Mayapan,
  Born of Heaven by name.

5226. The Maya are generally not fond of dogs, identifying them with an excessive appetite for food and sex.

*the Heaven Born. In this katun
there will return the beginning
of the animal sacrifices of 13
Ahau, a rather poor time. (5274)
    Then in 11 Ahau there will be
the thirteen followers of the
buggers, and the three-part Bull
will reach the judge, ordering
the return and distribution of*

Ti u hokol u y anal caan

  U y anal katun i
Bin manac u sut ichil a cahal ex

  Ti ma u cuchil e
Bin uchuc ocnal
  Kuchil
U kin ma ya cimlal bal cheob*

  Ca bin culac t u pop
Hun Sip u than
  Hun Sip u caan u Sip katun*

Ox tzuc u uah
  Oxil uah
Nicte katun kuch i*
  U kin u cutal
Ox lahun
  Y ti u pop
Ah calam chuuch
  Ah cal pach
Te ix u tal *bula* u ca ten tac*

  Ox pp*
Tii u manel *bula*
  Lai ca uli ix *ues*
Ualac xolte (8r) takin
  Ualac sac cib
Bin u uahite
  He x cib e

Which is the arrival of the existing
heaven,
  The existing *katun* then.
5265 It is going to pass its return in your
towns.
  It is not its burden then.
Then is to occur the coming
  And arrival
Of the day of painless death of
animals.
5270 Then he is to be seated on his mat.
One Zip the word,
  One Zip the teaching of the deer
  katun.
Breadnut his food,
  Breadnut food.
5275 The Flower *katun* arrives then,
  The day of his seating.
Thirteen
  Are the children of the mat,
Of the hole suckers,
5280 Of the asshole sinners.
There also arrives the Bull for the
second time.
  And in three parts.
That was the purchase of the Bull,
  Which then comes to the judge
5285 To return the sums of money,
  To return the wax candles.
It is to be distributed
  Together with those candles

5269. Animal rather than human sacrifice, presumably a concession to Christianity, reestablishing authority, as the next line states.

5272. Zip, the third month of the solar year, is identified by Roys with the deer god. This is the only thing in the passage resembling a date, but it doesn't quite make it. It does establish that 13 Ahau may have been the deer *katun*. See also note 1806.

5275. The Flower *katun* arrived on 11 Ahau 7 Uo, August 26, 1539; thirteen days later would have been 1 Zip (falling on 12 Ix). The end of the classical (Tikal) *katun* would have fallen four *uinals* after 11 Ahau on 11.16.0.0.0 13 Ahau 7 Xul, November 4, 1539 (Julian). In 1824 the Mayan new year fell on 10 Cauac 1 Pop, September 18, and 11 Ahau was the following day.

5281. There are two papal bulls that could be referred to here: Pius VII's *Vix nova a nobis* (1809) and Pius VIII's *Litteris alto* (1830). Both deal with mixed marriages (Fremantle 1956: 121, 124). It seems more likely, however, that the "Bull" was the announcement of the suspension of tribute by the Cortes of Cadiz in 1812. This important bit of news was finally and reluctantly released in Yucatan but was almost immediately revoked. Republican Mexico suspended Indian tribute definitively in 1821.

5282. I read *ox ppel*.

5284. I read *juez* for *ues*.

tribute and the establishment of Christianity. For justice now is blind. And they will preach about the world. 11 Ahau will end in pain and who knows what prophet! And it will end the yearbearer doctrine that has spread everywhere as the message of 11 Ahau. You will be decapitated for heresy by the Archbishop when he comes. You will flee to the forest and follow after Christ the merciful. And he will depart and his sacrifices will be designated and

Ti em *justisia* likul canal

   Nacebal *christianoil* ual e*

Uenel u u ic *justisia*
   Ti u natic cochom
Ca bin ticin
   Pecnac
Caan
   Y etel luum
Hach ya ix
   Bin tz'ocebal nicte katun e
Ma u uil
   Mac bin kuchuc t u than i
Ca bin chin chin polcinabac
   U tel chacil che
Ti tun u y uk ba peten
   T u lacal conolbil
Ua bin tz'ocbal
   U than nicte katun e
Ma uil bal u bel
   A tz'aic a pol ex ti *arsobispo* e*

Ca bim emec e
   Bin ix uil xic es
A bal a ba ex ti kax e
   Ua bin a tz'a ba ex i e

Bin ex
   Xic ex
T u pach hahal ku tal i
   Ti *Xp̄to*
Bin u kabat e
   Ti y anom cochom e
Ti tun ca bin tz'ococ
   U thibah a u ichil ex
Talel bin u cib
   U lil nicte*
Lai atan
   Bin u kabate*

To the descending justices raising on high
5290   The elevation of this Christianity again.
Sleeping is the eye of the justice
   Who understands it clearly.
Then will be spread
   The awareness
5295 Of heaven
   And earth.
Great pain too
   Will be the end of the Flower *katun*.
One can't see
5300   Who will arrive and speak.
Then will be loaded up to be carved out
   The fake rain tree
Which has spread itself to the country,
   To all the markets,
5305 As though it will be the ending
   Of the word of the Flower *katun*.
If you don't follow the road
   You'll give your heads to the Archbishop
Who may be coming down,
5310   And if you are to come,
You will route yourselves to the forest.
   If you are going to be taken there then,
You go
   And come
5315 Behind the True God who has come,
   Who is called Christ,
Who may be called upon
   To be merciful,
And then will have to finish
5320   His appearance within you.
There will be coming his candles,
   His shaken Flowers.
That is the payment
   Which may be designated

5290. There is a recurrent prophecy in these texts that the tribute paid to the Spanish was an indemnity for the wars of the conquest, to be paid off in a definite term, after which no further tribute would be required and what had been collected would be repaid. The Spaniards do not appear to have been aware of this expectation.

5308. "False prophets" are abundant in this history, and executions for heresy began in the early years of missionization. They are obliquely referred to as the hangings. Decapitation is not elsewhere mentioned.

5322. I read *u lol nicte*.

5324. Sacrifices other than human.

you will be converted. 13 Ahau
will end in suffering, for he will
prophesy and you will come to
God. For the sage who under-
stands the aim of true Chris-
tianity will rule 280 years
before the darkness. (5340)

Then will come the nobles
Don Antonio Martínez and
Saúl by name, who went to
heaven and to Tizimin, killed a
captain, and married a queen.
Seven times that year they di-
vided out the marriage license
fees and saved them, raising a
fleet of thirteen-sail ships

Ti x a natic ex
  Ca bin ticin pecnac can e

Hach ya bin tz'ocebal
  Nicte uinicil
Ti to ca bin thanac
  U tz'ib t u nak pak e
Ti x a u alc ex kuil xan
  Lei bin a u ocsic ex t a u ol kuil
Hi uil mac ah miatz
  Y an a u ichil ex
Bin natic
  T an hitz'il
U tamlil *xp̃tianoil*
  Bin natice halilil o
Lahu cam ppel katun c u ba tabil
  Ca tun batabac och e*
Ca bin uluc
  Al mehenil e
Dn Antonio Maltines
  Y (etel) *Xaul**
Lai
  U kaba
Ca luki
  Ti caan
Ti x bin i
  Tzimentan e*
Ti x y ilah hun tul ix ahau
  Ca ix cimi hun tul nacom
Ca ix y alah ix ahau
  Y ichamte
Uuc te
  Ti hab
U kamic (u *ca* e)*
  Ca heb i
U hol nail takin
  Ti can kas na
Etsab i
  Ti
Ca t u liksah u chem
  Ox lahun bak

5325 And when you understand
  Then will be spread the awareness
    of heaven.
Great pain will be the ending
  Of the Flower people,
For soon he will speak
5330   His writing near the wall
Where you also call upon the deity;
  That will bring the deity into you.
Should there be someone
  Who is a sage among you,
5335 Then he will understand
  That was the end,
The profundity, of Christianity.
  He will understand this truth.
For fourteen *katuns* he will rule:
5340   And then will rule the shadows.
Then will be the arrival
  Of the nobility:
Don Antonio Martínez
  Y Saúl.
5345 These
  Are their names:
Who ascended
  Into heaven
And who went
5350   To Tizimin.
And who saw a queen
  And then killed a captain;
And the queen said
  To her husband,
5355 "Seven rounds
  In the year
He gets married
  Then we divide up
The house door money
5360   Of the four-room house.
And it is placed
  In them."
Then his fleet is raised:
  It is of thirteen sails.

5340. Fourteen *katuns* from the end of 13 Ahau (1539) brings us to the end of the Spanish Empire: 11 Ahau (1824).

5344. Antonio Martínez y Saúl is unknown to history, but his story is remarkably parallel to that of Santiago Iman, who was imprisoned in Tizimin in 1838 (Reed 1964).

5350. *Ti tzimin* 'at the tapir/horse' is Nahuatlized as *Tzimentlan*.

5357. Roys reads *casamentoil* for *ca*. I believe he is right. The Chumayel text makes it clear that the "house with four rooms" was the marriage registry office.

against Havana, which was apostate. And God heard about the secret buggers inevitably, and that's what happened in Tizimin. And he was judged, and three days later jailed. (5384)

"But I shall save you, and you captains will follow me in travail and see the guns and the burning sea, and I shall take power. And when the firing stops, dust and foam will cover the sea and the face of the sun. And the captains will prepare, and a hurricane will drop rocks and earth, clanging like thir- teen-sail ships. And the cap-

Ca t u liksah katun
    Hauana u lumil*
Ti x y an u nup
    U than ahau *Hauana*
Ca ix tun alab u xicin ahau

    T u men u nup u than e
Ti y an u y ah tacil
    U hol t u pach
Ca bin i
    Y ubah ix u chucul xan i
Ti likul i
    Ca bin i
Te
    Tzimentan e
Ti chuc i
    Ti u xotah u than xan
Ti y ah chucil i
    Oxeh kin kuchl i
Lic tun u kuchul e
    Lic u kalal ti mascab
Tan muk tun in talel*
    T en bin luksic ech ti mascab
T ex c ex nacom e
    Ca tulil i
Bin tac t in pach i
    Nacsabac bolon ti ya
C u ilah tz'on e
    Bin ix elec kaknab
Bin in likebal
    Ti culan
Kak u tz'ocol i
    Bin likic
Sus
    Y etel yom ha
Bin ix tupuc u u ich kin
    T u men chac bul ikil e

Ti tun u
    U cenic u ba nacom i
Bin hu . . . lacal tunichob*
    Y etel luum t u men yk

C u cumta
    (8v) Lic u tal ox lahun bak chem

5365 When the *katun* is raised
        Havana is its country,
    For there is also opposition
        To the word of the lord in Havana.
    And so it was borne to the ears of the lord
5370   Because of the opposition to his word:
    Which was the secret
        Back holes.
    For it was going then
        To be heard, and that's that then;
5375 Which is what came up
        And went on
    There
        In Tizimin.
    It was finished
5380   And his word was also judged.
    The ghost was completed.
        Three days arrived,
    And since he had arrived
        He was clapped in irons.
5385 "Meanwhile then I am coming.
        I shall remove you from irons.
    You who are captains
        Are returning,
    And will shelter behind me
5390   To be returned great in pain,
    And see the guns.
        And the sea will also burn,
    And I shall be raised
        And seated.
5395 The firing will stop
        And will raise
    Dust
        And foam on the water
    And will cover the face of the sun
5400   Because of the strong filling of the winds.
    When there is a moon,
        The captains will dress themselves,
    And all the stones . . .
        And earth will be dropped by the wind,
5405 And be made to clang
        Like the coming of thirteen-sail ships.

5366. Havana was the habitual place of exile for deposed Yucatecan politicians in this period.
5385. I read *ta muk*.
5403. Some letters are missing.

tains will lead your fathers to kill the French." So says this man. (5412)

"Why fight for your fellow man? Because you will be told to. Press on after the lead ship with good wind and sail. For the sea will burn, and I will raise one sun and then another to destroy ships. Don't you believe me? I am your preparer. You will be twice born or my name isn't Martínez. (5434)

"For there are the seven priestly books compiled in three by Xopan Nahuatl, Kauil Ch'el, and Puc Tun, who also knew the seven books and his-

Ti u cenic u ba nacom i
  Ch'a a ba yumil ex e
Te u talel *Flanses* e
  Bin ix ciman t u men e   5410
Ci u than
  Uinic e
Bax u bil u lubul a muk

  T u men a u et uinicil e
Ca ix alabacte   5415
  C ex i to e
Xicen
  T in tz'al u hool chem chumuc

Uet lic ci
  Ix u ikal e   5420
El ix kaknab
  In binc i
Nocoi hi ix u u ich caan
  He tun ca emen e

Tak licil i
  U u ich ca sat chem e*   5425
Max a uinicil c u than t en
  Ix ma ok olal e
T en i
  Ah ch'aal t ex t en i   5430
Bin a ca put sihes e
  Ca ix y alah xan
Bin ix in tum t in kaba
  Lai *Maltines* in kaba
Ca ix t u hoksah uuc tz'acab *libro**   5435
  U xocob ah kinob
Ti ox ppel u mansic u ba ah kinob

  Ah *Xupan*
Y etel ah kin Ch'en
  Na Puc Tun   5440
Ti x ohelan uuc tz'acab *libro*
  Ti tem te

When the captains dress themselves,
  Your fathers will be taken.
There will come the French
  And will be killed by them."   5410
So says
  This man's word.
"What's the use of wielding your strength
  Because of your fellow man?
For also it is to be told   5415
  To you there as follows.
Go on:
  I have pressed the head ship in the middle.
The sail is raised,
  And the wind,   5420
And the sea burned.
  I am just going to raise
Also perhaps the eye of heaven,
  And then when it shall descend there,
Create another—   5425
  An eye to destroy ships.
Which of your people speaks to me
  And does not believe me?
Your preparer
  Am I.   5430
You will be twice born
  And mothered as well,
And I shall try in my name,
  My name which is Martínez.
For seven steps of books have appeared,   5435
  The accounts of the sun priests.
In three it was compiled by the sun priest
  Xopan Nahuatl,
And the sun priests Kauil Ch'el
  And Puc Tun,   5440
Who also knew the seven-step book
  In these steps,

5426. No such naval engagement is recorded.

5435. The *uuc tz'acab libro* 'seven-step book' may well have been a glyphic manuscript, possibly in seven chapters or folds. Here, Xopan Nahuatl and Puc Tun join Kauil Ch'el in preparing a new three-chapter version in the tradition of Ahau Pech and the Spokesmen of the Jaguar, probably sometime in 5 Ahau. The story of Antonio Martínez would be inserted at a substantially later date when the manuscript was recopied in the 1820s. Despite the prophetic preoccupation of the Mayan sun priests, their frequent citation of written precedents is a significant step toward modern history.

tories like those of Ahau Pech,
and the date of the katun.
(5448)

"That's not all. The mer-
chants have agreed to give me
their towns. Half of each town
is altogether mine, that you
must pay for. Do that for justice
and Christianity. So good
Christians will come secretly to
the holy city in the wilderness
in the designated place without
further notice at the beginning
of 9 Ahau. (5476)

"That will complete my
prophecy of the end of tribute
and suffering in the final katun

Heklai
    Potz'
Licil u payal chi ah kin
    Pech
Ti x tun
    T u katunil uchmal
Talom*
    Ma hauom in than
He ix u mansic u ba ob
    Ah belnalob e
Ti tun y alah
    U tz'a u cahal t en
Tan coch
    Tub y an a cahal
In cahal t u lacal
    C u than
Ti t a botic in cahal c en

    Xaul e
Lic u alic t ech
    Ti emi *justisia*
Uchebal u nacal x͞ptianoil

    Y etel bolon pixan
Lai bin ocebal nicte uinicil

    Ti u katabal than ti ob
Ti y ahaulilob cah
    Ua ma mac y ohel e ti u hokol
Ich lumil che
    Ich lumil tunich i
T u u y etz'tal
    Cah i*
Manan Ch'amac
    Bin chibalnac i
Lai t u kuchul
    T u bolon Ahau katun ual e*
Lai u binel tulah
    Pach in than
Ti kuchi t u kinil
    Bin ix emec patan
T u hitz' num ya
    Y etel t u hitz' chuchul chuch

Accounts
    And extracts,
5445 Like the predictions of the sun priest
    Ahau Pech,
And the *tun*
    When the *katun* period occurred.
Come
5450 But not ended is my word.
Thus they all got together too,
    These travelers,
And then said
    To give their place to me.
5455 Halfway
    Where your place is
Is my place altogether.
    It says
That you are to pay for my place for
me.
5460 So come then
As I have told you,
    For the descent of justice
Has brought about the rise of
Christianity,
    And the great soul
5465 That will be the coming of the Flower
people
    Who are desired to speak to them
In the lordship city.
    If no one knows that he is appearing
In the lands of wood,
5470 In the lands of stone,
In the designated
    Place,
There is no courting
    That will have been brought about.
5475 That is on the arrival,
    At 9 Ahau *katun* then.
That is who is going to complete
    The back of my word,
Which is coming at the time
5480 When he shall drop his tribute
And end the suffering,
    End the carrying of the load:

5449. A final syncretistic propaganda message asking for contributions for a secret "Christian" cult, the ideology of which is consonant with that of the Cruzob of the Caste War.

5472. Chan Santa Cruz perhaps? The first outbreak of the Caste War is identified with Tizimin, Valladolid, Ichmul, and Tihosuco (Reed 1964). They are all late Itza centers.

5476. That is, 1848 to 1872.

*of 4 Ahau. For the war indem-
nity it will not be a sun priest
in charge or a tax collector.
When the time comes for the
French to invade, there will be
no sun priest even secretly because of the Christian* katun.
(5498)

   *"That is the prophecy forever
for this* katun *from me, the
Spokesman of the Jaguar and
Spokesman of the True God,
the judge of the Itza nobles."*
(5514)

T u katunil ox lahun
   Ti can Ahau ual e*
Ti tz'oc u botic ob
   U liksah katun ca yumob ual e

Ma ix a u alic ex
   A u ahaulil ex katun c u talel e

Y ah cuchul a koch ex
   Ca natz'ac
T u kin uchmal e
   Lai kom cab e
Flanses e
   Lai katunob e
Manan ah kin
   Bin alic u cuch
Tupan u u ich
   T u men nicte katun
Lai u tucul
   Lei u naat
M an kin
   M an akab
T u nicteil katun ual e
   Halil e in u almah xicin t ex

Oktah
   Ben in than
C en
   Chilam Balam
Ca in tzolah u than hahal ku
   Ca bin uchuc u kin
U salhal
   U num ya
Y al
   U mehen Ah Itza e.*

In the *katun* period 13,
   In 4 Ahau again.
5485 Which completes their payment
   For the raising of the wars of these
   our fathers.
And don't say
   That it is your lordship of the *katun*
   that is coming,
The bearer of your taxes
5490   Who is to approach.
When the time is accomplished
   That is the digging of the land
By the French,
   That is the *katun* period
5495 Without a sun priest,
   Who will tell his burden
With his face hidden,
   Because of the Flower *katun* again.
That is his thought;
5500   That is his knowledge.
No day;
   No night
In the flowering of this *katun*.
   True enough, I am the spokesman
   to you
5505 In advance,
   And spread my word,
I,
   Spokesman of the Jaguar.
For I recount the word of the True God,
5510   Whose day will come
To help
   Or punish
The born
   And engendered children of the Itza."

5484. 4 Ahau will be the final *katun* in a significant sense—it will be the thirteenth *katun* after the Valladolid reform that shifted the calendar to a twenty-four-year *katun*, and it will be the twenty-fourth *katun* since the conquest. See also note 4940. The new chronology ran:

1752–1776 4 Ahau	1920–1944 3 Ahau
1776–1800 2 Ahau	1944–1968 1 Ahau
1800–1824 13 Ahau	1968–1992 12 Ahau
1824–1848 11 Ahau	1992–2016 10 Ahau
1848–1872 9 Ahau	2016–2040 8 Ahau
1872–1896 7 Ahau	2040–2064 6 Ahau
1896–1920 5 Ahau	2064–2088 4 Ahau

5514. Following this in the original manuscript is a note in a late hand: *aquí falta una hoja* 'page missing here'. The missing page (9r–9v) contained the fragmentary end of a version of the Antonio Martínez story, the prophecies of Chilam Balam and Puc Tun, and the first half of the prophecy of Kauil Ch'el, versions of which may be read in Roys 1967: 163–166.

Appendix: The Mayan Calendar

The *Book of Tizimin* counts time (as it says in chapter 38) in four systems: (1) the 260-day *tzol kin*, a permutative count of 13 numbers and 20 named days, (2) the 365-day *hab*, made up of 18 named *uinals* of 20 serially numbered days each plus 1 *uinal* of 5 days, (3) the 360-day *tun*, and (4) the Spanish *año* of 365 days plus leap years. The *tuns* were counted by twenties, 20 *tuns* being a *katun*. Larger intervals of time were counted in two systems: by twenties (20 *katuns* being a *baktun*) and by thirteens (13 *katuns* being a *may*). The *baktun* or Long Count dating system does not appear directly in the Tizimin (though it does in the Chumayel); the *may* is featured prominently.

The *Tzol Kin*. The numerological interaction of these cycles is complex, and the Mayan comprehension of it was masterly. The numerology of the *tzol kin* automatically produces cycles of 13 and 20 days. Among the permutations of the factors of these, the Maya were particularly impressed by cycles of 4 × 13, or 52, and 5 × 13, or 65, and they used those cycles (a fifth and a quarter of the *tzol kin* respectively) in divination and ritual. The *tzol kin* traditionally begins on 1 Imix, and it works out that Imix will recur 13 times within this cycle, or every 20 days. Because the count runs 1 to 13, then 1 to 7 (for a total of 20), Imix' second occurrence will have the coefficient 8, leading to the sequence 1, 8, 2, 9, 3, 10, 4, 11, 5, 12, 6, 13, 7 as the coefficients of any particular day. Thus the numerals 1 and 7 come to represent alpha and omega to the Maya. The same sequence applies to the *uinal* and the *tun* for the same reason, as both are based on 20-day counts.

The *Hab*. Because 20 goes into 365 18 times with 5 days left over, the first day of the year advanced by 5 days each year, and only 4 of the 20 days could begin the year (20 ÷ 5 = 4). These were the yearbearers (*ah cuch hab*) or the four changers (*can hel*). The yearbearer that began the first month, or 20-day *uinal*, also started all the others.

Different calendars used different yearbearers. The Zapotecs, for example, used their equivalents of Imix (+ 5 days later), Cimi (+ 5 days later), Chuen (+ 5 days later), Cib, or Type I yearbearers (in Zapotec Chilla, Lana, Goloo, Loo). The Quiche and the Classic Maya used Type II (Ik, Manik, Eb, Caban; or Ik, Ceh, E, Noh in Quiche). The Aztecs used their equivalents of Type III (Akbal, Lamat, Ben, Etz'nab; or Calli, Tochtli, Acatl, Tecpatl in Nahuatl). The colonial Maya used Type IV (Kan, Muluc, Ix, Cauac). And the Type V set (Chicchan, Oc, Men, Ahau) is the focus of the Yucatecan Burner cycle of fire ceremonies, which fall automatically one day later than the colonial yearbearers.

Since 13 goes into 365 28 times with a remainder of 1, the numeral coefficient of the first day of the year advanced by one each year, thus producing a cycle of 13 years, and the same day appeared with the same coefficient only after four such cycles, producing the 52-year *kin tun y abil*, or calendar round. In the colonial calendar used in the Tizimin, the calendar round began on 1 Kan in 1581, for example.

The Mayan *hab* of 365 days, sometimes called a vague year, had 18 *uinals* of 20 days each and 1 *uinal* of 5 days, the dreaded Uayeb (?'specter steps'). These 5 were called nameless days (*x ma kaba kin*), although they were numbered and named normally in the *tzol kin* count and in the *hab* count. This was the period of the year's end ceremonies, to be followed by those of the new year.

The *Tun*. The *tun*, a period of 360 days, was divided into 18 periods of 20 days each and always began on a day Imix. Consequently, it also ended on a day Ahau. The numeral coefficients of these days followed the same sequence as in the *tzol kin* (1, 8, 2, 9, 3, 10, etc.), repeating after 13 *tuns*.

The *Katun*. Tuns, however, were normally counted by twenties, and 20 *tuns* constituted a *katun*. Before 1539 the *katuns* always began on a day Imix and ended on a day Ahau, but in 1539 the system was changed so that they always began on a day Ahau and ended on a day Imix. In either case, the numeral coefficients of the Ahau days yield a cycle of 260 *tuns* or 13 *katuns*. The period of the *katun* (7,200 days) divided by 13 gives 553 cycles of 13 with a remainder of 11. Thus the sequence of the numeral coefficients of the *katuns* runs 13, 11, 9, 7, 5, 3, 1, 12, 10, 8, 6, 4, 2. The period of the half *katun* of 10 *tuns* (*lahun tun*), which was also ceremonially significant and which ran to 3,600 days, when divided by 13 gives 276 cycles of 13 with a remainder of 12. Thus if we count by half *katuns* we get a sequence of 13, 12, 11, 10, 9, 8, 7, 6, 5, 4, 3, 2, 1.

The *Baktun*. The Long Count dating system of the Classic Maya was based on periods of 20 *katuns*, each of which equals 1 *baktun*. A typical Long Count date might be transcribed as 11.16.0.0.0, meaning 11 *baktuns*, 16 *katuns*, no *tuns*, no *uinals*, no days. (All these units were counted vigesimally from 0 to 19 except for the *tuns*, which were counted from 0 to 17, thus totaling 18.) Not content with this rather elegant and precise dating system, the Classic Maya usually recorded important dates in "initial series" dating, giving the Long Count date, the *tzol kin* date, and the *hab* date, thus using all three of the basic cycles that have been described.

The *May*. For most purposes this elaboration was not required, and the Maya were content to count *katuns* by thirteens rather than by twenties. This gives us a period of 260 *tuns* (or 260 years minus 1,300 days, 160 days short of 256 years). This cycle was called the *may*, or the *kahlay katunob* 'account of the *katuns*'. The Maya stopped carving Long Count (*baktun*) dates on their monuments in 10.6.0.0.0 (948). What survived into colonial times was the *may*. A great deal of debate has gone into resolving the correspondence between the *may* dating and the *baktun* dates, an essential step in correlating the Mayan and Christian calendars, with a potential discrepancy of nearly 256 years always hanging in the balance.

The general relationship among these various cycles was well understood by the Maya. They realized that 73 *tzol kins* equaled 52 *habs* ($52 \times 365 = 73 \times 260$). They knew that 72 *habs* equaled 73 *tuns* ($72 \times 365 = 73 \times 360$). And they calculated that $9 \times 65 = 13 \times 45 = 585$, just one day more than the Venus year of 584 days! They concluded that they were right in thinking 9 and 13 to be important.

The Tikal Calendar. During the period represented by the *Books of Chilam Balam*, three different Mayan calendars were in use at different dates: the classical Tikal calendar from 692 to 1539, the Mayapan calendar from 1539 to 1752, and the Valladolid calendar from 1752 to 1848. Other calendrical proposals were made from time to time, but none seems to have caught on. The naming of these calendars is my own (Edmonson 1976), based on where they were first found or where they were inaugurated.

The Tikal calendar appears to have been used throughout Mayan country until 1539 except for certain aberrant inscriptions, largely in the Usumacinta Valley. It used Type II yearbearers, numbered the days of the *uinal* from 0 to 19, and counted *katuns* terminally. Its last *katun*, 13 Ahau, ended in 11.16.0.0.0 (1539).

The Mayapan Calendar. The Xiu and the Itza, both Mexicanized groups of elite lineages among the post-Classic and colonial Maya, disputed the proper use of the *may*, a cycle which they believed legitimized political power. The Xiu wanted to end the *may* in 8 Ahau, which appears to have been the Classic Mayan view; the Itza wanted to end it in 13 Ahau. In or shortly before 1539, there was a calendrical congress to resolve this issue, which resulted in the promulgation of a new calendar, initiated in 1539. The Xiu compromised by accepting 11 Ahau as the beginning of a new cycle. The Itza compromised by accepting initial dating of the *katun*. The date was dictated by calendrical considerations: the conjunction of the cycles was unusually favorable to the change contemplated. The result was that, 80 days before the end of 13 Ahau in 11.16.0.0.0, the Itza inaugurated a new (colonial) calendar at Mayapan. It differed from that of Tikal in adopting Type IV yearbearers, numbering the days of the *uinal* from 1 to 20, and naming the *katuns* from their initial days rather than from their final ones. The Xiu initiated the same system at their own date in Merida.

The result of this change was literally epochal. As in the case of the birth of Christ, Mayan dates before 1539 are counted backward from their endings, and those after 1539 are counted forward from their beginnings.

The Valladolid Calendar. As dated in the Mayapan calendar, *katun* 4 Ahau began in 1737. Five years before it ended, a new calendar was promulgated, apparently at Valladolid. By calendrical coincidence, in 1752 the name day of the *katun* (4 Ahau) fell on the second day of the Mayan year. The Itza sun priests, who were due to be obsolete in 1776, figured out that by redesigning the *katun* as a period of 24 *habs* instead of 20 *tuns* they could fix it so that the initiation of future *katuns* would always fall on the second day of the year. Tidy enough. But, if they also converted the 260-*tun* cycle (the *may*) into a "*katun*" cycle of 24 *katuns* of 24 years each, they (or their descendants) could remain in office until 2088! They therefore reinaugurated *katun* 4 Ahau on the 24-*hab* basis, ending it in 1776. In the Tizimin this system is used only in dates after 1752; in the Chumayel it was sometimes used retroactively, with disastrous (but traceable) effects on some of the dates.

The *Año*. The Maya thought it very clever of the Spanish to have a year of their own—they learned it rapidly and found it child's play. By the time Landa got around to asking them (in 1553) when their year began, they were able to give him a deceptively simple but correct answer:

Sunday, July 16. The 365-day cycle was nothing new to them, of course, and they had figured out how to handle leap years by reckoning them separately.

Every Christian leap year day fell in a Mayan year with the yearbearer Ix, and the day 1 Ix initiated the second half of the calendar round in 1555. In the only really direct correlational statement in the Chumayel, written in 1556, it is clear that the July 16 correlation is pegged to the year 1 Ix, 1555 (Edmonson 1976). The true Christian date can thus be reached by adding the number of Ix years for dates before 1555 or subtracting them for dates thereafter. The Maya did that in their heads but simplified matters by clinging to the July 16 correlation. It was not until the present century that the Europeans generally accepted the Goodman-Martínez-Thompson (GMT) correlation and acknowledged that the Maya were correct (Edmonson 1976).

The only direct correlational statement in the Tizimin, in a text written around 1618 to 1623, also dates the beginning of the Mayan year to July 16 but pegs this not to 1 Ix, the middle of the calendar round, but to 1 Kan, the beginning of it. This was 1581. But the priest who wrote this must surely have been aware that the true correlational date was half a calendar round (26 years) earlier (including 6 Ix years). All references to the Christian year in the *Books* are tied to the July 16 date for 1 Pop, the first day of the Mayan year. And that was true only for 1552 to 1555.

The Julian Calendar. All the European dates are in the Julian calendar. Despite the promulgation of the Gregorian calendar by the pope in 1582, the Maya clung to the Julian one throughout. It is only in some late marginal notes of the nineteenth century that they began using Gregorian dates, which add ten days to the Julian ones. Since the Gregorian reform was accepted promptly in the Spanish world, this is an interesting documentation of the autonomy of Mayan calendrical thought.

The Week. The Mayan reaction to the 7-day week merits special comment. They realized promptly that the days of the week acted as yearbearers, constituting (leap years ignored) a 7-year cycle. (That is, the 365-day year contains 52 weeks plus 1 day.) Eventually they figured out that because of leap year these Christian "yearbearers" occur in cycles of four, and it takes 28 years before any particular 4-year set will be repeated. The number 7 was already important in Mayan numerology, so they comfortably added the weekdays and their planetary associations to the native astrology and used them for divination.

The Mexican Calendar. The Mexican calendar was only partly parallel to the Mayan one; the Nahuas lacked the *tun, katun, may,* and *baktun.*

Maya	Mayan and Mexican Calendars	Nahuatl
xoc	day number	pohualli
kin	day name	tonalli
uinal	20-day cycle	cempohualtonalli
u	lunar month	metztli
tzol kin	260-day cycle	tonalpohualli
tun	360-day cycle	
hab	365-day cycle	xihuitl
katun	20-tun cycle	
kin tun y abil	52-year cycle	xihuitl molpia
may	13-katun cycle	
baktun	20-katun cycle	

These tables may help in understanding and calculating the numerous calendrical references in the text and notes. For a fuller discussion of the Mayan calendar see Thompson 1927, Morley 1946, and Satterthwaite 1965.

Yearbearer Type	Days (Kin)			
I	Imix	Cimi	Chuen	Cib
II	Ik	Manik	Eb	Caban
III	Akbal	Lamat	Ben	Etz'nab
IV	Kan	Muluc	Ix	Cauac
V	Chicchan	Oc	Men	Ahau

Note: These are counted permutatively: 12 Imix, 13 Ik, 1 Akbal, 2 Kan, etc.

Months (Uinals)			
Pop	Xul	Zac	Pax
Uo	Yaxkin	Ceh	Kayab
Zip	Mol	Mac	Cumhu
Zotz'	Ch'en	Kankin	Uayeb
Tzec	Yax	Muan	

Note: These are counted serially, as with our months: 19 Pop, 20 Pop, 1 Uo, 2 Uo, etc.

Sequence of Uinals (For a year 1 Kan)	Sequence of Katuns	Calendar Round Yearbearer Dates (1 Kan equals:)
1 Kan	13 Ahau	
8 Kan	11 Ahau	1529
2 Kan	9 Ahau	1581
9 Kan	7 Ahau	1633
3 Kan	5 Ahau	1685
10 Kan	3 Ahau	1737
4 Kan	1 Ahau	1789
11 Kan	12 Ahau	1841
5 Kan	10 Ahau	
12 Kan	8 Ahau	
6 Kan	6 Ahau	
13 Kan	4 Ahau	
7 Kan	2 Ahau	

Long Count Dates		
8 Ahau	9.13.0.0.0	692
13 Ahau	9.17.0.0.0	771
8 Ahau	10. 6.0.0.0	948
13 Ahau	10.10.0.0.0	1027
8 Ahau	10.19.0.0.0	1204
13 Ahau	11. 3.0.0.0	1283
8 Ahau	11.12.0.0.0	1461
13 Ahau	11.16.0.0.0	1539

Katun Dates

	Tikal				Mayapan	Valladolid
8 Ahau	692	948	1204	1461	1697	
6 Ahau	711	968	1224	1480	1717	
4 Ahau	731	987	1244	1500	1737	
2 Ahau	751	1007	1263	1520		1776
13 Ahau	771	1027	1283	1539		1800
11 Ahau	790	1047	1303		1539	1824
9 Ahau	810	1066	1323		1559	1848
7 Ahau	830	1086	1342		1579	
5 Ahau	849	1106	1362		1598	
3 Ahau	869	1125	1382		1618	
1 Ahau	889	1145	1401		1638	
12 Ahau	909	1165	1421		1658	
10 Ahau	928	1185	1441		1677	

Bibliography

ANCONA, ELIGIO DE
1878 *Historia de Yucatán.* 3 vols. Merida: M. Heredia Argüelles.

BARRERA VASQUEZ, ALFREDO
1948 *El Libro de los libros de Chilam Balam.* Mexico City: Fondo de Cultura Económica.

BLAIR, ROBERT W., AND REFUGIO VERMONT-SALAS
1965 Spoken (Yucatec) Maya. Mimeographed. University of Chicago, Department of Anthropology, Chicago.

BOOK OF CHILAM BALAM OF CHUMAYEL
n.d. Original in the Princeton University Library, Princeton. *See also* Gordon 1913; Roys 1967.

BOOK OF CHILAM BALAM OF KAUA
n.d. Original lost. I have used a partial photostatic copy in the Latin American Library, Tulane University, New Orleans, and a partial photostatic copy in the possession of Paulina Hartig, Hamburg.

BOOK OF CHILAM BALAM OF MANI
n.d. Original lost. I have used Pío Pérez n.d.

BOOK OF CHILAM BALAM OF TIZIMIN
n.d. Original in the Museo Nacional de Antropología, Mexico City. I have used a photostatic copy in the Latin American Library, Tulane University, New Orleans, and Roys n.d.

BRASSEUR DE BOURBOURG, CHARLES ETIENNE
1872 *Dictionnaire, grammaire et chrestomathie de la langue maya . . .* Paris.

BRICKER, VICTORIA REIFLER
1981 *The Indian Christ, the Indian King: The Historical Substrate of Maya Myth and Ritual.* Austin: University of Texas Press.

BRINTON, DANIEL G.
1882 The Maya Chronicles. *Library of Aboriginal American Literature* 1. Philadelphia.

CHAMBERLAIN, ROBERT S.
1948 The Conquest and Colonization of Yucatan, 1517–1550. *Carnegie Institution of Washington Publication* 582. Washington, D.C.

CHUMAYEL. *See* BOOK OF CHILAM BALAM OF CHUMAYEL

CIUDAD REAL, ANTONIO DE
1600? Vocabulario de la lengua maya. Copy in the Latin American Library, Tulane University, New Orleans.

CLOSS, MICHAEL P.
1976 New Information on the European Discovery of Yucatan and the Correlation of the Mayan and Christian Calendars. *American Antiquity* 41: 192–195.

EDMONSON, MUNRO S.

n.d.a Los Popol Vuh. *Estudios de Cultura Maya.* Mexico City. In press.

n.d.b U Chun Uchben T'an: Preliminary Lexicon of Roots of Historical Yucatec. MS in the possession of the author, Tulane University, New Orleans.

1971 The Book of Counsel: The Popol Vuh of the Quiche Maya of Guatemala. *Middle American Research Institute Publication 35.* New Orleans.

1976 The Mayan Calendar Reform of 11.16.0.0.0. *Current Anthropology* 17: 713–717.

EGGAN, FRED

1934 The Maya Kinship System and Cross-Cousin Marriage. *American Anthropologist* 36: 188–202.

FREMANTLE, ANNE

1956 *The Papal Encyclicals in Their Historical Context.* New York: Mentor.

GARIBAY KINTANA, ANGEL MARIA

1953 *Historia de la literatura náhuatl.* 2 vols. Mexico City: Porrúa.

GORDON, G. B.

1913 The Book of Chilam Balam of Chumayel. *University of Pennsylvania. The Museum Anthropological Publications 5.* Philadelphia.

KAUA. *See* BOOK OF CHILAM BALAM OF KAUA

LANDA, DIEGO DE

1929 *Relation des choses de Yucatan.* 2 vols. Paris: Genet.

MAKEMSON, MAUD W.

1951 *The Book of the Jaguar Priest: A Translation of the Book of Chilam Balam of Tizimin with Commentary.* New York: Schuman.

MANI. *See* BOOK OF CHILAM BALAM OF MANI

MARTINEZ HERNANDEZ, JUAN

1929 *Diccionario de Motul. Maya-español.* Merida.

1940 *Crónicas mayas.* 2d ed. Merida: Carlos R. Menéndez.

MOLINA, ALONSO DE

1944 *Vocabulario en lengua castellana y mexicana.* Madrid: Ediciones Cultura Hispánica.

MORLEY, SYLVANUS G.

1946 *The Ancient Maya.* Stanford: Stanford University Press.

MOTUL DICTIONARY. *See* CIUDAD REAL, ANTONIO DE

PACHECO CRUZ, SANTIAGO

1969 *Hahil Tzolbichunil Fan Mayab.* Merida: the author.

PIO PEREZ, JUAN

n.d. Book of Chilam Balam of Tizimin. Transcription, partial translation, and notes in the Latin American Library, Tulane University, New Orleans.

1866–67 *Diccionario de la lengua maya.* Merida: Molina Solís.

1898 *Coordinación alfabética de las voces del idioma maya.* Merida: Imprenta de la Ermita.

REDFIELD, ROBERT

1941 *The Folk Culture of Yucatan.* Chicago: University of Chicago Press.

REED, NELSON
1964   *The Caste War of Yucatan.* Stanford: Stanford University Press.

ROYS, RALPH L.
n.d.   Book of Chilam Balam of Tizimin. Transcription, partial translation, and notes in the Latin American Library, Tulane University, New Orleans.

1931   Ethno-Botany of the Maya. *Middle American Research Institute Publication* 2. New Orleans.

1935   Place-names of Yucatan. *Maya Research* 2: 1–10.

1940   Personal Names of the Maya of Yucatan. *Carnegie Institution of Washington Publication* 523, contribution 31. Washington, D.C.

1957   Political Geography of the Yucatan Maya. *Carnegie Institution of Washington Publication* 613. Washington, D.C.

1965   *Ritual of the Bacabs.* Norman: University of Oklahoma Press.

1967   *The Book of Chilam Balam of Chumayel.* Norman: University of Oklahoma Press.

SANCHEZ DE AGUILAR, PEDRO
1892   Informe contra idolorum cultores. In Francisco Paso y Troncoso, ed., *Tratado de las idolatrías, supersticiones, dioses, ritos, hechicerías y otras costumbres gentílicas de las razas aborígenes de México*, pp. 181–329. Mexico City: Editorial Fuente Cultural.

SATTERTHWAITE, LINTON
1965   Calendrics of the Maya Lowlands. In R. Wauchope, ed., *Handbook of Middle American Indians* 3: 603–631. Austin: University of Texas Press.

SOLIS ALCALA, ERMILO
1949   *Diccionario español-maya.* Merida: Editorial Yikal Maya Than.

SWADESH, MORRIS, MARIA CHRISTINA ALVAREZ, AND JUAN RAMON BASTARRACHEA
1970   *Diccionario de elementos del maya yucateco colonial.* Mexico City: UNAM.

THOMPSON, J. E. S.
1927   A Correlation of the Mayan and European Calendars. *Field Museum of Natural History, Anthropological Series* 17, no. 1. Chicago.

1951   Review of Maud W. Makemson, *The Book of the Jaguar Priest: A Translation of the Book of Chilam Balam of Tizimin with Commentary. American Anthropologist* 53: 546–547.

1958   Research in Maya Hieroglyphic Writing. *Pan American Union, Social Science Monographs* 5: 43–52. Washington, D.C.

TIZIMIN. *See* BOOK OF CHILAM BALAM OF TIZIMIN

TOZZER, ALFRED M.
1941   Landa's Relación de las Cosas de Yucatan. *Papers of the Peabody Museum of American Archaeology and Ethnology, Harvard University* 18. Cambridge, Mass.

VILLA ROJAS, ALFONSO
1945   The Maya of East Central Quintana Roo. *Carnegie Institution of Washington Publication* 559. Washington, D.C.

Index

Entries in the index are primarily to
the notes and are cited by line
number. Included are (1) all Spanish
and Nahuatl words occurring in the
text, (2) all proper names, calendrical references, dates, and social
statuses, (3) unusual expressions
and rhetorical forms (metaphors,
kennings), (4) all plants and animals, and (5) a topical, analytical,
and primarily ethnographical cross-
referenced listing of the contents of
the notes, which may also serve to
indicate the location of particular
topics in the text. Abbreviations are
Lat., Latin; Nah., Nahuatl; and Sp.,
Spanish.

3637, 4159, 4210, 4866, 4940, 4974
day, count, 2284; name, 787, 4973 (Maya:
   Imix, Ik, Akbal, Kan, Chicchan,
   Cimi, Manik, Lamat, Muluc, Oc,
   Chuen, Eb, Ben, Ix, Men, Cib, Caban,
   Etz'nab, Cauac, Ahau; Nahuatl:
   Cipactli, Ehecatl, Calli, Cuetzpallin,
   Coatl, Miquiztli, Mazatl, Tochtli, Atl,
   Itzcuintli, Ozomatli, Malinalli, Acatl,
   Ocelotl, Cuauhtli, Cozcacuauhtli,
   Ollin, Tecpatl, Quiahuitl, Xochitl);
   number 1–13 (Maya: *hun, ca, ox,*
   can, ho, uac, uuc, uaxac, bolon,
   lahun, buluc, lah ca, oxlahun;
   Nahuatl: *ce, ome, yey, nahui, ma-*
   cuilli, chicuace, chicome, chicnahui,
   matlactli, matlactlionce, ma-
   tlactliomome, matlactliomey)
de (Sp. 'of'), 3109
De León, Ponce, 346
death, 460, 462, 1628, 3053, 3356, 3360,
   3423, 3441, 3449, 4478; deer, 5256;
   and destruction, 2636; God, 4095,
   4397 (*see also* Ah Puch); painless
   (*see ma ya cimlal*); red stone (*see* sacrifice); wood and stone, 2500; yellow,
   395. *See also* burial; burning; dart;
   decapitation; famine; hanging; medicine; plague; sacrifice; throat;
   uprooting
decapitation, 5308
Deceiver, 1238
December, 3469
decoration, 196, 634
deep, 953
deer, 836, 1418, 1838, 1922, 1948, 3071,
   3262, 3337, 5250, 5272; death, 5256;
   katun, 2124, 5272; people, 3071,
   3337. *See also* Ceh; Zip
deity, 5332
descent, 655, 685
desire, 2144, 2259, 2984, 3945
destruction, of burden, 1934; of city, 41,
   66, 647, 2431; of Emal, 648; of governor, 114; of homes, 72; of Mayapan,
   118, 119; of road, 88; of world by fire,
   5515 ff.; of year, 2427
devil, 518, 524, 526, 534, 1500, 3099
diciembre (Sp. 'December'), 3469
difracismo (Sp. 'diphrasing'). *See* kennings
dig, 1001
Dios (Sp. 'God'), 826, 1336
direction, 16, 738, 1550, 2987; color, 930,
   1578; symbolism, 930, 973
distance, bend, 1784, 1852; day, 4156;
   shot, 228, 324, 1784, 1852, 2074;
   shout, 1184, 2074, 3974, 4184; sleep,
   2323; stop, 1183, 3974, 4184. *See also*
   measuring stick; pace; rest; step
distribution. *See* bearer; begging; boat;
   borrowing; market; merchant; selling; stealing; trade; travelers
ditch, 2323
divination, 426, 2415, 2856, 3049, 4723,
   4772; by cast, 411; eclipse, 2419; far
   seeing, 2418; fire, 2415; holy day, 412;
   katun, 5086; *kin tun y abil,* 5086;

DATE DUE

FEB. 27. 991			
APR. 03 1991			
MAY 08. 1991			
GAYLORD			PRINTED IN U.S.A.